Patrick Chamoiseau
Recovering Memory

Contemporary French and Francophone Cultures 8

Contemporary French and Francophone Cultures

Series Editors

EDMUND SMYTH
Manchester Metropolitan University

CHARLES FORSDICK
University of Liverpool

Editorial Board

LYNN A. HIGGINS
Dartmouth College

MIREILLE ROSELLO
University of Amsterdam

MICHAEL SHERINGHAM
University of Oxford

DAVID WALKER
University of Sheffield

This series aims to provide a forum for new research on modern and contemporary French and francophone cultures and writing. The books published in *Contemporary French and Francophone Cultures* reflect a wide variety of critical practices and theoretical approaches, in harmony with the intellectual, cultural and social developments which have taken place over the past few decades. All manifestations of contemporary French and francophone culture and expression are considered, including literature, cinema, popular culture, theory. The volumes in the series will participate in the wider debate on key aspects of contemporary culture.

1 Chris Tinker, *Georges Brassens and Jacques Brel: Personal and Social Narratives in Post-war Chanson*

2 Debra Kelly, *Autobiography and Independence: Selfhood and Creativity in Postcolonial African Writing in French*

3 Matthew Screech, *Masters of the Ninth Art: Bandes dessinées and Franco-Belgian Identity*

4 Akane Kawakami, *Travellers' Visions. French Literary Encounters with Japan, 1881–2004*

5 Nicki Hitchcott, *Calixthe Beyala: Performances of Migration*

6 Jane Hiddleston, *Assia Djebar: Out of Africa*

7 Martin Munro, *Exile and Post-1946 Haitian Literature: Alexis, Depestre, Ollivier, Laferrière, Danticat*

MAEVE McCUSKER

Patrick Chamoiseau

Recovering Memory

LIVERPOOL UNIVERSITY PRESS

First published 2007 by
Liverpool University Press
4 Cambridge Street
Liverpool L69 7ZU

This paperback edition published 2011

British Library Cataloguing-in-Publication data
A British Library CIP record is available

ISBN 978-1-84631-048-5 cased
978-1-84631-686-9 limp

Typeset by XL Publishing Services, Tiverton
Printed and bound in the UK by Marston Digital

Contents

Acknowledgements   vi

Abbreviations   vii

Introduction   1

1 Beginnings: The Enigma of Origin   21

2 'Une tracée de survie': Autobiographical Memory   47

3 Memory Re-collected: Witnesses and Words   76

4 Memory Materialized: Traces of the Past   101

5 Flesh Made Word: Traumatic Memory in
Biblique des derniers gestes   127

Afterword   150

Notes   157

Bibliography   174

Index   183

Acknowledgements

I would like to thank colleagues in Queen's University Belfast, former and current, for their guidance and good will. Jennifer FitzGerald, Nigel Harkness, Chris Shorley and Isabel Torres read sections of the manuscript, which is immeasurably improved for their input; shortcomings remain of course my own responsibility. I am also grateful to Peter Broome, who first introduced me to Chamoiseau's work, to Janice Carruthers, for her practical and moral support, and to Claire Moran, Evelyn Mullally, Lorraine Browne and Denise Toner, for their unfailing generosity. Thanks are also due to the staff in QUB library, and in particular to Florence Gray.

The encouragement of colleagues and friends elsewhere in French and Francophone studies has been greatly appreciated: Derval Conroy, Catriona Cunningham, David Murphy and in particular Charles Forsdick, whose support for this project has been crucial. I feel particularly indebted, for reasons that go far beyond a shared interest in postcolonial writing, to Aedín Ní Loingsigh, Mary Gallagher and Lorna Milne. The latter's generous reading of the manuscript, as the (not so anonymous) reviewer for Liverpool University Press, was invaluable in the final stages of writing. At LUP, the constructive comments of the readers of proposal and manuscript, coupled with Anthony Cond's efficiency and patience, greatly lightened the venture.

Family and friends provided sustenance and distraction when the going got tough: Brian Hollywood, Claire Campbell, Jill Cush, Marie-Clare Crawford, John and Alessandra McIlduff, Mairéad and Siobhán McCusker, Deirdre and Áine Gormley and, in particular, Peter Rosser. My parents have been unstinting in their support and it is to them that the greatest debt is due.

A section of Chapter 4 appeared in *Ici-là: Place and Displacement in Caribbean Writing in French*, edited by Mary Gallagher, and Chapter 5 draws on some of the insights explored in my article 'Carnal Knowledge: Writing the Body in Patrick Chamoiseau's *Biblique des derniers gestes*', forthcoming in *Violence and Identity in the Francophone Ex-Colonies*, edited by Lorna Milne. I would like to thank both editors for permission to reproduce this material.

Abbreviations

The most frequently cited works will be abbreviated as follows:

Chronique des sept misères: CSM
Solibo Magnifique: SM
Lettres creoles: LC
Eloge de la créolité: Eloge
Antan d'enfance: AE
Chemin-d'école: CE
A Bout d'enfance: BE
L'Esclave vieil homme et le molosse: EVH
Ecrire en pays dominé: EPD
Cases en pays-mêlés: CPM
Biblique des derniers gestes: BDG

Introduction

> All of the Antilles, every island, is an effort of memory; every
> mind, every racial biography culminating in amnesia and fog.
> Pieces of sunlight through the fog and sudden rainbows, *arcs-en-
> ciel*. That is the effort, the labour of the Antillean imagination.
>
> Derek Walcott, *What the Twilight Says*

Since the early 1990s, the islands of the French-speaking Caribbean – the
départements d'outre-mer, Martinique and Guadeloupe, as well as Haiti,
the first Black republic – have been the site of a heightened and intense
debate around historical memory. These islands – and notably
Martinique – have already witnessed a long-standing tradition of theoretical self-analysis and identitarian debate, and have produced a number
of thinkers (Frantz Fanon, Aimé Césaire, Edouard Glissant) who have
anticipated and contributed to what we now call postcolonial discourse.
Yet the contemporary centrality of the concern with collective memory,
its pervasive and almost obsessive force, is nonetheless remarkable, even
by the standards of a literary and cultural hotbed such as Martinique.
This current centrality derives in part from a number of deeply contested
anniversaries, which served in recent years to reinforce the peculiarities
of a supposedly postcolonial situation. As the millennium loomed,
Antilleans were successively enjoined to commemorate the 500th
anniversary of Columbus's discovery of the Americas (1992), the 50th
anniversary of departmentalization (1996), and the 150th anniversary of
the 'abolition' of slavery (1998) – all events which are fraught with
complex and ambivalent associations in the Caribbean imaginary.
Unsurprisingly, this last anniversary was of particular significance, a fact
attested to by several publications from the period.[1] In addition, and
emphasizing a *devoir de mémoire* of a quite different nature, 2004
marked the bicentenary of Haitian independence, an anniversary which
would also encourage the *départements* to reflect on their very different
historical destiny.

Implicitly linked to these heightened moments of remembrance, and
reflecting the atavistic umbilical link which endures between *départements* and metropole, the 'loi Taubira'[2] was ratified in the French
parliament on 10 May 2001. This law finally recognized slavery as a

crime against humanity, and provided for a day of remembrance in the metropole. (France remains, incidentally, the only country to have made such a declaration to date.) Jubilation was, however, short-lived, as the government appeared slow to act on instituting the principles enshrined in the law. More recently still, the polemic around the law of 23 February 2005 has further energized, and to some extent polarized, the debate around postcolonial memory. This law – which was mainly concerned with the colonial legacy in North Africa, and in Algeria in particular – demanded in its fourth article that the 'positive' effects of colonization be taught in French state schools. The stipulation, which was widely criticized by academics, journalists and historians in the Maghreb, France and elsewhere, was rejected with particular vehemence in Martinique and Guadeloupe, islands which in fact are not even mentioned in the text.[3]

That the law of 23 February, quickly christened the 'loi de la honte', had such an enormous impact in the Antilles can be explained by a number of factors. First – and in contrast to the vast majority of colonial territories once owned by France – Martinique and Guadeloupe remain an integral part of the French state. In terms of their political status, they are, notoriously, only problematically postcolonial. This means that, unlike in Algeria, Tunisia or the other states with which the law was more explicitly concerned, the centralization of the French education system would inevitably require Antillean children, along with their French peers, to learn about the advantages of colonialism. This attempt to reconstruct colonial history according to a narrative of progress and enlightenment – reminiscent perhaps of the notorious imposition of the formula 'nos ancêtres les Gaulois', ludicrously repeated by schoolchildren throughout the French empire – was deemed unacceptable by all shades of local political and artistic opinion. Secondly, there is undeniably a distinction to be drawn between a postcolonial state, in which the colonial presence is a relatively discrete, if painful, interval in a continuous past, and an ex-slave society whose very foundations are wrought through genocide, oppression and exploitation. However inappropriate it may seem to celebrate the benign or ameliorative effects of colonization in Algeria or Senegal, there is something particularly uncomfortable about this gesture in a culture in which enforced expatriation and ritual humiliation were the dominant experience for the vast majority of inhabitants. A third factor, I would suggest, is precisely the heightened political consciousness outlined above. Memory – its manipulation, reinvention and repression – has been a constant theme in political and cultural debate in the Antilles over the last twenty years, a fact which ensures that any political insensitivity on the part of the metropole will be immediately and confidently exposed.

The current prominence of memory, as subject and as rhetorical trope, is largely driven by the writers of the Antilles, who frequently combine a prolific literary output with a strong political presence, ensuring that they play an active part in shaping collective memory. Aimé Césaire, whose dual role as statesman and poet is of course well known, is only the most obvious example of the imbrication of literature and politics in the islands. More recently, the Guadeloupean novelist Daniel Maximin was coordinator of the commemorations of abolition in Martinique and Guadeloupe in 1998. His countrywoman Maryse Condé is president of the 'Comité pour la mémoire d'esclavage', instigated in the wake of the 'loi Taubira'.[4] Writers such as Chamoiseau, Glissant and Césaire have been highly vocal commentators on the importance of memory in the Antilles, and were forthright critics of the French state in the wake of the 'loi de la honte'.[5] In January 2006, the French president Jacques Chirac finally (many would say belatedly) announced 10 May as the date for the commemoration of slavery in metropolitan France. In the presence of Condé and her committee, he entrusted to Edouard Glissant – whom he described, without a trace of irony, as an 'homme de mémoire et de l'universel' – the preliminary preparations for the establishment of a national centre devoted 'à la traite, à l'esclavage et à leurs abolitions'.[6] Tellingly, there is still no substantial museum dedicated solely to colonization or slavery in Martinique or in Guadeloupe.

But it is through writing itself that these figures make the strongest impact on the memorial landscapes of Martinique, Guadeloupe and beyond. Since the 1980s, Caribbean authors have acquired a new prominence on the world stage, and one of the main characteristics of this dynamic tradition is its explicit concern with collective and, increasingly, individual memory.[7] Paradoxically, then, despite the frequent proclamations by Antillean writers that memory has been erased, repressed or shattered, it remains their most persistent preoccupation, central, as both source and theme, to their literary output. And undoubtedly, one of the key reasons for the contemporary prominence of writers such as Glissant and Chamoiseau is their theoretical writing, which has provided such a rich – and, in our current theory-driven age, marketable – complement to creative texts. It should be emphasized, however, that the distinction between the theoretical and the creative is itself broken down in the self-conscious, experimental and generically promiscuous approach exemplified in texts such as Glissant's *Poétique de la relation* or Chamoiseau's *Ecrire en pays dominé*. The extent to which such writers and thinkers in the French Caribbean have anticipated, contributed to, and frequently challenged or confounded the ongoing theoretical debates around memory is indeed remarkable. Their reflections coincide with developments in both metropolitan French and postcolonial theory, operating alongside, and occasionally ahead of, more celebrated achievements elsewhere. More than in most other postcolonial societies, after all, Antillean writers bear the cultural and theoretical imprint of the metropolitan centre, however vociferously they may assert their difference from its institutional networks. Edouard Glissant's *Le Discours antillais* appeared within two years of Lyotard's *La Condition postmoderne* (1979) and, like the more famous essay, promotes the value of the lower-case *histoire(s)* over the metanarrative expressed in *Histoire* – a distinction frequently mobilized by Chamoiseau. The *Eloge de la créolité* (1989), with its emphasis on hybridity and syncretism, and its expressed distrust of ethnic absolutism, prefigures both Paul Gilroy's *The Black Atlantic* (1993) and Homi Bhabha's even more influential *The Location of Culture* (1994). Furthermore, trauma studies acquired an unprecedented currency during the 1990s, although Glissant was already exploring notions of traumatic memory, repression and amnesia in *Le Discours antillais* (1981).

Amnesia and Anamnesis

The attention to cultural memory exhibited by Caribbean writers has to be considered, then, in the context of a remarkable and widespread acceleration in the study of memory since the 1980s. Memory has become one of the defining terms of contemporary thought, largely the result of the ongoing attempts to deal with the traumas of World War II, and particularly with the memory of the Holocaust. Many of the key texts of 'memory studies' derive directly from, or deal directly with, this context. For example, Marianne Hirsch's influential *Family Frames* is inspired by the Holocaust, and in particular by her family's experience as immigrants to the United States.[8] Dominick LaCapra's work, too, is principally concerned with this event, as is evidenced in titles such as *Representing the Holocaust* (1994) and *History and Memory after Auschwitz* (1998). Henri Rousso's reappraisal of the traumatic memory of France's occupation, *Le Syndrome de Vichy*,[9] diagnoses a succession of stages, drawn from psychoanalysis – 'deuil inachevé', 'refoulement', 'le miroir brisé', 'obsession' – in the recovery of a nation ill from the hangover of its own past.[10] While one should be wary of mapping any such neat typology onto a radically different postcolonial situation, it could be argued at the very least that Antillean culture has demonstrated, often simultaneously, symptoms of all four of these stages. And, as the highly mediatized commemorations of the 1990s attest, the contemporary age could be described as one of 'obsession'. The increasing significance of slavery as a theme in the writing of Chamoiseau and others can be seen as a return of the repressed, and writers have both reflected and shaped the memorial process, attempting in particular to challenge the partiality of French commemoration.

The paradigmatic status of the Holocaust, then, means that it figures at once as impetus and touchstone for the contemporary upsurge of interest in memory. This positioning has involved its own distortions and exclusions, simultaneously overshadowing and stimulating memory of other traumatic historical events, and most notably, I would argue, that of slavery. Any comparative discussion of atrocities such as the Holocaust and slavery is of course a futile venture, which risks degenerating into a competitive view of suffering, bogged down in issues of scale, uniqueness and transcendence. There is also the danger of over-valorizing victimhood at the expense of agency, or of pandering to what the Saint-Lucian poet Derek Walcott calls a 'literature of recrimination and despair'.[11] And yet inevitably, one catastrophe has recalled, and been defined in relation to, the other. Already in his *Discours sur le colonialisme*, Césaire had remarked of the Holocaust that it was not the crime in itself which caused such outrage, but rather the humiliation of the white man, and the fact of having applied in a European setting 'des procédés colonialistes dont ne relevaient jusqu'ici que les Arabes d'Algérie, les coolies de l'Inde, les nègres d'Afrique'.[12] In *Ecrire en pays dominé*, Chamoiseau describes the slave trade as 'l'holocauste des holocaustes, une sorte de nazisme avant l'heure, dont la conscience humaine ne se souvient même pas' (*EPD*, p. 122). The comparison has inflected critical discourse as well. Ana Douglass and Thomas A. Vogler conclude their introduction to *Witness and Memory*, a collection principally concerned with the Shoah, by stating that 'the time when we celebrate the opening of our first Native American Holocaust Museum, or our African Diaspora or slavery museum seems far in the future'.[13] Likewise, Michèle Praeger notes that

> [unlike] the Holocaust, the horror of abduction and enslavement has never been acknowledged publicly by Westerners. No day of atonement, no spectacular gestures such as Willy Brandt's redemptive kneeling at the monument

> to Warsaw's former ghetto, no scandalous act such as Ronald Reagan's visit
> to an SS cemetery, no museums of slavery, no memorials, no monuments,
> no memories, no remorse. [...]. Their [the African slaves'] Holocaust spread
> over more than three centuries.[14]

Whatever the pitfalls of this comparative tendency, its prevalence is unavoidable. While, however, the experience of slavery can clearly be considered a 'limit event', to use Dominick LaCapra's term,[15] the writing of the French Caribbean has only rarely been brought into significant dialogue with the branch of memory studies which has emerged directly from these theorizations of Holocaust memory, trauma theory. Theorists of trauma, and the critics who draw on their work, have tended to privilege the writing of 'living memory' and to foreground accounts by individual survivors (primarily of the Holocaust, but also of Vietnam, and similarly of abuse). The shadows of the Caribbean past, on the other hand, can *only* be recreated imaginatively. For this reason, Marianne Hirsch's concept of postmemory is particularly valuable. Postmemory, she argues, is 'the relationship of survivors of cultural or collective trauma to the experiences of their parents', experiences that they only remember at second hand, but that are so powerful, so monumental, as to 'constitute memories in their own right'. Crucially, she suggests that this form of memory 'is not mediated through recollection but through an imaginative investment and creation',[16] a notion that chimes with the views expressed repeatedly by both Chamoiseau and his characters.

Memory Fatigue?

Even this short survey of contemporary cultural studies confirms that the general enchantment with the *theme* of memory, discernible since the late 1980s, shows no signs of abating. Memory has been debated and dissected, prodded and probed, corralled and critiqued, from almost every conceivable angle, and the term has been applied so broadly and so indiscriminately as to render it at times almost meaningless. Inevitably, then, the sheer prevalence of the term means that there is some evidence of a backlash. A recent special issue of the journal *Representations* – the journal in which, incidentally, Pierre Nora's influential introduction to his *Lieux de mémoire* project first appeared in English[17] – provides a useful distillation of some of the reservations being voiced in certain quarters. The collection criticizes the 'industry' that has sprung up around memory, and registers a general sense of what we might call memory fatigue. In his polemical contribution to the volume, for example, Kerwin

Lee Klein criticizes the colonizing force of the term, and the lack of rigour in its definitions and applications: 'Where we once spoke of folk history or popular history or oral history or public history or even myth', Klein argues, 'we now employ memory as a metahistorical category that subsumes all these various terms'.[18] Moreover, the new 'materialization' of memory elevates it to the status of a historical agent, so that 'we enter a new age in which archives remember and statues forget'. Klein's reservations, however, do not only refer to taxonomic sloppiness or to the tendency to hypostasize memory. He is principally concerned with the apparent 'softening' or domestication of cold hard facts which our vogue for memory entails. Klein insists that 'if history is objective in the coldest, hardest sense of the word, memory is subjective in the warmest, most inviting senses of that word. In contrast with history, memory fairly vibrates with the fullness of Being'.[19] He continues, in a mischievously dichotomizing vein, 'History is modernism, the state, science, imperialism, androcentrism, a tool of oppression; memory is postmodernism, the "symbolically excluded", the body, "a healing device and a tool of redemption"'.[20] Such an unthinking substitution of one term by the other is also criticized by Thomas W. Laqueur, who concludes his introduction to the same volume by stating that 'a bit less memory and a bit more history would not be such a bad thing. Or to put it differently, we might want to concentrate more [...] on the history of the political and moral failures, for example, that produced the Holocaust rather than the memory of its horrors.'[21]

These observations provide a useful context for this study of the representation of memory in Chamoiseau's work, as much for the ways in which they do not fit the subject under discussion as for the light they shed on it. In their own exclusions and emphases, these critical counterpoints will help us to define the particularities of postcolonial, and particularly Antillean, memory. Klein and Laqueur suggest, for example, that the rise of memory has somehow been at the expense of history. They yearn for a return to a more dispassionate and objective way of dealing with the past, and to an ethics of remembrance which is less grounded in the subjective, the contingent and the therapeutic. If, as Fredric Jameson famously suggested in the *The Political Unconscious*, 'history is what hurts',[22] Laqueur and Klein would counter that in contemporary literature and culture, memory offers the false promise of healing. And yet, such neat binaries have to be radically rethought when dealing with the subject of memory in the Caribbean. This is a society whose history, after all, is defined more by its gaps and fissures than by its presences or certainties, and in which such vast swathes of the past have been wiped out as to render history impossible and memory, also, peculiarly impoverished. Four and a half thousand years are glossed in *Texaco*'s opening chronology as 'Galibis, Arawaks, Caraïbes occupent les îles françaises'; the existence of these peoples is not described, and even their decimation is absent from the account. Subsequently, the absolute historical invisibility of the slave, coupled with a willed amnesia surrounding slavery, means that the trail of historical consciousness has been definitively and repeatedly eroded. In *L'Esclave vieil homme et le molosse*, the old man's history begins and ends with the empty signifier of the navel, whose knot symbolizes a dead end rather than a vital link to the past: 'sa généalogie, sa probable lignée de papa manman et arrière-grands-parents, se résume au nombril enfoncé dans son ventre, et qui zieute le monde tel un œil coco-vide, très froid et sans songes millénaires. L'esclave vieil homme est abîme comme son nombril' (*EVH*, p. 22).[23] In *Texaco*, not only has Esternome lost all connection to his pre-plantation roots, but he deliberately avoids his daughter's questions about slavery. This process, repeated over generations, means that the narrative can only be reconstructed through the imaginative workings of memory. If the initial traumas of transplantation, the middle passage and slavery irrevocably fractured collective memory across the Caribbean, the extreme dependence resulting from the decline of the plantation economy and *départementalisation* have accelerated a sense of historical and cultural amnesia. That Antillean writers are so invested in the recuperation of memory, rather than of history, testifies to the unusually complete decimation of any historical trace of their past. From this perspective, then, the criticisms of an excessive recourse to memory can be refuted.

This complex relationship with the past means that contemporary writers simultaneously strain to escape what Derek Walcott has called the New World 'servitude to the muse of history'.[24] Caught in a creative double bind, they are subject to the overwhelming and debilitating presence of the past, while at the same time being conscious of its apparent dereliction or absence. That this paradoxical attitude has its origins in slavery is underlined in the opening paragraphs of *L'Esclave vieil homme et le molosse*, when the assertion that 'les histoires d'esclavage ne nous passionnent guère. Peu de littérature se tient à ce propos', is followed by the apparently contradictory acknowledgement that 'nous nous sentons submergés par ce nœud de mémoires qui nous âcre d'oublis et de présences hurlantes' (*EVH*, p. 17). Chamoiseau here gestures towards a tentative distinction between 'histoires' and 'littérature' on the one hand,

and 'mémoires' on the other. The distinction registers a fault line between the public and official domain of the written record, and the private and intimate nature of intergenerational memory. For if the stories or histories of slavery have been neglected by the unidentified and amorphous 'nous' of the diegesis, so too has literature, in a parallel but complementary suppression, tended to overlook or to elide this narrative. And yet the knot of (private) memories which co-exists with and counteracts such erasures is itself constituted by screaming presences *and* by absences, 'oublis'. The emotional and cognitive resistance to memory ensures that there can be no straightforward connection to the past, and even that which is remembered comes freighted with bitter oblivion. As the title of this study suggests, any attempt to recover collective memory will also, by definition, be an attempt to recover *from* that very memory, a paradox of reluctant anamnesia.

Plenitude and Loss: *Créolité* Reconsidered

The insights of French theorists such as Pierre Nora and Henri Rousso – while concerned with specific metropolitan contexts – have some relevance for my analysis of memory in the French Caribbean. Nora's approach, although it takes scant account of the role of the colonies in shaping 'national' identity, privileges memory, and suggests that history can only ever be an incomplete reconstruction of the past. This perspective coincides with much work done in the Caribbean, notably around the death of the oral tradition. In *Les Lieux de mémoire*, his seminal study of the construction of the French past, Nora states that we speak so much of memory because there is so little of it left.[25] He thus suggests that 'pure' and integral memory, taken for granted by people in the past and generated and transmitted through the oral tradition, has been displaced by the deliberate and often ironic representations of a postmodern world. Eric Hobsbawm, in a similar vein, suggests that 'the destruction of the past, or rather of the social mechanisms that link one's contemporary experience of the past to that of previous generations, is one of the most characteristic and eerie phenomena of the late twentieth century'. Hobsbawm suggests that in contemporary times people 'grow up in a sort of permanent present, lacking any organic relation to the public past of the times they live in'.[26]

Like Nora, Hobsbawm – whose 'organic relation' resonates with the terminology of *Les Lieux de mémoire* – regrets a particular kind of direct and uncontaminated connection with the past. Leaving aside for the moment the specificities of postcolonial memory, it is of course questionable whether in the metropolitan context which is of primary (indeed almost exclusive) interest to Nora, or in the Europe discussed by Hobsbawm, such a sense of untroubled memorial plenitude ever in fact existed. For the observations of both Nora and Hobsbawm are predicated on what Ann Rigney has described as a 'plenitude–loss–restoration' model of collective memory, according to which the willed, deliberate (and usually written) preservation of memory at once counteracts and aggravates the loss, 'by carrying "lived" or "internal" memory into what Halbwachs calls the "external" sphere of history'.[27] Such notions of plenitude and loss have been repeatedly mobilized, to varying effects, in the Antillean context. The *négritude* movement, for example, considered the African continent as the site and source of memorial plenitude, and saw the Middle Passage as a memorial severance, creating a traumatic sense of loss, lack and absence from which the slave was never to recover. The *créolité* writers revise this view, however, complicating the narrative of inevitable degeneration favoured by *négritude*. Their nostalgia is no longer directed towards a prelapsarian Africa; rather, their writing articulates a profound sense of loss and regret for an 'authentic' and localized Caribbean identity. While conceding the brutal fracture to memory caused by the forced expatriation from Africa, they focus on the remaking of memory on the plantation, pointing like Walcott to the exhilarating creative force unleashed by transplantation to the New World: 'Where there was nothing, there was everything to be made. With this prodigious ambition one began'.[28] From this perspective, the plantation offered a new space in which memory was forged and fermented, notably through the Creole language itself. For the *créolistes*, then, it is imperative to rediscover what they describe as the 'true' memory of the Caribbean, 'cette mémoire-sable voltigée dans le paysage, dans la terre, dans des fragments de cerveaux de vieux-nègres, tout en richesse émotionnelle, en sensations, en intuitions' (*Eloge*, p. 38). This overtly nostalgic conceptualization, emphasizing memory's fragmentary and aleatory qualities, and its spontaneous emotional charge, should however be read against the rhetorical grain of a manifesto which seeks to impose its frequently exclusionary view of 'la mémoire vraie'.[29]

The 'loss' of this Creole memory, a loss initiated with the fall of the plantation system and accelerated in the aftermath of *départementalisation*, is seen by the *créolistes* as a further traumatic blow. To adapt Rigney's paradigm, writers such as Chamoiseau and his fellow *créoliste*

Raphaël Confiant would argue that Antillean memory has followed a trajectory which we might describe as loss–recreation–loss. For them, it is with loss rather than plenitude – bluntly put, with the Middle Passage rather than with Africa – that the Caribbean experience begins. For this reason, the term 'anamnesis', with its suggestion that forgetting precedes remembering, is perhaps particularly appropriate. And it is in the context of the latest, contemporary stage of loss, seen as one of cultural and economic stifling by the metropole, and of passive dependence on the part of the Antillean population, that the *créolité* writers' revalorizing of Creole culture is to be understood. From this perspective, a particularly strong nostalgia inflects the presentation of the early decades of the twentieth century, the twilight era of Creole culture. This nostalgia has a distinctly literary dimension as well. However critical he may be of Césaire's political legacy, for example, Chamoiseau regrets his own belated position in relation to the literary forefather. In *Biblique des derniers gestes*, the explosive verse of Aimé Césaire ('ces vers terribles, chargés de puissance, de raideur et de force', *BDG*, p. 767) is wistfully evoked. Both Chamoiseau and Confiant concede that their region has escaped the brutal violence of the decolonization process in Africa and elsewhere. However, the 'silent domination' which operates in the French Caribbean today, and which is the subject of *Ecrire en pays dominé*, is deeply insidious in its apparently benign effects, creating its own sense of despair and frustration. Chamoiseau's ironic beatitude, '*Heureux ceux qui écrivent sous la domination de l'âge dernier: leurs poèmes peuvent faire des balles*' (*EPD*, p. 18, italics in original) is at once a recognition of literary belatedness, and an urgent acknowledgement of the threat that the relative political and economic (dis)ease poses to the artist. The contemporary Antillean, after all, 'n'affronte[s] qu'une mise sous assistances et subventions' (*EPD*, p. 18), a state which stifles, and yet for this very reason mandates, the move towards self-expression.[30]

One of the most striking aspects of the *créolité* movement is this confused temporality, an ambivalent mix of projection and retrospection, of prophetic proclamation and nostalgic regret. In reclaiming for the future the culture of the past, the *créolistes* find themselves perhaps in a typically postcolonial double bind. In *The Location of Culture*, Homi Bhabha describes a form of cultural reinscription that moves *back to the future*. 'I shall call it a "projective past", a form of the future anteriority'.[31] The pessimistic orientation of much of the fiction, which mourns the passing of traditional Creole traditions and customs, and suggests no real hope of their continuation in the future, sits uneasily with the forward-looking and projective tone of the *Eloge*. This time lag, heralded in the essayistic writing, is extensively played out in Chamoiseau's fiction, and will be discussed in more detail in the course of this study. For the paradox at the heart of the *créolistes*' writing is that in attempting to recover the 'mémoire vraie' of their native land, they run the risk of alienating the very local population whom they seek to celebrate. Meanwhile, they could be accused of providing an exotic sense of local colour for the French readership, while pandering to nostalgia rather than to genuine historical understanding. With specific reference to the literary endeavours of the *créolistes*, Richard and Sally Price speak for many when they suggest that their literary works are 'complicitous with the celebration of a museumified Martinique, a diorama'd Martinique, a picturesque and "pastified" Martinique that promotes a "feel-good" nostalgia for people who are otherwise adjusting to the complexities of a rapidly modernising lifestyle'.[32]

Of course, such nostalgia could be described as symptomatic of our contemporary postmodern condition. As theorists such as Fredric Jameson have pointed out, 'the insensible colonization of the present by the nostalgia mode' is a defining symptom of contemporary culture.[33] There is however an important distinction to be made between the postmodern as imagined by the *créolistes* and that which has more general currency. Writing specifically in the context of a post-Holocaust Germany, Eric Santner has identified 'a metaphorics of loss and impoverishment' as central to the (European) postmodern project, arguing that postmodern discourses mourn the absence of an already definitively lost organic society, and promote a 'perpetual leave-taking from fantasies of plenitude, purity, centrality, totality, unity and mastery'. Santner argues that the postmodern critic invites the reader

> to learn to tolerate the complexities and instabilities of new social arrangements as well as more hybrid, more 'creole', forms of personal, sexual, cultural, and political identity. It is a matter of learning to live as a nomad, as one disabused of notions of roots and rootedness and as one who has learned that survival is a constant improvisation.[34]

Santner's assessment is a very useful one in helping us to locate the faultline between the practice of the postmodern in the European and in the post-plantation society. For the values he identifies as the ones we must now 'learn to tolerate' are precisely those that have historically defined the Caribbean. As Martin Munro explains, 'the countries of the Caribbean have missed out a stage of wholeness of identity which began with the nineteenth-century nation states, and which was only later dismantled by the realities of cultural heterogeneity'.[35] This means that the prevalent sense of a deconstructed identity in Caribbean writing is generated less by the sense of a *loss* of wholeness, than by the sense that such plenitude never in fact existed. For it is the dereliction of secure origins, and therefore the absence of cultural stability, which is adduced by critics such as Antonio Benítez-Rojo as evidence of the Caribbean's supremely postmodern credentials.[36] Raphaël Confiant has stated that '[le] terme "Créole" est donc éminemment moderne [...] et même post-moderne dans le sens où il signale l'émergence d'une nouvelle identité qu'on pourrait appeler "multiple" ou "mosaïque"'.[37] Similarly, J. Michael Dash persuasively explains the particular applicability of a term which is often seen to be exclusively of relevance to Western society: 'There is a practice of the postmodern in the Caribbean that is not related to the concept of postmodernity in industrialized societies. The turbulence, the diversity, the indeterminacy left in the wake of the collapse of the plantation as a production site is no doubt the key to the application of the postmodern to the Caribbean archipelago'.[38] And it is precisely *towards* the Creole, the hybrid and the unstable that nostalgia is directed in the works of Chamoiseau and Confiant, who would argue that fantasies of purity or totality have not been lost, but rather have had little purchase in the Caribbean, and for whom the homogenizing tendencies of contemporary culture and media represent the greatest threat to what Chamoiseau has termed *diversalité*.

And yet, the celebration of hybridity does not in itself guarantee a radical poetics or politics. In *Colonial Desire*, for example, Robert Young sounds a cautionary note when he observes that 'today's self-proclaimed mobile and multiple identities may be a marker not of contemporary social fluidity and dispossession but of a new stability, self-assurance and quietism. Fixity of identity is only sought in situations of instability and disruption, of conflict and change'.[39] If we apply Young's insights to the contemporary Caribbean, it could be suggested that the free-floating signifier *créolité* functions as something of a cover-up, an excessively celebratory gloss. The fervour with which the apparently democratic ideal of *créolité* is upheld and celebrated could be said to distort or to airbrush out the realities of contemporary Antillean society, characterized by mass unemployment, drug abuse, economic paralysis and the increasing cultural and political stranglehold of France. This tension, between a theoretical rhetoric of celebration, and an often-evoked reality of stagnation and dependence, will be a recurrent concern in this study.

Locating Chamoiseau

The contemporary vitality of Antillean literature is frequently linked, by both writers and critics, to Patrick Chamoiseau's emergence. In addition to his creative output, he is a major postcolonial theorist, working directly in the tradition of Edouard Glissant, but having affinities with a number of postcolonial thinkers. His works have been widely translated into English, and are almost obligatory inclusions in courses on post-colonial literature, and on comparative Caribbean writing.[40] In a curious anomaly, perhaps, it is in fact Chamoiseau's fiction which is frequently cited in general comparative studies, while his more theoretical endeavours remain largely ignored by postcolonial theory, to its detriment. To date, and particularly since the award of the Prix Goncourt for his 1992 novel *Texaco*, he has been the subject of numerous scholarly articles and chapters. However, until very recently, no full-length study had been devoted to his work. Lorna Milne's *Patrick Chamoiseau: espaces d'une écriture antillaise* appeared as this study was nearing completion,[41] and marks a significant contribution to the growing body of criticism devoted to Chamoiseau's work. Milne's insightful reading foregrounds space as a persistent concern in Chamoiseau's writing. I hope that my approach complements hers in its privileging of the 'other' pole of this central nexus, time. In any case, despite the growing popularity of Caribbean writing, both in the United States, Canada and the UK and in the English-speaking Caribbean, this is the first full-length English-language study of Chamoiseau's work.

In the opening lines of his preface to Chamoiseau's first novel, *Chronique des sept misères*, added to the second edition of the novel, published in 1988,[42] Edouard Glissant declares that '[la] littérature antillaise de langue française qui avait beaucoup d'éclat *prend désormais corps*' (*CSM*, p. 3, my italics). It is no coincidence that in a recent interview Maryse Condé, in retrospective rather than projective mode, identifies 1985 as a turning point in French Caribbean writing, a moment she implicitly links to the incipient *créolité* movement.[43] Although frequently critical of Chamoiseau's theoretical work, Condé hints at his pre-eminent literary status in her autobiography, in a section whose title, 'Chemin d'école', is an intertextual *clin d'œil* to Chamoiseau's autobiography of the same name: 'La littérature des Antilles ne fleurissait pas encore. Patrick Chamoiseau dormait informé au fond du ventre de sa maman'.[44] H. Adlai Murdoch describes his writing as the 'pinnacle of contemporary francophone fiction writing',[45] while the critic Joseph

Nnadi is yet more explicit: 'Dire qu'une école littéraire se forme actuelle-ment autour de Patrick Chamoiseau, c'est sans aucun doute peu dire. Car il est évident que le nom "Chamoiseau" symbolise dans la Martinique des années 1990, plus encore qu'une école littéraire, un mouvement poli-tique, idéologique'.[46]

Chamoiseau is one of the contemporary writers who exhibits the most explicit and far-reaching concern with memory, a term which permeates his writing and which looms large even in his titles. His theo-retical interventions can be considered critical, if neglected, contributions to postcolonial theory, and in particular to the ongoing debates around postcolonial memory. His work (five novels, three autobiographies, several important theoretical essays and significant shorter pieces) explic-itly and consistently engages with the key debates in this highly contested field: the relationship between private and public memory, the border-line between history and fiction, the significance of repressed and traumatic memory, the processes and problematics of autobiographical memory, the relationship between the body and memory, the role of the witness and the archive in storing, transmitting and (de)forming memory, the lure of nostalgia, the commodification of memory. The symmetry in the titles of Chamoiseau's earliest novel (*Chronique des sept misères*, 1986) and his latest (*Biblique des derniers gestes*, 2002) registers a conti-nuity, even a coherence, in the concern with memory, a continuity which is borne out in patterns and consistencies which emerge from one work to the next: a preference for elderly (and usually childless) protagonists, who are vectors of popular memory and often personifications of a particular tradition now lost to the Antilles; an ongoing exposé of the wiping out of the past by the present in contemporary Martinique, an exposé often figured in a highly metaphorical way; a strong concern with intertextual memory and with literary precursors. It could be argued moreover that his preference for the novel form in itself signals an interest in temporality, memory and the reconstruction of past time. Fiction is the genre most closely associated with the accommodation of a histor-ical consciousness, and one whose extended scale allows for a grappling with the problematics of time through narrative. And, as Edward Said explains, novels are 'æsthetic objects that fill gaps in an incomplete world: they satisfy a human urge to add to reality'.[47] This impulse to add to or supplement reality has particular appeal in a context in which the sense of the past has been descisively ruptured; the desire to counteract the incompletion, or to 'fill in the blanks', of the past, may explain the domi-nance of fiction in contemporary Caribbean writing.

The key theoretical texts of the *créolité* movement were produced in collaboration, suggesting a sense of hybridity in the very genesis of the writing, as well as in its thematics.[48] Recently, this collaborative principle has been more pronounced still, in Chamoiseau's production of a series of works in conjunction with the Martinican photographer Jean-Luc de Laguarigue: *Elmire des sept bonheurs* (1998), *Tracées de mélancolies* (1999) and *Cases en pays-mêlés* (2000).[49] This collaborative practice injects a principle of hybridity into the very conception of the creative act, breaking down any sense of the impermeability of art forms and genres.[50] Indeed, not only are text and image juxtaposed in these works, but Laguarigue's background, as a member of the white *béké* caste, inflects the collaboration with a sense of racial and social hybridity. These works can be described as 'photo-texts', a term coined by Jefferson Hunter to describe a genre of 'composite publications evoking a land-scape or recording a history, celebrating a community or mourning a loss'.[51] Although in novels such as *Solibo* and *Texaco* photography is shown to be a highly suspect art, manipulated by characters to authenticate spurious truths, and generally implicated in a touristic and exoticizing gaze, it acts here as a powerful supplement to the written word. For, as Susan Sontag has argued, photography is a form particularly suited to the global postmodern. 'It is a nostalgic time right now', she writes, 'and photographs actively promote nostalgia'.[52] She continues,

> Photography is an elegiac art, a twilight art. Most subjects photographed are, just by virtue of being photographed, touched with pathos... all photographs are *memento mori*. To take a photograph is to participate in another person's (or thing's) mortality, vulnerability, mutability. Precisely by slicing out this moment and freezing it, all photographs testify to time's relentless melt.[53]

The photographs in works such as *Elmire des sept bonheurs* (often black-and-white portraits of aged Creole people, or colour images of privileged sites of Creole identity – the plantation, the distillery, the house) are highly elegiac in quality. In the combination of a nostalgic tenor and an obvious referentiality (names, locations, dates and even times are frequently specified), these works in many ways can be seen to express *both* plenitude and loss.

Finally, if memory is an explicit theme of Chamoiseau's writing, there is also a sense in which, at the textual level, the reader's memory is being repeatedly activated and stretched. The remarkable coherence of the project means that one's attention is continually drawn to striking similarities of plot and theme, as well as to recurrences of characters, events and indeed of intertextual networks from one work to the next. This nexus of interrelations, echoes and doublings means that most novels reference other Chamoiseau novels, heralding those under preparation or referring back to already published works. This self-referential reach breaks through the fact–fiction boundary, so that in *Biblique*, for example, the writings of Sarah-Anaïs-Alicia, the 'Livret des lieux du deuxième monde', bears a remarkable similarity to the (real) short text released at the same time as *Biblique*, the *Livre des villes du deuxième monde*.

But, more significantly perhaps, there is a strong linguistic and stylistic dimension to this ongoing appeal to the reader's memory. Pierre Gamarra, in an early review of Chamoiseau's work, observes that 'on constatera au fil de la lecture un phénomène intéressant. Sans qu'il soit toujours besoin de notes, de glossaire ou d'explications extérieures, nous pénétrons de mieux en mieux cette langue, *nous apprenons à lire*'.[54] Such an initiation is of course itself an effect of memory. Gradually, as individual works progress, and particularly in the cumulative effect of reading across works, the reader has the sense of being initiated into a linguistic as well as a fictional world. Like someone learning a new language, there is a sense of satisfaction at absorbing and recognizing unfamiliar vocabulary – by osmosis and informed guesswork, rather than by explanation and definition – and at being able to find one's way around this linguistically obscure *œuvre*. This is at least partly because Creole itself is, as Glissant has shown, an opaque language of resistance and detour. While English translations of the work have attempted to be faithful to this opacity, there is an inevitable loss of obscurity in the recasting of these works not only into another language, but into a language which has no ideological investment in the deliberate practice of linguistic camouflage. In any case, the active engagement of the reader's memory is one of the most pleasurable aspects of reading this dense, playful and highly self-aware work.

Writing in a recent companion to postcolonial literatures, Benita Parry argues that 'the emergent canon of postcolonial writing has created its own exclusions and blind spots'. She continues, 'the privileging of postcolonial styles which animate a postcolonial identity as fissured, unstable and multiply located can be related to the manifest preference in the postcolonial discussion for mestizo or creolized formations, the corollary of which is a tendency to scant the intelligibility, mutability and inventiveness of the indigenous'.[55] Parry specifically mentions Chamoiseau, along with figures such as Salman Rushdie, Gabriel García

Márquez and Ben Okri, as responding to our contemporary taste for magic realism rather than realism, and as exemplifying the decision to write in a dominant language rather than a dominated one. Moreover, she argues that the experimental styles and audacious word-play that characterize such texts means that they fit nicely the 'linguistic turn' that characterizes much postcolonial criticism. And yet I would argue that Chamoiseau's success is evidence of much more than linguistic or stylistic play. At its best, his work is a deeply political attempt to explore the compelling momentum of modernization in the Caribbean, while simultaneously recreating the culture of the past. In the course of this study, the interplay of language and politics, of ethics and æsthetics, in the forging of a highly distinctive memorial literature, will be at the heart of my analysis.

The continuity in the preoccupation with memory is of course remarkable, and each of Chamoiseau's texts could be read through the optic of loss and nostalgia which we have been exploring above. This applies as easily to the autobiographies, which profess a sense of loss of the magical childhood apprehension of the world, as it does to individual novels, which lament the demise of the oral tradition, or the local market culture, or the sense of community forged in, and sustained by, the dynamics of the Creole *quartier*. And even the latest novel, whose very title connotes a sense of nostalgia (we are in the presence of the 'derniers gestes' of an old man) essentially explores two distinct, and polarized worlds: the 'pays officiel' and the 'pays enterré'. The contrast between an official, but superficial, dominant culture, and a repressed authentic variant, remains a structural as well as a thematic principle.

This study will follow a broadly chronological sweep. This structure is not simply a convenient organizational principle, however. Although the first and the last chapters focus on a single work, most chapters counterpoint several texts, so as to suggest recurring and significant themes and issues. It is hoped that this approach will give a sense of Chamoiseau's consistent return to particular concerns, while bringing out the development of his work as an *œuvre*, and highlighting its increasingly experimental style and its growing ambition. The memorial aspirations of the most recent novel – at 789 pages, the longest in the Caribbean tradition – are particularly noteworthy: this text evokes in some detail the Middle Passage, and indeed the beginnings of the universe itself, although it is ostensibly set in contemporary Martinique. Moreover, the novel marks a departure for Chamoiseau, moving outwards in space, and evoking many major anti-colonial struggles elsewhere in the world. This novel, while carrying through many familiar preoccupations, could be seen in terms of scale, scope and ambition as a culmination and a realization of an artistic and political vision developed over fifteen years.

Chapter 1, 'Beginnings: The Enigma of Origin', argues that Chamoiseau's first novel, *Chronique des sept misères*, constitutes an extended meditation on the notion of 'beginnings', announcing and crystallizing many of the ideas explored in later works. This chapter will introduce trauma theory as a way of exploring the presentation of slavery in the text. The 'unremembered' nature of slavery does not invalidate the work of theorists like Dominick LaCapra or Cathy Caruth; indeed criticism of women writers of the Black diaspora has been hugely influenced by work on trauma.[56] However, this body of theory has until now remained marginal to analyses of the French Caribbean. Chapter 2 examines the three volumes of autobiography that Chamoiseau produced between 1990 and 2005, arguing that his marked preference for the genre is further evidence of an obsession with beginnings, and, more generally, with memory. Chapter 3 will examine the representation of historical memory in Chamoiseau's work, drawing on postmodern theories of history, and examining the presentation of archives and orality in *Texaco* and *Solibo Magnifique*. Chapter 4, in contrast with the emphasis on orality in the previous chapter, looks in some detail at the growing significance of *physical* relics of the past – in particular the house, and the stones and bones which become increasingly prominent in later work – as evidence of a yearning for a more material, ontologically grounded connection to the past. The final chapter is devoted to Chamoiseau's most recent novel, and his most experimental to date, *Biblique des derniers gestes*. This chapter will return to the theories of trauma introduced in Chapter 1, in an attempt to explain the hallucinatory and excessive nature of this novel, and to identify slavery, a seemingly marginal feature of the novel, as being in fact at its traumatic core.

The subtitle of this study, 'Recovering Memory', does not suggest any definitive or settled retrieval. Its present participle gestures towards a provisional, tentative and continuous process, rather than towards the absolute 'recovery' of any original memory or identity. Moreover, 'recovering' should also be read as an adjective; the traumas of slavery, as I suggested above, have not until relatively recently found an outlet in writing. This study will discuss how, in Chamoiseau's work, attempts to recover (bring back) the memory of the past have contributed to a collective and individual coming to terms with, and, potentially, a recovery from, its effects. It is hoped that in bringing the theme of memory to the forefront of my analysis, and in considering this highly memorial writing alongside work done in a wider context, insights will be generated which will have resonance in the broader field of postcolonial literary studies.

CHAPTER 1

Beginnings: The Enigma of Origin

Chronique des sept misères, Chamoiseau's first novel, establishes many
of the key concerns which will be further explored in his later writings.
It deals throughout, and in a very direct way, with the confrontation
between memory and oblivion, and presents a pessimistic diagnosis of
the possibilities for memory, and hence self-knowledge, in contemporary
Martinique. The novel is structured around a fall from grace: it traces
the island's transition from an economy based on the local Creole market
in the early twentieth century to its brutal entry into the world of modernity, consumerism and global capital in the aftermath of World War II.
In many ways, this is a move from diversity to uniformity, a decline
signalled even in the names of the French supermarkets (Prisunic;
Monoprix) springing up on the island. In this new world of consumerism
and non-production, the local market has been usurped by global
economic interests; the instinctive, wily knowledge of the collective
protagonists, the *djobeurs*,[1] along with the 'agencement imperceptible'
of the marketplace, have become surplus to requirements. Thus, in its
concern with the Western values of development and progress *Chronique
des sept misères* – whose title will echo in two later works, *Elmire des
sept bonheurs* and *Biblique des derniers gestes* – inaugurates a body of
work which will be consistently critical of the stifling of Creole culture
by the (neo)colonial process.

And yet *Chronique* is also atypical of subsequent writings in several
significant ways. The creolization of French, which will become such a
signature device of *Solibo Magnifique* and *Texaco*, is not yet in evidence;
rather, conventional explanatory footnotes or bracketed translations,
clarifying Creole expressions and filling in local historical or botanical
knowledge for the (presumably French) reader, punctuate the text. More
significantly for the purposes of this chapter, *Chronique* does not feature
the *marqueur de paroles*, the authorial alter ego found in all the other
novels, whose reflections on the act of writing have provided such fertile
ground for critics interested in metafiction and postmodern narrative. It
is precisely this metafictional dimension which facilitates or signposts the
explicit foregrounding of memory in other texts. Its absence in *Chronique*
has ensured that this theme (and, as I will argue, the memory of slavery

in particular) has been somewhat overlooked in critical analyses. Existing criticism underplays, for example, the novel's ending, in particular the importance of the ghost-slave Afoukal, and concentrates heavily on the theme of departmentalization, thereby sidelining the significance of slavery. And while important analyses of symbolic locations (the market-place and, by extension, the town) have been produced, these studies have tended towards an overly positive, and indeed unduly positivistic, reading. Richard Burton sees the novel's characters as cunning tacticians of daily life, enterprising and adaptable creatures who, while implicitly aware that they will never manage to overturn the structures of power, succeed in opposing the system from within.[2] Valérie Loichot suggests that the dynamic of the novel, and in particular its division into two sections, 'Inspiration' and 'Expiration', does not necessarily indicate an inexorable progression towards the erasure of Creole culture: 'On peut cependant y voir la binarité rythmique [...] où l'herbe bleue importée de Métropole finit toujours par être remplacée par l'herbe bleue des campagnes'. She argues that this cyclical dynamic of inspiration/expira-tion might imply an ongoing, eternally renewable rhythm: 'à l'expiration succède l'inspiration, à l'hivernage le carême'.[3]

This chapter will pursue a different line, arguing that *Chronique des sept misères* is, as its title suggests, an essentially pessimistic work, one in which a widespread melancholic reverence towards a lost (recent) past acts as a screen memory for a much more traumatic and unrecoverable origin. In other words, in lamenting the decline of the market as a site of memory and of 'authentic' Creole culture, the novel's characters (like its critics, to a certain extent) marginalize and repress the story of slavery, a story which acquires an increasing importance as the story progresses. Chamoiseau's first full-length narrative is itself, then, a meditation on the insecurity of beginnings, a story in which origins, and by extension endings, are especially precarious. On a structural level, complicated genealogical patterns, pronominal shifts and convoluted, wayward narratives contribute to this sense of fragility, so that the instability of narrative form can be seen to reflect both the characters' fractured sense of selfhood, and their contemporary social and economic reality. The fragility of individual and collective memory, and the inability to remember or make sense of the past in all its forms, make for a debili-tating precariousness of identity, so that characters have an unsatisfactory relationship to themselves, to others and to history more broadly. This weakened subjectivity and the lack of self-presence are epit-omized by the *djobeurs'* observation that 'nous étions là sans être là' (p.

218). In this respect, *Chronique* can be distinguished from later works such as *Texaco*, in which, as Lorna Milne has rightly observed, 'individuality, the sense of self and innate personal characteristics are presented as an essential given of the subject'.[4] The story of the collective 'beginning' is the lacuna which explains the instability of the narrative voice, and the voided identity and lack of authority of the novel's characters. And it is this unremembered 'beginning' which Pipi will inadvertently uncover, however unsatisfactorily, in his relationship with Afoukal. Despite its contemporary setting and concerns, then, *Chronique* in fact carries through a perennial preoccupation with what René Depestre calls 'le naufrage ontologique de l'homme dans les plantations'.[5]

The Redundancy of Memory

Early in their disjointed narrative, the *djobeurs* declare that 'notre participation à la vie du marché n'avait point, comme pour les tôles du toit, les grilles ou le ciment des établis, *la confortable certitude d'y être indispensable*' (p. 15, my italics). Their narrative is itself a study of redundancy and insecurity; very little in this story, on either a thematic or a structural level, is comfortably certain or clearly indispensable. Rather, the precarious socio-economic, cultural and political condition of the community (and in particular the hand-to-mouth existence of the *djobeurs*) is conveyed on a narrative level by redundancy and a sense of randomness and improvisation. Names, unsurprisingly in a plantation context where, historically, they were bestowed by the white master, are frequently unreliable indicators of identity in Caribbean writing. Here, however, their function is particularly unstable and random. They are occasionally markers of a character trait, serving to fix or reflect identity (Théophile Paville is indeed devout), and are sometimes ironically inappropriate (despite the sunny connotations of his name, Félix Soleil is a miserable bully). But names tend most frequently to have an inbuilt redundancy, whether it be the empty, hyphenated repetition of Anatole-Anatole or the tautology of Chine le Chinois, the Beckettian symmetry of Pipi and Gogo, the legion *ManMans* and *Papas*, empty signifiers attached to tenuous signifieds, or the plodding reverberation of Didon and Pin-Pon. Names tend, moreover, to be multiple, and are adopted and then shed with an ease which befits this tenuousness. For example, Héloïse becomes Man Elo; Elyette becomes Man Paville, and later in life is known as Odibert, while the character known as Bidjoule for most of the novel turns out to have been christened Daniel.

The diegetic time of the narrative hinges on Martinique's departmentalization (1946), the event which separates the two halves of the novel, 'Inspiration' and 'Expiration'. And it is in the precise context of departmentalization that the decline of the old market acquires its fullest metaphorical charge. For, as Celia Britton has argued, assimilation – which was enshrined in and accelerated by the 1946 law – is also a digestive metaphor.[6] While the Caribbean islands are associated, in the popular imagination, with the export foodstuffs (rum, pineapples, bananas), the reality of the contemporary Antilles is in fact that the traffic is going overwhelmingly in the opposite direction. The Antillean people are now feeding on over-priced metropolitan food mainly purchased in French-owned supermarkets, and have forgotten local traditions of sourcing and cooking food. The opening lines of 'Expiration' are therefore particularly poignant:

> Messieurs et dames de la compagnie, à mesure que passait le temps, les avions et bateaux de France augmentaient. Ils amenaient des caisses de marchandises à bon marché, des pommes et raisins exotiques à nous chavirer le cœur, des produits inconnus en conserves, sous cellophane, ou en sachets sous vide. (p. 133)

Everything in this description suggests artificiality, sterility and a rupture with natural rhythms and lifespans, from the 'exotic' fruit (apples and grapes, which displace the local mangoes and letchies), to the preserves and the cellophane packs which, by sealing out air, prolong the shelf life of the imported product. The journey has been foreshadowed, moreover, by another ghostly trans-Atlantic crossing. The contemporary boats and planes retraverse an axis of the triangle of trade initiated by the slave ship, a vessel which also carried, in bulk, a cargo of exotic and alien products: African slaves. Like these new commodities, the slave cargo was cheap, tightly packed, and was to a chilling extent 'sous vide', emptied out of memory and identity.

As in other novels, contemporary Martinique is caught up in the unstoppable march towards modernity, and is much more beholden to the tourist souvenir than to any authentic and organic memory. This loss of memory is explicitly linked to the island's rapid assimilation; the first page of the second section, evoking the immediate aftermath of the 'coup de loi' conferring departmental status, describes a new and sterile cityscape of plastic shop façades, neon lights and shoddy apartment blocks. Likewise, *Chronique* resonates with references to tourism, an industry shown to be deeply injurious to memory, and yet which is the only area of the Martinican economy to have flourished in recent years. The Creole market, a crucible of community and orality (people come certainly to 's'acheter le manger du jour', but more importantly to 's'aiguiser la langue sur disputes et paroles inutiles', p. 49), degenerates into a spectacle to be consumed by sightseers (p. 140), and has by the end of the novel become a parody of its former self, a kind of theme park with its 'carafes à touristes et [...] babioles made-in-et cætera' (p. 215). There is a particular irony in the fact that the giant yam, the transport of which confirmed Pipi's status as 'roi des djobeurs', becomes a celebrated attraction at a time when the community is starving. The tourists who descend upon the market are there not to purchase any of its produce, but rather to view the overgrown root and to pay to photograph it. In other words, the vegetable has become an article for visual rather than oral consumption and, as we will see in the course of this study, the 'visualization' of culture (photography, television, museums) can have disastrous consequences for memory.[7] As Susan Sontag reminds us, 'Whatever the moral claims made on behalf of photography, its main effect is to convert the world into a department store or museum-without-walls in which every subject is depreciated into an article of consumption, promoted as an item for æsthetic appreciation'.[8] Thus, it is the copy which has economic value rather than the original, and what Sontag calls the 'article of consumption', in this case the yam, is merely a visual or an æsthetic commodity, entirely divorced from its original nutritional function.

The terms used to describe the new kind of transaction occasioned by the yam, in their tongue-in-cheek suggestion of productivity and economic activity ('*L'industrie* dura quelques mois jusqu'à ce que l'igname ne devienne une crème véreuse'; '*La récolte* de billets étranges que donnaient les touristes...', p. 97, my italics), serve only to underline the extent to which this production economy has lapsed into one of passive *re*-production, epitomized in the obsession with photographs. This degeneration from primary to tertiary industry is clearly symptomatic of the fate of the country as a whole. Moreover, it is not coincidental that the new 'industry' threatens to destroy the market altogether (the stench of the rotting vegetable is such that had it not eventually been removed, the *djobeurs* would have had to abandon the market), nor that it is only the intervention of the council authorities, the avatars of colonial control in the city, which finally resolves the problem. For, as will be seen in more detail later, one of the most pernicious effects of departmentalization is the infantilization of the Antillean people, which perpetuates a sense of dependency, helplessness and redundancy. By the second half of the novel, the site of the market is unquestionably one of spectacle rather than of memory, and the objectifying impulse of the touristic gaze has become entirely normalized. For example, the advice offered by a young student about crop rotation and diversification is dismissed as an empty performance, having no more effect than 'un charabia de haute-taille pour touristes' (p. 135). Later, the *djobeurs* casually observe that they have become curios in their own land, displaying themselves as an absurd commodity in the market 'en vue d'une séance de photos avec des savants canadiens' (p. 140).

By the novel's end, most of the major characters are dead (Pipi, Chinotte, Bidjoule, Man Goul, Ti-Joge), and the Creole market, the space around which their activity was concentrated, has been definitively destroyed. In contrast to other novels, there is no triumph or redemption, however mitigated (the perpetuation of Solibo's wisdom; the survival of Texaco) or reconciliation (the return of the old warrior in *Biblique*). Rather, in the 'Annexe' which closes the novel, the 'Note de l'ethnographe' laments: 'Aujourd'hui: plus un seul djobeur dans les marchés de Fort-de-France. Plus une seule brouette. Leur mémoire a cessé d'exister' (p. 243). This memory is doubly obliterated: both the memory possessed *by* the *djobeurs* themselves (the skill of making and handling the wheelbarrow, of ingratiation with a particular *marchande*, of negotiating the streets of Fort-de-France), and any collective popular recall, by the community at large, of their very existence, have vanished. In other words, and in a manner symptomatic of tradition in Martinique generally, the aged *djobeurs* have forgotten their contemporary reality and are forgotten by it.

On a diegetic level, the threat of amnesia is insidious and all-pervasive; at times it threatens to stall narrative entirely. Spontaneous individual recall is rare, and when it occurs it is figured as a bringing back to the surface of long-buried or distant material. Clarine finds 'dans une case fraîche de sa tête' (p. 57) the shards of the past that Pipi will reintegrate in narrative form, while Man Goul, on the arrival of Anastase, resurrects from a 'trou perdu de sa tête' (p. 119) the ability to laugh and smile; the use of the word 'tête', moreover, emphasizes the corporeal rather than intellectual activity of memory, a point to which we shall return later. But more frequently, characters forget each other's existence, and fail to recall even major parts of their own past. Forgetting, as we will see in the case of Clarine, can be mobilized deliberately, to quell the pain of the past and to assume control of the present, or invoked as a strategy to better ensure the preservation of certain other memories.[9] But it tends more often to operate in a sporadic, all-encompassing and ultimately debilitating manner. Fanotte, as her name suggests, simply fades out of existence. Her body cannot be located when her husband is buried years later, and Anatole-Anatole's comment – 'Hébin, je l'avais oubliée' (p. 32) – is typical. Amédée, Ti-Joge's mother, has already forgotten the name of his sailor-father by the time he is born (p. 70). And the *djobeurs*-narrators are, like the collective consciousness they represent, equally susceptible to oblivion. They comment at one point, 'quant à Anastase, le monde de ce morne l'oublia' (p. 117), and immediately reiterate this forgetting, as though they had already forgotten their own amnesia. The politically active student, intent on imparting her views to the community, is similarly forgotten (p. 136), and even a fairly major character such as Ti-Joge would have been forgotten 's'il n'avait surgi parfois à sa fenêtre, cheveux blanchis, pâle et défait' (p. 139). The female elders, so often in Caribbean fiction the primary transmitters of collective memory, are particularly prone to oblivion. Man Goul's memory is described as 'fatiguée' (p. 109), while Manman-Doudou, 'qui n'avait aucune mémoire de ses paroles' (p. 48), trots out the same stories to Héloïse day after day. Their effect on the younger woman, in turn, is to help her to '*oubli*[er] ses propres malheurs' (p. 48, my italics). At such moments, narrative itself is undermined or engulfed by oblivion, and amnesia functions not only to anæsthetize characters against their past, but also to leave gaps in the narrative which cannot be filled by the reader.

Narrative is further destabilized in that it refuses to settle into a singular, monologic version, and doubt and uncertainty are integral to the storytelling activity. But this uncertainty is not explicitly signposted as in *Texaco* or *Biblique*, novels whose postmodern credentials make them overtly sceptical towards empirical truth. Rather, in *Chronique*, a low-level and unsettling randomness prevails. Frequently, information is provided and then rendered redundant by a subsequent undermining clause. At one point, for example, the *djobeurs*, who claim to have witnessed the scene in question, comment that 'Anatole-Anatole embrassa son fils durant plusieurs secondes, ou beaucoup moins, comment savoir?' (p. 45). Likewise they describe Anastase's imprisonment for stabbing Zozor Alcide-Victor, but conclude: 'Elle doit encore y être, ou elle n'y est plus, quelle importance?' (p. 221). Later Man Goul recounts the story of Ti-Choute and Féfé, concluding that '[elles] sont encore dans cette case, ou elles n'y sont plus, c'est possible' (p. 117). Facts are thus established and then cancelled out with an unsettling immediacy, calling into question the truth value of the narrative more generally, and making it difficult to locate a stable position from which to read and interpret. And the fact that these 'facts' are in themselves fairly insignificant or contingent – if not completely irrelevant – to the overall development of the plot only serves to make their inclusion all the more puzzling. At the end of the novel the *djobeurs* declare that the only certainty is their imminent disappearance: 'Nous disons et redisons ces paroles, ces souvenirs de vie, avec la certitude de devoir disparaître. Vous en donner cette version nous a fait un peu de bien, si vous venez demain vous en aurez une autre, peut-être plus optimiste, quelle importance?' (p. 240). Any account is provisional and can be undone by a subsequent retelling. Empirical evidence is thus invoked and then dispensed with, so that incompleteness and reversibility dominate the telling. But the casual randomness with which this is effected makes this an unsettling reading experience, one in which the situations and events evoked are frequently incidental, and in which accident appears to be the norm.

The novel puts subjectivity and psychological realism under strain, so that self-knowledge, motivation and self-assurance are repeatedly undermined. Thus, none of the characters can be considered fully constituted discursive subjects. With the exception of Pipi and Bidjoule, the eponymous *sept misères* have an entirely unindividuated status, commenting at the end of the novel that they are 'incapables du Je, du Tu, de distinguer les uns des autres, dans une survie collective et diffuse' (p. 240). Characters frequently do not know why they behave in certain ways (p. 72; p. 78; p. 96; p. 99), and the absence of an omniscient perspective means that such narrative lacunæ remain unfilled. Throughout the text, many characters are introduced only to be written out or forgotten with hyperbolic frequency, often in flukish circumstances that stretch credibility. Théophile Paville is crushed by a car in the garage where he works; Gogo dies in a freak accident at sea; Odibert, Gogo's wife, is reduced to dust before the eyes of the assembled crowd. Even characters who have not figured significantly in the diegesis meet unlikely ends. Emma is carried away by a cyclone, and Anastase's grandmother is trampled to death in a Calcutta riot. However, the affective economy of the novel works against the exploration of any kind of inner emotional life, and in particular the expression of grief or sentiment. The outrageous fate of many characters means that they tend to be unindividuated in terms of psychological depth, and have such a fragile purchase on affective depth – and hence on narrative security – that they are dispensed with casually and rarely mourned or even missed. Characters are literally self-effacing; the *djobeurs* declare at the end of the novel that they are 'victimes d'une gomme invisible' and that 'nous nous effacions de la vie' (p. 216). This means, inevitably, that the reader's memory is in turn called into question or undermined. The sheer number of characters, plots and subplots, the weakened sense of subjectivity of characters 'under erasure', the convoluted relationships which obtain between characters, and the shifting or multiple names, all challenge the memory of even the most attentive reader. Equally, there are frequent slippages in narrative perspective, so that narrators give way to and supplant each other, weakening the 'hold' they have over the story being told: all of these factors combine to undermine realist notions of coherence, causality and the autonomy of the individual self, and in so doing undermine the reader's grasp of the story.

Frequently, too, the facts of the plot are insufficient to explain the behaviour of characters, teasing but not entirely satisfying the 'sense-making' agenda of the reader. We are told, for example, that Clarine and Gogo have sex once and then never again, but no reason is given for this (p. 63). General de Gaulle is introduced as an 'espèce de vakabon sans foi ni loi', but a page later has been transformed, inexplicably, into the more familiar hero 'Papa de Gaulle' (pp. 54–55).[10] Elsewhere, blatant inconsistencies emerge. In a typical disjunction between the narrative of the *djobeurs* and the evidence afforded by the text, we learn that for Pipi 'l'absence de père avait sans doute toujours vrillé sa chair' (p. 52). And yet the young child has been described in a manner that emphasizes physical and mental strength, giving an impression of unusual solidity and wellbeing. He is 'calme, avec des gestes ronds' (p. 50); he matures quickly, and he readily adapts to the rules of his environment. At another point, we are told that unlike Ti-Joge, Pipi is 'insoucieux du passé' (p. 94), a statement which openly conflicts with the latter's already well-established quest for collective memory. Similarly, the aphorisms and proverbs which pepper this text sit uneasily with the events recounted. Many of these sayings refer to generational continuity and perpetuation, while the text itself works to undermine such notions of linear transmission and inheritance. At the start of the novel, for example, the narrators explain that their forefathers have instilled in them the skill of the *djob* ('ils se bâtirent et nous héritâmes de leur science', p. 16), while they have specifically highlighted, a page earlier, their very lack of ancestry. When Pipi meets his *dorlis* father, the narrators comment 'quand le sang rencontre le sang il n'y a plus de barrières' (p. 52), and later we are told that 'les petits du tigre ne naissent pas sans griffes' (p. 101). Yet throughout the novel, as we have seen, blood ties are extremely fragile and easily undone. Such aphorisms, then, which imply a continuity in – and perpetuation of – memory across generations, are undercut by the events in the novel, and demonstrate the fallibility of the narrative voice.

One of these aphorisms stands out, however, for its applicability not simply on a circumstantial and thematic level, but equally for its pertinence to form and structure. In one of the many references to fate in the text, we are told that 'Le destin met toujours un *milieu* et un *bout*' (p. 108, my italics). What is missing from this formula, however, is precisely the 'beginning' of the story. The difficulty of beginning, and the absence of beginnings, in collective, familial and individual terms, will be explored in the next section of this chapter.

Difficult Beginnings, Enigmatic Origins

If the elusiveness of secure beginnings – genesis, initiation, foundation – characterizes all experience, then this insecurity is all the more pressing for the postcolonial, and in particular the diasporic, writer. Edward Said argues that 'whether an interest in beginnings is practical or highly theoretical, there is an imperative connection to be observed between the idea of a beginning and an aboriginal human need to point to or locate a beginning'.[11] With specific reference to the Caribbean, Mary Gallagher identifies the 'difficulty of locating the beginning' as one of the distinguishing features of the Caribbean condition, and an obsessive concern in the region's writing.[12] Kathleen Gyssels, too, argues that the predilection for paratextual density displayed by so many Caribbean writers is evidence of an 'entrée en écriture difficile': 'Tout se passe comme si les Antillais ont la plus grande difficulté à commencer'.[13] Indeed Chamoiseau himself, in a later novel, acknowledges the tortuous difficulty in locating a fixed or satisfactory starting point: 'ici on ne commence pas […] on diffracte soudain' (*BDG*, p. 33). And, as I discussed in the Introduction, narrative prose is itself a medium that seeks to fill in gaps in temporality, and to explore history and origins.

Chronique des sept misères, as a first novel, is a narrative beginning for Chamoiseau in a very literal sense. And it opens, significantly, with a series of false starts: in addition to title pages, it includes (at least in its second edition) a preface from Glissant, a number of dedications signed PC, an epigraph from *Le Discours antillais*, a preamble from the *djobeurs*, and then finally, and somewhat ironically, a heavily signposted 'beginning': 'au démarrage, prenons le commencement, donc sa mère'. As we have seen, this is a text in which characters strive for legitimacy, security and ancestry, yet in which they frequently remain ignorant of their own individual and collective genesis. Their insecurity can therefore be seen to have a strong metafictional corollary in the 'surcharge paratextuelle' which surrounds *Chronique*.[14] While this novel is less freighted with epigraphs and dedications than some, Glissant's 'priority', in both senses of the word, as an interruptive and deferring presence, is inescapable. The older writer, an important (overbearing?) precursor, is given quite literally the first word in the Preface, which interestingly was added to the second Folio edition of the novel, and entitled 'Un marqueur de paroles'. In other words, even though the novel had achieved not inconsiderable success in its first edition, the presence of Glissant bolsters the legitimacy of the product. Moreover the first section of the text, significantly entitled 'Inspiration', opens with an epigraph from *Le Discours antillais*. It is striking that a novel so concerned with absent and substitute parents opens with such a blatant legitimising strategy, signalling affiliation to the literary father. For, as Jay Clayton explains, 'Both narrative and authority are grounded in notions of a generative beginning, a source that can control its issue and maintain the continuity of its course. Narrative creates authority, but at the same time one must have authority to begin to narrate'.[15] In the absence of a secure, long-standing literary tradition within which to work, and at the threshold of Chamoiseau's career as a novelist, the author-ity of Glissant is twice invoked, and will continue to inflect Chamoiseau's literary career.[16]

While its title promises a chronicle, by definition a 'register of events in the order of their occurrence' (OED), a fully-drawn developmental account, the narrative weave of *Chronique des sept misères* is a tangled one, dominated by gaps and fissures and by the pervasive force of forgetting. The Book of Chronicles, the novel's biblical pre-text, opens with an extended series of genealogical lists, tracing the regal lines, from father to son, of kings such as David and Solomon. *Chronique*, however, foregrounds the maternal genealogy of its protagonist Pipi Soleil, described in mock-heroic terms as the 'roi de la brouette'. And yet this is clearly no straightforward matrilineal inversion or mirror image of the family tree. While the opening flirts with the notion of 'beginning at the beginning' ('au démarrage...'), and pays lip service to chronological continuity, the reader is cast into a diffuse and rhizomatic narrative which branches far from the direct lineage of Pipi to trace the family trees of Clarine, Ti-Joge, Chinotte and Kouli, among many others. Stories pile up, collide, re-emerge and overtake each other, to such an extent that the novel, in its disjointed, non-linear form, can be said to be structured like memory itself. Indeed in one of the annexes to the novel, 'Paroles de djobeurs', Chamoiseau states that an earlier version was marked by an even more chaotic structure: 'Le texte initial était d'une complexité qui voulait *rappeler le fonctionnement normal de la mémoire*, fonctionnement jamais linéaire, tout en ruptures de temps, de lieux, de tons et de manières' (p. 247, my italics). Not only, then, is memory a central theme of the novel, but the text's very structure, although apparently now 'ordonné' by the writer, nonetheless stems from an attempt to replicate the meanders, circularity and unpredictability of memory.

Narrative, in its proliferating tangents and its rhizomatic, paratactic structures, reflects the profound disturbance in genealogy and lines of descent. Although the novel continually foregrounds the notion of origins, *Chronique* is haunted by parental absence, oblivion, neglect and indifference, clearly metaphors for the lack of memory, and obscurity of origins, of the Antillean people more generally. The absent father is of course a stock character in Caribbean fiction, and indeed is a prominent figure here: Alphonse Antoinette 's'enfuit en zigzag' on realising his imminent paternity (p. 60); Clarine's father is as distant as the horizon (p. 57); Pipi's paternity is a taboo; most hypocritically, Zozor Alcide-Victor's father swears that he will never forget his son ('qu'Allah me terrasse si jamais je l'oublie', p. 121), before proceeding to do exactly that. Such paternal irresponsibility pervades Antillean writing. What is more surprising is the extent to which *all* filial bonds – and in particular the mother–child dyad – have been disrupted here. For in this novel, unusually, mothering becomes the site of a two-way oblivion, in that children (and particularly daughters) forget their mothers and mothers, ostensibly at least, reciprocate this forgetting. Thus the young Héloïse, who lives with her domineering and misogynistic father, finds no compensatory comfort in the maternal relationship. Rather she, like her father and eight sisters, 'avait fini par oublier Fanotte, tellement discrète parmi les hardes de la paillasse' (p. 28). Clarine abandons and instantly forgets her mother, Emma, after the latter has brought her to a witchdoctor for an abortion – an intervention which in itself aims to interrupt genealogy, to obstruct lines of descent and to dissolve the past. Later, Clarine's second pregnancy is characterized by its *not* awakening any ancestral maternal instinct (p. 68), and the child remains 'anonyme'. She eventually abandons the baby in order to remake herself ('se faire neuve') for her new lover, and leaves her son 'le pas presque léger, le cœur ouvert sur Ti-Joge' (pp. 72–73). Hence her designation as a 'mère oublieuse', a title which recurs somewhat obsessively in the text (p. 56; p. 57; p. 63) and which is eventually shortened to 'L'Oublieuse'.

This presentation of the mother–child relationship – precisely because it hinges on neither rejection nor acceptance, but rather on disengagement, apathy and oblivion – radically rewrites one of the primary sustaining myths of black womanhood. It is the female characters' casual *indifference* which most directly subverts the affective economy of this supposedly matrifocal society. For it bears repetition that in Antillean writing motherhood has often figured as the central pillar of female identity, either the root of oppression – hence often actively rejected through its association with the slave past – or the wellspring of women's strength. That mothers can beget and then forget, or that a daughter can nonchalantly overlook her mother's disappearance, is symptomatic of a profound malaise. Indeed, from this perspective, it could be argued that Clarine complicates the very paradigm which she seems initially to epitomize. For it is precisely the deliberateness of her decision – a pragmatic, hard-headed choice to conceal her past in order not to jeopardize her new romance – which sets her apart from the other indifferent mothers and daughters. Her very designation as 'L'Oublieuse' points to a whole-hearted assumption of an identity, as well as to an unusual sense of agency. Moreover, Clarine never quite forgets her son; as Pipi wryly comments to the now dead Daniel/Bidjoule, 'c'est l'oublieuse qui paya ton cercueil' (p. 140). To the extent that her forgetting is voluntary, Clarine is less a victim than an agent of amnesia; in order to forget as a deliberate strategy, one has to remember (to forget).

In any case, the fracturing of the parent–child relationship is deeply rooted in the collective imaginary, and is most consistently explored on the discursive and metaphorical level. Richard Burton has studied in detail the remarkable persistence of a familial discourse in the conceptualization of the (post)colonial relationship between Martinique and France, and in particular the internalization of these very terms by the colonized population.[17] Evidence of this internalization runs throughout *Chronique*. Just as the *djobeurs* are 'dispersés, anonymes et sans clans' (p. 50), so the Martinican people are frequently presented as orphaned, and in search of a meaningful relationship with that sexually doubled figure, the *mère-patrie*. The narrators declare at the outset that the novel is the 'histoire des anonymes' and ask 'Comment connaître qui furent nos pères?' (p. 15). Later, they celebrate the advent of departmentalization 'avec la frénésie qu'ont généralement les orphelins quand une mère les recueille' (p. 134). But any sense of recognition from a generous and beneficent mother-figure is inevitably short-lived. Soon afterwards, as the euphoria of departmentalization gives way to a realization of increased dependency, they comment that 'Notre seule mère c'est la déveine, le courage notre père' (pp. 139–40).

As the novel progresses, the community invests a succession of transitory and inadequate father figures with excessive but short-lived devotion.[18] These men, all of whom bear ostentatious signifiers of authority and masculine power in their various titles (Admiral Robert, Marshal Pétain, General de Gaulle, Deputy Césaire and his deputy, le père Aliker, and even the witchdoctor, Papa Feuilles), become the objects of an ongoing, but ultimately doomed, quest by the people for identification and authority. As World War II takes hold, a striking passage explains that Pétain's aim was to 'mettre le pays dans un œuf afin de pouvoir l'étouffer ou le couver à sa guise', while a few lines later his High Commissioner in the Antilles, Admiral Robert, 'mit le pays sous coquille, et les Américains le couvèrent d'un blocus' (p. 54). Ironically, then, these archetypal 'übermales' – soldiers, marshals, admirals – are associated with such quintessentially female symbols as the egg and the seashell. Moreover, the repetition of the verb 'couver' (to hatch, brood or over-protect) emphasizes their nurturing instincts, and reinscribes the immaturity and dependency of Martinique. But their s/mothering attentions are of course, like so much in this novel, highly ambivalent and uncertain. The *djobeurs* do not know whether Pétain aims to protect the country or to stifle it entirely, and they seem characteristically unperturbed either way. The breathy excitement of the very next sentence, ('ce Maréchal Pétain, dieu vivant sur la terre, nous voilà, nous voilà, ô Papa de nous tous auquel il fallait obéir'),[19] with its slippage from the third person 'neutral' perspective into the immediacy of the first person plural, reflects the Martinican people's frantic quest for a dominant authority, however objectionable or dangerous, whom they could invest with respect and unquestioning obedience. The seamless substitution of Pétain by de Gaulle as the object of desire and impossible identification is all the more striking given the radical *volte-face* it represents on an ideological level: 'aiguillonés par les appels de Papa-de-Gaulle (un mois de 24 juin, il s'adressa à nous, à nous oui! à nous directement!)' (pp. 55–56). If excess is a strategy to mask lack, these desperate, fickle overstatements of filial piety gesture towards a deep-seated anxiety at the heart of Antillean identity. That Pétain, Robert and de Gaulle all feature, in a practically indistinguishable and undifferentiated way, as symbolic white fathers from whom recognition and approval is sought, is symptomatic of the fragile, unfixed identity of the 'child', caught in an unending process of displacement and substitution.

'Papa Césaire' is in many ways the Black equivalent of these authority figures, not least because his pretentiousness aligns him with French values and tastes. Césaire features in almost all of Chamoiseau's novels, and his extra-textual position as an overbearing literary precursor has been amply studied elsewhere.[20] While the poet-statesman is generally characterized quite negatively, it is perhaps in this novel that he is presented in the most damaging light. His benign but patronizing visit to Pipi's garden is excruciatingly misjudged; in kissing Pipi and declaring him a *'Martiniquais fondamental'* (p. 200), Césaire reduces the successful gardener to a child-like state, sweating and stuttering. More seriously, however, his intervention is directly responsible for the garden's decline, and as such he works *against* the perpetuation and transmission of memory. Pipi has learnt his skills from the Rastafarians, a group who have managed, unlike their compatriots, to 'renoue[r] l'ancestrale connivence de l'homme avec la terre' (p. 195). In a novel so deeply concerned with the impossibility of connecting to the past, words such as 'renouer' and 'ancestrale' carry particular weight. The Rastafarians' primordial and innate understanding of the land suggests that they are the only true 'fathers' capable of transmitting any form of organic memory. Their 'humilité' and 'simplicité' are in direct contrast to the arrogance of Césaire and the 'nègres savants' who accompany him, and who attempt, in a 'français redoutable', to initiate Pipi into the caricatural Latinate world of 'convolvulacées, de dioscorea, de xanthosoma saggitæfolium' (p. 202). More damagingly still, the scientists force Pipi to read a number of documents in order that he acquire the vocabulary necessary for the transmission of his knowledge. Here, as so frequently in Chamoiseau's fiction, the imposition of the symbolic order of writing works against the transmission of memory. Pipi's sudden sense of self-consciousness and shame, occasioned by his awareness of his own literary inadequacy, brings about the end of the garden's fertility. In this sudden fall from grace, which takes place in a plentiful and peaceful garden, there is no doubt an echo of the lapsarian moment. Pipi's Adamic innocence has been interrupted by the world of culture and cultivation. However, the somewhat simplistic opposition explored in this scene (land/memory; writing/death) will in turn be deconstructed in subsequent novels, where the figure of the *marqueur de paroles* and other writer figures allow the exploration of a more complex and nuanced relationship to the written word.

Tragedy, Treasure, Trauma

Of all Chamoiseau's novels, *Chronique des sept misères* lays the strongest claim to a tragic status. Admittedly the name Pipi, with its unheroic connotations of bodily function, childishness and waste, deflates any seriously tragic stature, just as the fact that the narrative is mediated through the unreliable *djobeurs* means that we have limited access to Pipi's motivations and deepest feelings. But the *djobeurs* have strong affinities with the chorus of classical tragedy: they introduce the situation in prologue, bridge the gap between audience and character and, in their more reflective interventions, contribute to a heightened lyrical mood. The novel's title announces a series of miseries, and it charts the rise and catastrophic fall of the Creole market, and with it the fortunes of Pipi Soleil, king of the wheelbarrow. The story is cast in the heightened – indeed hyperbolic – terms of tragedy, a tragedy explicitly linked to the loss of ethnic memory ('Seul l'ethnographe pleure les ethnocides insignifiants', p. 243), and the demise of the market is figured throughout in murderous terms ('extinction', p. 134; 'génocides', 'hécatombes', p. 269). References to an arbitrary fate and to impending doom saturate the text and, again consistent with classical tragedy, the misfortune of the characters tends to be greater than anything their deeds have provoked. Moreover, if the precariousness and casual randomness of the narrative, as well as its scant respect for psychological realism, would seem to work against the tragic code, the incompatibility is more apparent than real. The twin emphases in this novel on the 'accidental' and the 'predestined' can be seen as complicit, in that both radically question the power of human beings to mould their own destiny.[21]

Like that of many Chamoiseau protagonists, Pipi's heroic status is confirmed by the supernatural circumstances surrounding his conception and birth. His mother Héloïse was raped by a *dorlis*, an eerie figure of Caribbean folklore who violates unsuspecting virgins as they sleep. Pipi, then, is quite literally a child of trauma. Like the best tragic heroes, he is at once exceptional (in the circumstances of his conception), superior (in his innate skill in negotiating the streets of Fort-de-France), and yet essentially representative of his people, described by the *djobeurs* as an archetype: 'comme une seule mangue dit les essences de l'arbre, ce qu'il fut nous le fûmes' (p. 17). And as the novel progresses, Pipi can be read as metonymically representative of Martinique itself. The shame and uncertainty surrounding his conception, the violence of the rape inflicted upon his mother, his temporary jubilation in the period of departmentalization and then his profound disillusionment and economic failure can all be read on an allegorical level. Pipi's tragedy is that of his fellow islanders more generally, and his fate is inescapably bound up with theirs.

Against the backdrop of endemic and widespread forgetfulness, Pipi is however unique in his thirst for historical knowledge and collective memory, and in his attempt to delve beneath the layers of collective amnæsia. This will to remember is the most significant aspect of his heroic status. Already as a child, he discovers Elmire the *pacotilleuse*,[22] and encourages her to tell her stories of 'des terres, des peuples et des ciels inconnus' (pp. 51–52). He motivates Clarine, too, to recount her past. We are told that she tells her disparate memories so often to Pipi that he can soon 'les ordonner et lui réciter la première longueur de sa vie...' (p. 57). The six-page section which follows, in which Pipi relays Clarine's own story (or more precisely, the typically elusive *beginning* of her story, 'la première longueur') back to her, is entitled '*Dit de Pipi sur la vie de Clarine, future mère oublieuse*'. Clarine's story begins in the second person singular ('Tu es née au Lamentin') and, although still voiced by Pipi, it slips seamlessly into a more conventional third person narrative. The fact that Pipi is more capable of telling her story than Clarine herself, and that the pronominal shift is from 'tu' to 'elle', thus bypassing the 'je' entirely, gestures towards her very fragile sense of possession of her past. Moreover, the scene enacts a key configuration of Chamoiseau's fiction, in that a young male character becomes the agent shaping the 'raw material' of a woman's memory. Pipi motivates and interprets, gives meaning to the past, and in this unequal collaboration Clarine becomes the object rather than the subject of her own story or chronicle, a point to which I shall return in Chapter 3, with specific reference to *Texaco*. Later in the novel, the *djobeurs* are keen to hear over and over again the same story: 'Malgré les protestations de Pipi, nous suppliâmes Man Goul de nous redire, et de nous redire encore l'histoire de Kouli'. Pipi, however, wants to escape this continually stalled narrative, and attempts to propel the story forward: 'Pipi protestait: Et la manman d'Anastase? La manman d'Anastase qu'est-ce qu'elle est devenue?' (p. 109). Even then his prompting produces an unsatisfactorily perfunctory response ('elle accoucha'). His second attempt is met with the lumbering repetition of the temporal conjunction ('après, après, après, après, après'), a repetition which signals the effort involved in piecing together the narrative of the past, and specifically in connecting past to present. These examples show that Pipi prefigures the character of the *marqueur de paroles* in the quest for collective memory, and in the interpretative, ordering role to which he aspires. But Pipi is at once cipher, source and subject of these stories, while the role of the *marqueur* is largely a secondary one of recording and transmission. When he reveals to the *djobeurs* the truth of Bidjoule's paternity, for example, there is a sense in which he is endowed with a superior store of memory: 'Pipi nous ouvrit alors sa mémoire' (p. 139). In a novel in which the power of forgetting is shown to be much more potent than the capacity to recall, this sense of memory's plenitude and availability is unusual.

Fate and flaw are two further essential ingredients of tragedy. As we have seen, references to fate and destiny permeate the text, particularly in reference to Pipi. Most notably, the mysterious words which the *dorlis*-father utters on meeting his son – 'Tu sauras parler à la jarre, mais la Belle te mangera' (p. 53) – inscribe predetermination and foreboding at the heart of the story. The deciphering of this prophecy will constitute the last movement of the text, and is the ultimate proof that Pipi's fate is inescapable.[23] But if Pipi's destiny is established, albeit elliptically, from early in the novel, his 'fatal flaw' emerges much later, in his conversations with the elders of the community. As poverty continues to blight the island, the old men tell Pipi the story of Afoukal, a faithful slave who, after the declaration of emancipation, was duped and murdered by his master as he was helping the *béké* bury his valuables. The zombie Afoukal now stands guard over the treasure. This narrative of buried *béké* gold is an enduring popular legend, and one which often features in Antillean literature.[24] But the jar's status is more metaphorical than real, holding out the reassuring, but illusory, promise of economic reparation for the ex-slave population. In his quest for this gold, Pipi fails to recognize the legend for what it is, or is simply too literal a reader of the legends of the past. In privileging the quest for material gain over the quest for memory, Pipi does not realize that the real treasure is in fact the 'memory bank' which the ghost of the murdered slave represents. This is spelt out at the end, when Afoukal comments: 'Les vieux nègres d'ici croient encore que toutes les jarres plantées en terre contiennent des trésors… ils ont raison, mais ils oublient que toutes les richesses ne sont pas d'or: *il y a le souvenir*' (p. 238, my italics).[25] And it is precisely the story of slavery which is revived, if not restored, through Pipi's relationship with the ghost, a figure of the uncanny and of an unquiet, disturbed, memory. This story, despite, or perhaps because of, its apparent marginalization, is belatedly revealed as being at the traumatic core of the novel.

Prior to the encounter between Pipi and Afoukal, what few references there have been to slavery have inflected characters' language on an apparently subconscious level, for example through haunting images of chains and dogs. Several characters are described as having left 'sans indiquer la longueur de [leur] chaîne' (p. 116; p. 218). Pipi, in his decline, is a 'chien en mal de maître' (p. 98). Slavery is most frequently invoked, however, in the description of sexual relationships and their inequalities: Chinotte is described as the *quimboiseur*'s 'nouvelle esclave', underlining the exploitative nature of their relationship (p. 85); Anastase is described as Zozor Alcide-Victor's 'esclave d'amour' (p. 220); and conversely, in its happier stages, the relationship between Pipi and Marguerite is figured as 'un amour sans chaînes' (p. 189). Thus, slavery is a shadowy memory, which occasionally surges to the surface to inflect discourse on a proverbial, metonymic and imagistic level, but which is otherwise unverbalized and repressed. Pipi's quest for gold will lead not to any material riches, but to the attempted disinterring of this traumatic past.

In setting off to look for the treasure Pipi, armed with shovel and oil lamp, resembles a miner or an archæologist, and indeed his quest is described as a 'fouille' (p. 148).[26] When he discovers Afoukal, he immediately and instinctively identifies with the murdered slave, in empathetic terms that highlight the similarity in their experience. He is explicitly linked to Afoukal through a series of images of burying and splitting. Both characters dig holes: the former was coerced to bury the relics of the past for their subsequent retrieval, while the latter attempts, belatedly and unsuccessfully, to excavate them. Just as Afoukal was murdered by his master splitting his skull with a cutlass, so Pipi announces, 'Oui c'est moi, Pipi, djobeur de déveine comme toi Afoukal, je creuse des trous sans savoir s'il s'agit de ma tombe et chaque jour quelque chose *me fend la tête*' (p. 150, my italics). Moreover, Afoukal's story is told from the 'tu' perspective, directly interpellating the addressee, Pipi. The two are described as having 'une curieuse complicité' (p. 175), and the increasingly blurred boundary between them is reinforced when, in a description which again mobilizes imagery of burying and splitting, Afoukal's narrative is shown to counteract Pipi's own oblivion and repression: 'C'est par là que Pipi remonta *sa propre mémoire* fendue d'oubli comme une calebasse et enterrée au plus loin de lui-même' (p. 151, my italics). Given the identification between Pipi and Afoukal, and given that, as we saw earlier, Pipi's identity is metonymically linked to that of Martinique in general, the implication is that Afoukal's wounding and trauma continue to affect the collectivity in the present. Indeed at one point, the wounding metaphor is explicitly extended to encompass the entire population:

'Dans cette vie où chaque homme est la croûte d'une blessure, comme il est difficile de reconnaître les sèves du désarroi' (p. 139). The scab, a protective layer of oblivion, nevertheless prevents any easy reconnection with the vital source, the sap, of Caribbean collective memory, a memory described as 'désarroi', disturbance. While it is Afoukal who has been directly subject to the experience of trauma (slavery, murder), the inability of subsequent generations to absorb the reality of this past has resulted in the sense of historylessness which pervades the text.

If, at first sight, the imagery mobilized in this section appears to combine Fanon's predilection for splitting and disintegration with Glissant's emphasis on repression, a closer examination confirms that Chamoiseau has much more in common with the latter's theorizing of Antillean identity.[27] The split Caribbean psyche is not really the primary subject of Chamoiseau's fiction, which deals less with individual psychological pathology and neurosis than with collective dysfunction. Indeed, there is scant evidence in Chamoiseau's writing of Fanon's fundamental argument that 'Subjectivement, intellectuellement, l'Antillais se comporte comme un Blanc';[28] in a sense, the characters of *Chronique* are too lacking in awareness of *both* self and other, and too oblivious to, and remote from, the power dynamics which regulate their world, to identify, even subconsciously, with the culture of prestige. Such identification would require a mimetic drive, an aspirational energy which, however harmful, is lacking in the subjectivities explored in the novel. Chamoiseau would seem to endorse, rather, Glissant's view that the Caribbean experience is one of blockage, of an unarticulated trauma that precludes the consolidation of a collective identity in the present. The contemporary Antillean condition is thus formed, as Glissant explains, 'sous les auspices du choc, de la contraction, de la négation douloureuse et de l'explosion'.[29] The pervasive images of splitting link not, then, to a divided or conflicted psychological state, but rather to the effects of shock, to the wounding of trauma. For Chamoiseau, as for Glissant, the collective, transgenerational unconscious of Martinique is based in the repressed memory of slavery itself, figured metaphorically in *Chronique* as a subterranean deposit, the irretrievable jar.

If Chamoiseau is working very explicitly in the tradition of Glissant, the work of theorists of what we now call 'trauma studies' is also eminently applicable to his fiction. In a now classic definition, Cathy Caruth defines trauma as 'an overwhelming experience of sudden or catastrophic events, in which the response to the event occurs in the often delayed and uncontrolled repetitive appearance of hallucinations and other intrusive phenomena'.[30] Trauma, then, is a structure of subjectivity split by the inaccessibility of part of its experience which cannot be remembered, causing a 'fundamental enigma concerning the psyche's relation to reality'.[31] Afoukal's repeated interventions, in Pipi's dreams, have a strong hallucinatory quality. But the 'fundamental enigma' – ostensibly, the location of the *jarre de provence* – is in fact the history of Martinique itself, the lost narrative which explains the blockages and slippages of the present, and which is only partially and temporarily retrieved here. The process of anamnesis which the Pipi–Afoukal relationship sets in motion emphasizes the force of repression, the 'enterré', and seems, initially at least, to offer the possibility for what Caruth calls 'unclaimed experience' – a particularly apt description of the story of slavery in this novel – to be claimed. For in *Chronique*, the slave ghost is belatedly given the opportunity to testify, on behalf of subsequent generations, to his experience. Afoukal's 'dix-huit paroles' explore many of the most brutalizing scenes of slave suffering, and the testimony bears the trace of post-traumatic witnessing. For example, Afoukal demonstrates a strong sense of identification with the aggressor, stating that 'je ne pouvais plus envisager ma vie sans lui' and stating that he understood him when he cracked open his skull on the jar (p. 168). In therapeutic terms, then, as Ruth Leys has argued, the recovery of the primary experience should precede and make possible the recovery of the damaged self, and thus enable psychological reintegration.[32]

The community's reactions to the story of slavery, when it is finally brought to the surface by Pipi, conform to many of the classic symptoms of traumatic shock. For example, it is a key tenet of Caruth's theory that traumatic experience cannot be assimilated directly into the psyche, but instead is encoded in the body, revealed through physical sensation rather than through language. Pipi's first visit to Afoukal's tomb provokes a highly sensual onrush: 'Il n'y rencontrait qu'une détresse sans nom, des bruissements de chaînes, des puanteurs de cales sombres, des clapotis de vagues amères' (pp. 150–51). And, when Pipi transmits what he has learned to his contemporaries, he does so in a way that links oblivion to self-harm: 'et se cognait le front en maudissant l'oubli' (p. 170). In turn, the response of the community is primarily a physical one: Sirop spins around, Sifilon adopts the look of a blind person, Didon scratches his head with both hands, his eyes tightly shut. As Elmire sobs, 'c'est *un vieux souvenir de chair* qui nous fait ça' (p. 170, my italics). In other words, the effect on the community is described in primarily corporeal terms, a kind of reflex action which transcends the cognitive or the intellectual.

Slavery is thus shown to remain inscribed on the flesh, if not in consciousness. Characters do not so much remember as embody memory, just as trauma cannot so much be remembered as re-experienced. Moreover, these physical responses have a (self-)destructive quality, and suggest a desire to ignore or further repress the story being told, rather than confront it. The community is thus shown to vacillate between states of hyper-arousal and numbing, staggering around in what Caruth describes as 'the complex relation between knowing and not knowing',[33] unable to achieve connectedness to the past or to exorcize it through narrative.

Pipi however, initially at least, seems fortified by the testimony: he is described as having 'le regard en bonne saison de ceux qui, pour la première fois, possèdent une mémoire' (p. 169). This sense of well-being and reintegration, through the apparent recovery of memory, is short-lived, however; he quickly becomes consumed by the story to the point of madness, isolating himself from the community in a haunted and remote clearing. In the vocabulary of trauma theory, Pipi's response is a negative one of 'acting out', rather than the healthy and therapeutic process of 'working through'. This is seen most clearly in his relationship with the children of his concubine, Marguerite Jupiter, with whom he acts out in a very literal way: in recounting to the children the story of slavery, he becomes carried away by his own proficiency, and is dubiously described at one point as being 'content' with his own performance. Moreover, in his use of the figure of the rebel slave, Séchou, as the protagonist for his stories, the slave experience is instrumentalized by Pipi, and transformed, or rather deformed, into a number of clichéd set pieces: 'Séchou contre la chaîne magique'; 'Séchou attaque la grande habitation'; 'Séchou prisonnier'. Pipi's enthusiasm to bear witness, to pass on the horrors of slavery, is shown to be a self-indulgent and solipsistic activity, whose fictionalizing devices are empty rhetorical gestures: 'Cette façon de dire une époque se révélait plus efficace que les sombres exactitudes historiques révélées auparavant' (p. 194). Pipi thus succumbs to a mythologizing and sacralizing tendency, and the story is reconstructed to render it more palatable: the children are described as drinking Pipi's words, and appear at times to be intoxicated by them. They respond, moreover, with unseemly excitement to the barbarity of the tale: 'Les enfants, fauves cruels, se délectaient à l'écoute des tortures ou des abîmes de détresse, et dansaient frénétiquement quand Pipi, *ses effets soigneusement dosés*, assassinait le méchant maître et dévastait l'habitation' (p. 194, my italics). What Pipi has done (in a more exploitative way, incidentally, than in his treatment of women's stories, mentioned above) is to assume narrative mastery over Afoukal's story, and in so doing to turn it into just another story of slave revolt. Veracity and faithfulness to the 'sombres exactitudes' is dismissed in favour of a rhetoric of efficiency and effectiveness.

The ethics of remembering are therefore called into question through Pipi's storytelling. We have already noted Pipi's remarkable sense of identification with Afoukal. Through his performance, the children also 's'identifiaient mieux aux nègres rebelles dans leurs jeux de guerre et de courage' (p. 195). The disparate slave stories are thus converted into redemptive narratives which highlight heroism and rebellion. But Pipi's gesture could in itself be read as an act of violence, a 'totalized, settled, understood and closed account' which, as Shoshana Felman has argued in her study of the ethics involved in narrating trauma, constitutes 'a speech act of disposing of the bodies'.[34] Moreover, Dominick LaCapra cautions against an overly keen identification with the victim, arguing that unchecked identification implies

> a confusion of self and other which may bring an incorporation of the experience and voice of the victim and its reenactment or acting out. As in acting out in general, one possessed, however vicariously, by the past and reliving its traumatic scenes may be tragically incapable of acting responsibly or behaving in an ethical manner involving consideration for others as others.[35]

It is significant that Pipi's mythologizing narrative is pointedly undercut, from the 'real world', by the cries of hunger of Marguerite's children. The scene seems to suggest that an excessive investment in the mythology of the past is an irresponsible act which leaves one disconnected from the present. Pipi is guilty of what La Capra has identified as the tendency to convert trauma into the sublime, 'by transvaluing it and making it the basis for an elevating, supraethical, even elated or quasi-transcendental test of the self or the group'.[36]

In his reading of *Hamlet* at the beginning of *Spectres de Marx*, Derrida suggests that spectral plots may become relevant precisely at the moment in which they have been put to rest for ideological reasons.[37] In *Chronique des sept misères*, the dominance of the social narrative of progress and modernity necessitates more than ever the return of the island's eclipsed, unquiet past. As Ranjana Khanna reminds us, the ghost is at once a reminder and a remainder.[38] It is crucial, then, that in terms of the narrative structure, Afoukal's first-hand narrative of suffering remains separated from the weave of the text, sectioned off in the '18 paroles', so that the memory of trauma is not embedded in the narrative. As a distillation of the most brutal sites of wounding in the slave imaginary, the section remains somehow intact, integral, unassimilated into the narrative. As such, it stands as a criticism, perhaps, of conventional historical or fictional narratives (such as those produced by Pipi), while at the same time intimating that history survives, as Homi Bhabha has argued with reference to the slave-ghost in Morrison's *Beloved*, 'in the deepest resources of our amnesia, of our unconscious'.[39]

In *Writing History, Writing Trauma*, LaCapra describes an 'ideal scenario' in terms of working through the traumas of the past and laying to rest its ghosts:

> When the past becomes accessible to recall in memory, and when language functions to provide some measure of conscious control, critical distance, and perspective, one has begun the arduous process of working over and through the trauma in a fashion that may never bring the full transcendence of acting out (or being haunted by revenants and reliving the past in its shattered intensity), but which may enable processes of judgement and at least limited liability and ethically responsible agency. These processes are crucial for laying ghosts to rest, distancing oneself from haunting revenants, renewing an interest in life, and being able to engage memory in more critically tested senses.[40]

Crucially, in *Chronique*, language provides no sense of control. The ghosts of the past are not laid to rest, and Pipi's relationship with the revenant fails to achieve any sense of what LaCapra calls 'critical distance'. The story of slavery, strikingly unassimilated at a textual level, also remains unabsorbed into the collective psyche, and unintegrated by the community. It sits particularly uncomfortably with the trappings of high capitalism that have taken over the island, and with the products that the 'nouvelles marchandes' wish to sell ('poulet-frites des fast-food ou les hamburgers des snacks de cinéma', p. 170). Indeed, it is precisely *after* the uncovering of the story that terminal decline sets in; the revelations of slavery are described as having snatched and poisoned the dreams of the community which, in another metaphor linking back to the slave experience, is now approaching the 'grand naufrage' (p. 171). At the end of the story, even Pipi appears to have learned nothing, obsessively repeating to Afoukal his request for the gold. This continued inability to relate fully (to) the horrors recounted poses a number of questions: is it possible to know or to relate such an event? How can the horrors of the past be reconstructed through language? And, by virtue of their status as trauma, are they beyond the limits of the knowable, the relatable, the assimilable? Pipi experiences the imperative to counteract the general oblivion of his community, and yet the painfulness of the material in question, and the reluctance of the collectivity to confront it, is perhaps proof of Toni Morrison's assertion, in *Beloved*, that slavery is 'not a story to pass on'. The legacy of slavery can neither be transcended nor transformed, and there has been in *Chronique* no reinforcement of agency or authority through insight.

Towards *Créolité*?

As a future theorist of *créolité*, whose joint-authored manifesto, the *Eloge de la créolité*, will appear three years later, it is hardly surprising that Chamoiseau in this first novel categorically and repeatedly undermines the role of Africa as 'homeland', or as the primary scene of loss. For example, in his initial attempts to identify the precise African origin of his countrymen ('Congos, Bambaras, Mandingues fils d'Afrique tous', p. 169), Pipi's gaze is described as being that of a tourist. His desire to return to the roots of this culture is shown, in two successive encounters with significant elders, to be obsessive, speculative and futile. The witch-doctor asks how one can possibly know the provenance of things: 'L'herbe monte des racines, mais d'où viennent les racines? Les racines sortent de la graine? Mais la question est: d'où vient la graine, et la graine de la graine?' (p. 185). In other words, the search for stable roots and origins is a spurious quest, and the attempt to locate an identifiable 'beginning' simply leads, in 'chicken and egg' fashion, to a continually deferred answer. When the witch-doctor asks '-scusez, Monsieur Pipi, mais où, où c'est l'Afrique?', Pipi 'ne put répondre hak à la question posée' (p. 186). Later in the novel, Afoukal undermines the significance of the continent in terms of contemporary Antillean culture: 'Quoi? Quelle Afrique? s'exclamait le zombi. Y'a plus d'Afrique fout'! Où c'est d'abord, l'Afrique? Où sont les sentiers, les tracées du retour? Y'a des souvenirs de chemin sur les vagues?' (p. 213). The experience of transportation creates such a fundamental split or break in identity that any reassuring sense of a homeland is radically dispensed with, and there can be no straightforward reconnection with the African continent.

In *L'Ecriture et la différence*, Derrida links trauma and nostalgia, arguing that trauma expresses 'the nostalgia for origins', and is experienced from the scene of loss.[41] In dismissing Africa as the source of ontological and empirical certainty, Chamoiseau does not entirely dismantle the notion of origins, but rather displaces the scene of loss from the Africa of *négritude* to the plantation itself. Somewhat ironically, slavery – however traumatic its nature, however repressed its memory – becomes itself the site of nostalgia, in the absence of any more primal culture to lay claim to. In *Chronique*, through an extended metaphor developed in Afoukal's narrative, the slave ship is figured as a uterine space from which were birthed entirely new creatures. And within this metanarrative of beginnings, the inception and inauguration of other aspects of the slave world are evoked as new beginnings in a world of multiple newness: the emphasis is on incipience and foundations. Thus, the origins of the Creole language are highlighted, for example – 'ils inventèrent le *début de ta parole*' (p. 151, my italics) – as is the encounter with the white man's religion: the 'grand conte de la messe' is '*la première chose* qui nous glissait des lèvres hors de notre propre langue' (p. 157, my italics). This nostalgia for origins also takes the form of mourning for lost slave traditions of resistance: orality, dance, *marronnage*. Just as Pipi tries to forge a retrospective connection to the past, so Afoukal's parallel – and equally futile – enterprise is to connect forward in time, through the interrogatives which close most of his eighteen 'paroles' ('Ça a changé?', 'Est-ce que cela s'est perdu?', 'Est-ce encore comme ça?'). Both the analeptic and the proleptic gestures, which attempt to create a sense of historical connection, are futile in their quest for a continuous historical narrative. The unspoken answer to Afoukal's questions is that, in its current state of passivity, dependence and repression, Martinique has definitively lost touch with the memory of such customs. And yet their importance is such that it is precisely such an urgent reconnection which is needed; the quest for the past is driven by the deficiencies of the present.

Indeed, the novel ends on something of an impasse, caught between the urgent need to remember and the inadequacy of the memorial process and its rewards. It is perhaps for this reason that the slave experience will be marginal in Chamoiseau's next two novels, *Solibo Magnifique* and *Texaco*, only coming again to the fore in the 1998 text *L'Esclave vieil homme et le molosse*. It is for this reason, too, that the *marqueur de paroles* emerges in the next novel, *Solibo Magnifique*, and will remain such a consistent – if uncertain – voice in subsequent texts. The vexed status of writing itself, neither straightforwardly expressive or representational, nor successfully transcendent, will be foregrounded in subsequent fiction. Pipi's anxiety regarding the inadequacy of witnessing and of storytelling is assumed in later fiction by the key figure of the *marqueur de paroles*. The *marqueur* is an ambivalent and self-reflexive voice, whose liminal status (at once outsider and insider), works against the overwhelmingly negative prognosis for the future of memory in *Chronique des sept misères*.

CHAPTER 2

'Une tracée de survie': Autobiographical Memory

The previous chapter explored the ways in which the absence of any sense of a stable, identifiable beginning, whether historical or mythical, motivates narrative and inflects form in Caribbean fiction, and specifically in *Chronique des sept misères*. In many ways, the autobiographical impulse expresses much the same need, in that it represents a quest for origins of a particular, but similarly elusive, nature. While, as we will see in later chapters, the elderly fictional protagonist is a privileged source of both the personal and the collective past, Chamoiseau's autobiographies foreground the child as a vector of individual memory, although in both genres the fallibility of testimony is underlined. His triptych of autobiographical narratives (*Antan d'enfance*, 1990; *Chemin-d'école*, 1994; *A Bout d'enfance*, 2005),[1] along with the essay *Ecrire en pays dominé* (1998), which also has a strongly autobiographical quality, can be seen to have initiated and sustained something of a 'boom within a boom' in the French Caribbean: in this same period, most of the major writers from the region (Raphaël Confiant, Gisèle Pineau, Maryse Condé, Daniel Maximin, Ernest Pépin, Emile Ollivier) would produce autobiographies which concentrate on childhood.[2] But in this contemporary burgeoning, Chamoiseau is at once the earliest of practitioners (chronologically, and in terms of age), and the most prolific.[3] It is he who has been most insistently drawn to the genre, and in his work the role and mechanisms of private, intimate, 'living' memory are explored on a uniquely extensive scale. His autobiographies stress the depletion of childhood memory, the inadequacy of language, and the extent to which the intensity and plenitude of early experience has necessarily been tarnished in the process of growing up. And yet, for Chamoiseau, this period remains so rich in 'raw materials', and so uncontaminated by the self-conscious urge to record or to memorialize, that it is at once an irretrievable period, and one which demands active rediscovery.

The exclusive and intense focus on childhood both enriches and inhibits the memorial quest, a tension conveyed by Chamoiseau's allusive and elliptical style. These are highly self-conscious and poetic texts, which in their linguistic richness unapologetically privilege *graphein*, writing, over *auto* (self) and *bios* (life). In keeping with this emphasis, precise dates and reliable temporal markers are generally absent in the three volumes. We are not aware of the protagonist's exact age at any point; time is instead experienced as an open continuum according to which events can be grouped in 'elastic bands', ordered according to the consciousness or sensibility of the child. To this end, the titles of the three volumes trace a progressive movement, a memorial trajectory which attempts to coordinate the beginning, middle and end of childhood. *Antan d'enfance* bears as the first word of its title one of the privileged signifiers of *créolité*, suggesting a backward-looking, highly nostalgic perspective on a definitively lost period. This volume is largely rooted in the domestic sphere, and is concerned with the magical, ethereal quality of early childhood. It is perhaps unsurprising, then, that this is the text in which memory is most frequently addressed, and in which the poetic and lyrical soundings of memory are more significant than their rewards. The second work, *Chemin-d'école*, explores the socialization and schooling of the child. It follows his experience beyond the domestic sphere, as he progresses through the education system, and focuses particularly on the clash between metropolitan French and Creole culture in the schoolroom. The series ends with the sense of termination, closure and even exhaustion signalled in the title *A Bout d'enfance*, a text which explores the *négrillon*'s dawning awareness of sexual difference (the word 'bout', as well as signalling the end, refers to the 'ti-bout', the penis, which is the source of some obsession in this work). The period of childhood is thus plotted through an overarching teleology, which traces a progression from delight, magic and mystery to mourning, and from inauguration to culmination.

While the individual works stand alone as self-contained texts, it is therefore as a triptych that they can be read most satisfactorily, and it is only this wider context that yields the intertextual echoes from one work to the next, as well as the coherence of the project more generally. Beyond the authorial quest for memory which is the explicit subject matter of the project, the reader's memory is more subtly activated through a tissue of continuities and recyclings, in which stories are developed, and episodes and lines are repeated or completed. To take but the most obvious example, *Antan d'enfance* closes with the unfinished sentence, 'mes frères O, je voudrais vous dire', a line which appears to tail off, but which is taken up, relay-like, and completed by the incipit of *Chemin-d'école*, 'mes frères O, je voudrais vous dire: le négrillon commet l'erreur de réclamer l'école' (*CE*, p. 17). Early in the first volume, the narrator initiates his own autobiographical pact with memory: 'Mémoire, passons un pacte le temps d'un crayonné' (*AE*, p. 12), a contract immediately followed by an appeal to origins: 'Où débute l'enfance?' (*AE*, p. 13). This pact is concluded and terminated in *A Bout d'enfance*, in which an obsession with endings has superseded the emphasis on incipience and initiation which was so central to the first volume.[4] The narrator announces that it is time to close the pact, and continues, 'Dis-moi, où, comment, pourquoi, à quel moment mon négrillon s'en va? Où défaille l'enfance?' (*BE*, p. 29). Some pages later, he announces that the pact has been terminated (*BE*, p. 42). By the end of this text, he states that he is out of breath, out of memory and *à bout d'enfance*, at the end of childhood.

The first two volumes – like *Chronique des sept misères* – are structured according to a simple binary division. *Antan d'enfance* consists of two parts, 'Sentir' and 'Sortir', while *Chemin-d'école* progresses from 'Envie' to 'Survie'. The symmetry extends beyond the assonance and alliteration ('Sentir' finds a half-rhyme in 'Envie', while 'Sortir' resonates in 'Survie') which phonetically pair the first and second sections of each work. The parallel has a semantic dimension as well, which reinforces the sense of a cyclical trajectory. Both texts begin with a primal, almost instinctual state of interiority and anticipation (feeling or sensing; desire), and proceed to propel the subject outwards and onwards (going out; survival).[5] Whether this progression is to the outside world beyond home and family (neighbours, shopkeepers) in the first volume, or whether it denotes the encounter with the republican school and its aggressive promotion of French culture in the second, the dynamic suggests, simultaneously, both projection and contraction, expanded horizons and loss, a classic transition from innocence to experience. *A Bout d'enfance*, on the other hand, has an intricate and complex framework. It is composed of eight sections, whose subtitles ('Ordre et désordre du monde', 'Contraires et antagonismes') signify an already more sophisticated and intellectual view of the world, and one which has a stronger investment in logic, clarity and order. And as the memorial journey reaches its end in this third volume, the rhetoric of closure and of culmination ('disparition', 'achèvement', 'mort', *BE*, p. 20; 'Où as-tu disparu?', *BE*, p. 42) becomes more pronounced. The sense of an imminent or encroaching ending is not, however, linked solely to the end of childhood. Rather, the dual perspective of autobiography is brought starkly to the fore as the present-day narrator simultaneously reflects, through recurrent italicized inserts, on the recent death of his mother. This loss inflects the entire third volume, and resuscitates in turn memories of the father's death. Moreover, a parallel between the loss of a loved one and the disappearance of an earlier self is suggested. Like his dead father, for example, his younger self is both departed from and omnipresent in the narrator's life (*BE*, p. 118). Most poignantly, the struggle with autobiographical memory, and the tension between childhood experience and adult amnesia which has been so central to the three works, becomes imbued in *A Bout d'enfance* with a particularly painful charge. The cruel devastation of Man Ninotte's memory in old age – her sense of confusion, disorientation and loss – provides a poignant parallel to the task of the now middle-aged author-narrator, also grappling, on the textual level, with the defectiveness and unreliability of memory.

Memory: Contracts, Pacts, Negotiations

> All autobiographies should be written in the third person. The pretext of confession, whose real purpose is not exploring but ennobling life, is the supreme fiction ... So the lie, once we have created this trance of style, of finding progress and illumination where there was really luck or repetition, multiplies once we begin. Henceforth, 'I' should be known as 'him' – an object distant enough to regard dispassionately... The true autobiographer will cultivate the schizophrenic gift.[6]
> Derek Walcott

It is often stated that the postcolonial subject has a troubled relationship with autobiography, a genre frequently viewed as inherently Western.[7] Glissant has argued that, for the Antillean artist, '[l']intime est inséparable du devenir de la communauté'.[8] And Sandra Pouchet Paquet, writing in the context of the anglophone Caribbean, notes that 'there is a clearly-defined tension between the autobiographical self as a singular personality with psychological integrity, and the self as a way into the social and political complexities of the region'.[9] One index of this tension in the French Caribbean is the marked reluctance on the part of many autobiographers to use the first person pronoun. Both of Raphaël Confiant's *récits d'enfance* adopt the second person, as does Daniel Maximin in *Tu, c'est l'enfance*. For his part Chamoiseau, in apparent sympathy with Walcott's call to arms in 'Another Life', privileges the third-person perspective of *le négrillon*. If the narrative occasionally proceeds to brief recuperations of the 'je' persona, such moments usually express a sudden intuition in the present, activated by the immediate moment of writing ('C'était, je crois, l'inexprimée inquiétude de l'enfance...', *AE*, p. 38; 'j'ai oublié le son de ta voix', *CE*, p. 41; 'Je suis au plein midi de l'âge et l'addition se fait', *BE*, p. 25).[10] So, while all three volumes share a marked degree of pronominal flux, moving through first, second and third person (singular and plural) perspectives, it is the third person which is generally dominant. This device appears to undercut the primacy of the 'je', and to posit an alternative subjective economy through which *le négrillon*, a racially marked diminutive, might be seen as a representative of the black child more generally. But it could equally be argued that, rather than distancing the subject under construction, or suggesting any kind of representativity, this shift is geared towards better retrieving the intensely personal and individual perspective of the child. And to this extent, the use of the diminutive 'le négrillon' can be seen as one example of a device mobilized by autobiographers throughout the ages. Citing such comparable instances as Duras's 'la petite blanche' or Sarraute's 'Tachok', Michael Sheringham argues that the desire for shape and definition means that the writer

> may fix on particular manifestations of selfhood and, by a kind of synecdoche, make them stand for an abeyant totality. Autobiographers often convey the impression that their textual effigies have the attraction of miniatures or scale models, an appeal which may be associated with the mind's disposition to classify and order. The autobiographical manikin or homunculus (which may be linked with an image 'in the mind's eye') is amenable, portable, available to scrutiny, a 'transitional object' to be cherished in the context of an otherwise unpromising environment.[11]

The figure of the little black boy, *le négrillon*, can be seen to exemplify the fetishistic impulse of the autobiographer, who 'fixes on and overvalues something small and graspable which can be dominated and possessed' as a substitute 'for the real and intangible object of desire'.[12] *Le négrillon* thus represents a kind of embryonic, concrete and static entity, more 'amenable' and 'portable', to return to Sheringham's terms, than the slippery and constantly evolving 'je'. This iconic imprint of the childhood self acts, then, as an *aide-mémoire*, a visual stimulus to reconnection with the past.

Sheringham goes on to differentiate between two conflicting versions of autobiographical memory. The first, strongly associated with the West, insists on the fusion of 'mémoire' and 'personne' (Georges Gusdorf's now discredited terms). It posits memory as 'rassemblement' and self-unity, and tends 'to exclude or attenuate the possibility of conflict, doubt, ambivalence, pain, or definitive loss'.[13] Conversely, as we have seen, Chamoiseau (in common with a host of modern autobiographers) privileges what Sheringham terms the 'otherness' rather than the 'sameness' of memory. His autobiographies are indeed shot through with a sense of loss (particularly the disappearance of the privileged perspective of childhood), and with a certain 'anxiety of authorship' which constantly underlines the insecurity of ownership over the past. In his work, memory has to be constantly cajoled, and not only are its rewards fluctuating and uncertain, but its very relationship with the self is the source of some anxiety. Near the start of *Antan d'enfance*, the narrator asks 'Est-ce, mémoire, moi qui me souviens ou toi qui te souviens de moi?' (*AE*, p. 12). Towards the end of the text, he reiterates this question of agency: 'Mémoire, qui pour toi se souvient? Qui a fixé tes lois et procédures? Qui tient l'inventaire de tes cavernes voleuses?' (*AE*, p. 157). The 'moi', quite literally subsumed into the word 'mémoire', struggles to assert its own autonomy, and for the hesitant and self-doubting narrator, whose inability to control memory is one of the main themes of these texts, the precarious borderline between selfhood and memory is the site of a fraught struggle for power.[14] Memory remains, moreover, as mysterious and as secretive at the end of the text as at the beginning. At times it seems defunct, exhausted. At such points the frustrated narrator apostrophizes it as if to 'egg it on', coaxing it to come up with the goods: 'Il y a l'image du papa-cordonnier. Elle est incertaine. Qui parle, mémoire? Quel rôdeur se souvient?' (*AE*, pp. 96–97). After an uninterrupted flow of recalled events, memory seems almost to run away with itself; the narrator asks, 'Mémoire, tu t'emballes?' (*AE*, p. 156). Such profusion, however, is short-lived. Within a few pages, memory is invoked in a spirit of resignation, emphasizing its depletion: 'Il n'y a pas de mémoire, mais une ossature de l'esprit, sédimentée comme un corail, sans boussole ni compas' (*AE*, p. 158). The shell which the mature narrator has formed around himself prevents any easy access to his former self. These frequent suspensions of narrative, seeking to engage directly with memory, testify at once to the vivid intensity of lived experience, and to the inability of memory to retain such qualities. The process of remembering, however, has been as important as its rewards.

Memory is therefore presented throughout all three texts as a locus of struggle, due to the dialectical relationship between experience and narrative, between narrated and narrating self. The epigraph from

Glissant with which *Antan d'enfance* opens, and which therefore heralds the entire project, encourages the narrator to '*trouver en soi non pas prétentieux, le sens de cela qu'on fréquente, mais le lieu disponible où le toucher*' (*AE*, p. 7, italics in original). In all three texts, the exploratory will be privileged over the explanatory. The imposition of fixed meanings and sewn-up connections will be secondary to an attentiveness to the 'lieu disponible', a kind of open disposition which will resist the lure of closure – fixed meanings, definitive conclusions, clearly demarcated 'events' – and will allow rather multiple (and often conflicting) versions to be negotiated. The opening paragraphs of this first volume reflect, at some length, on the operation of memory:

> Peux-tu dire de l'enfance ce que l'on ne sait plus? Peux-tu, non la décrire, mais l'arpenter dans ses états magiques, retrouver son arcane d'argile et de nuages, d'ombres d'escalier et de vent fol, et témoigner de cette enveloppe mentale construite à mesure qu'effeuillant le rêve et le mystère, tu inventoriais le monde? Mémoire ho, cette quête est pour toi. (*AE*, p. 11)

The interrogative form of the incipit, a direct address to memory, establishes a sense of hesitancy from the very outset of the project. Memory is figured as a defective, unreliable, yet occasionally creative faculty. The second paragraph continues in the interrogative mode:

> Et quel est ce recel, que veut dire cette ruine, ces paysages vides, faussement déménagés? L'Oubli, sur place, agrippe encore (impuissant) et traque l'émotion persistante du souvenir tombé. A quoi sert-il, qui dénude tes hautes branches, ce nouvel effeuilleur? (*AE*, p. 11)

Here, the tightly impacted syntax suggests (and indeed actualizes) the dense and shifting nature of the autobiographical task. Forgetting is shown to operate by stealth, its surreptitious manœuvres stripping bare the high branches, the most remote reaches of memory. Confronted with the mental reality of the 'paysages vides', the temptation is to attempt to re-cover their lost plenitude in the impulse towards coherence and totality. The narrator concedes, for example, that he has mixed up periods and ages, laughter and the illusion of having laughed (*AE*, pp. 11–12). Memory, however, furnishes only a tantalising series of partial and incomplete retrievals and, like the metaphorical ruins, is subject to restoration and even falsification.

The particular form of the autobiographical pact established at the outset of *Antan d'enfance*, in keeping with the Glissantian epigraph, signals instead a commitment to approach the task in a spirit of intoxication and delight:

Mémoire, passons un pacte le temps d'un crayonné, baisse palissades et apaise les farouches, suggère le secret des traces invoquées au bord de tes raziés. Moi, je n'emporte ni sac de rapt ni coutelas de conquête, rien qu'une ivresse et que joie bien docile au gré (coulée du temps) de ta coulée… Passons un pacte. (*AE*, p. 12)

This conspiratorial overture proposes a flexible and non-coercive approach, coaxing memory into letting down its guard. By dispensing with sword and swag bag, metaphors for (written?) language itself, always a potentially threatening and violating force, the narrator surrenders his right to any definitive purchase on the past. He thus embraces a more open-ended version which would defy capture and containment. In *Chemin-d'école*, the semantic field of piracy and looting is again mobilized to suggest the possibly destructive effects of mapping language onto memory; the *répondeurs* (an enigmatic plural voice, which dialogues with the narrator as the work takes shape, and which will be discussed more fully later in the chapter) are invited to laugh at the younger self, 'pilleur d'épaves délaissant l'argenterie royale, pas très sûr au filet, peu habile à l'hameçon' (*CE*, p. 28). The narrator contrasts this ineptly acquisitive self, plundering the shipwreck of memory in order to seize upon a tangible relic of the past, with his current instinctual and non-possessive approach: '…et vois maintenant, mémoire, comme je ne t'affronte plus, je te hume dans l'envol d'un arroi de poussières changeantes et immobiles' (*CE*, p. 28). He thus pledges not to come – from the outside, and from another partially absorbed culture – as a plunderer and exploiter, but rather to be respectful of, or even subservient to, the complex, unpredictable and only half-digested dictates of an original memory and the reality it guards. Invoking his predecessor (and celebrated chronicler of Caribbean childhood) Saint-John Perse, Chamoiseau vows to be 'attentif non pas à soi, mais au mouvement continu de soi' (*CE*, p. 28). Thus identity (and its elaboration through language) is envisaged as a dynamic, responsive and constantly evolving construct, rather than as a fixed and stable essence. Childhood is not a resource to be exploited, but rather a period to be revisited and recreated in full awareness of its irreducible otherness.

Countless incidences testify to the slipperiness of memory. One of the most emblematic is the sense of frustration as the adult tries to remember the death of an old rat he had tormented as a child. Reproaching his selective memory, he asks himself 'dans quels combles as-tu rangé sa mort?', and envisages several possible death scenes for the rat. Concluding that it is after all possible that the rat never actually died (or rather that the child that he was had no memory of such an event), the fate of the rat comes to represent that of all such forgotten moments: 'Il s'est peut-être campé entre deux rêves, et il reste là, momifié dans une insomnie devenue éternelle. Mémoire, c'est là ma décision' (*AE*, p. 49). The first-person possessive pronoun comes almost as a shock in this address to memory, itself inserted into a predominantly third-person narrative, and strikes an unusually assertive note. In the imperative to settle on 'a' version of the past, drawn from the unruly, inchoate raw material of memory, the pronominal shift signals a determined return to self-possession as a kind of *pis-aller*, in the absence of a fuller capacity for retrieval and ownership. A similar compromise is effected in *Chemin-d'école* when the narrator recalls (or fails to recall) the schoolboy competition for the attention of the schoolmistress: 'Allons, c'est décidé: malgré les autres j'étais son seul vaillant' (*CE*, p. 41). Later, he is unable to visualize the master's face, and admits that his vision is an incomplete and inaccurate one, overlaid with the features of all the schoolmasters he has subsequently known: 'C'est décidé, j'annule le temps et les étages' (*CE*, p. 54). But paradoxically, the appeal to decisiveness nonetheless weakens any sense of authorial control. Indeed, these interjections reveal memory to be less a neutral or authorized representation than a set of claims imbued with varying degrees of validity. In reinforcing the somewhat arbitrary or random reconstruction of the text, identity's constructedness is underlined, undermining the sense that it could be definitively constituted or immediately accessible.

If written language is generally treated with suspicion, associated with the threat of capture and containment, it is at certain points perceived in more positive terms. In describing his mother's fear that her pig would be stolen, the narrator comments, 'mais à l'écrire, j'ai soudain souvenance que rien à l'époque ne se volait' (*AE*, p. 51). Here, the rigidity of the written text facilitates a more authentic rediscovery which adjusts, corrects or belies a false perspective or an arbitrary memory. It is as though the narrator over-hastily settles on the most obvious explanation for his mother's concern. While such a distortion would no doubt pass unnoticed if recounted orally, the permanence of the written word demands more careful consideration and a greater degree of precision: the narrator acknowledges that if his mother was indeed worried, 'c'était sans doute d'une extinction de ce capital sous un pneu de voiture, compromettant ainsi le Noël à venir' (*AE*, p. 51). The writing process thus becomes a place of discovery, permitting discrepancies to be unearthed and different versions to be negotiated. And yet, perhaps inevitably, it is that which has not yet been written, the memory which has not been reduced to language, which provides the most intense pleasure. In a passage which deals with the smells of childhood, the narrator interrupts his own flow: 'Ô bazar d'émotions toujours justes, affectées dociles aux espaces vides de l'écriture à faire' (*CE*, p. 147).[15]

The creation of an open-ended, dialogic quality is largely due to such insights into the construction of the finished work, a process which mirrors the construction of the subject itself. At several points, the reader is presented with a number of possible accounts, none of which is privileged: 'mais il est aussi possible que...' (*AE*, p. 38); 'Une autre version [...] est possible' (*AE*, p. 41). Through such parenthetic remarks and digressions, strewn throughout the text, (written) language creates spaces through which memory is activated there and then, perhaps in conflict with and disputing the course of its original flow. At these moments, two levels or 'times' of memory are at work, one feeding and informing the project, acting as its background, the other (somewhat raw, unassimilated) triggered by the formulation of the text itself. There is no central adjudicator to choose between competing testimonies. Indeed, the seeming guarantor of the veracity of these memories, Man Ninotte (referred to at several points as 'la haute confidante') is also invoked explicitly to deny their validity ('Pour la Haute Confidante cette sornette est une baboule', *AE*, p. 34).[16] Paradoxically, however, such interruptions and corrections reinforce our sense of confidence in the narrator. As Philippe Lejeune has shown, while the 'exactitude' of the 'information' conveyed may be in question, the reader has a real sense of the writer's desire for the 'fidélité' of the text's 'signification'.[17] For, as Lejeune suggests, autobiographical truth resides not in a pedantic or obsessive attention to factual detail and objective accuracy; it inheres rather in the integrity of the approach to the quest, in a sense in the 'lieu disponible' identified in the epigraph from Glissant at the outset. In eschewing what Nathalie Sarraute, in *Enfance*, would call the 'prefabricated' and immediately retrievable account, and by refusing to paper over the cracks caused by oblivion, but rather in foregrounding their depletion, the narrator underlines his active engagement with his own past.

Thus, the texts continually stress the disparities between *mémoire* and *souvenir*, conflated in the English term 'memory'. Indeed *mémoire* as raw material and as active, critical process is consistently privileged over its end product. The narrator is haunted by the lure of the 'beaux souvenirs d'enfance', treated with such suspicion by Sarraute in *Enfance* (clichés, convenient or plausible explanations of motivation, retrospective additions or elaborations which reconstruct the imperfect autobiographical narrative into a 'well made story'). The ready-made *souvenir* must be held up to continual scrutiny, given memory's propensity to reconstruct and to falsify. The narrator concedes, for example, that it is doubtful that he knew moments of solitude, 'même si les souvenirs de son enfance s'amorcent, immanquablement, par des immobilités solitaires' (*AE*, p.17). Later, on taking his leave of his primary school teacher Man Salinière, he highlights precisely the absence of a consolatory ending which would round off this particular episode: 'Il n'y a pas de départ, pas d'adieu. Elle ne dit pas: *mes enfants, vous allez partir.* Elle ne dit pas: *Pensez à moi dans la grande école*' (*CE*, p. 46, italics in original). Memory furnishes no fond, sentimental farewell from this beloved teacher, nothing which could convert this event into a clearly differentiated or momentous 'turning point'. The temptation of transcendence and closure, of soft focus or mawkish nostalgia, is decisively resisted, and is shown to be the phoney privilege of a retrospective reframing.

Forgetting, on the other hand, is not diametrically opposed to memory. It threatens, paradoxically, both to disrupt identity and to stabilize it. For example, the very fact of having forgotten Man Salinière liberates memory: 'tout cela nourrit la splendeur muette d'une tendresse que je ne sais pas écrire' (*CE*, p. 41). Such amnesia allows a freewheeling, improvised approach to the past, one less constrained by the demands of accuracy. And the most extended intervention from the *répondeurs* in *Chemin-d'école* is a meditation, over four stanzas, on the importance of forgetting: 'Mémoire/tu te façonnes/à petites touches/d'oublis/et/chaque oubli/consolide ce qui reste' (*CE*, p. 148). The capacity for forgetting is intrinsic to the successful operation of memory, and acts as a sort of guarantor for the integrity of what remains. To remember everything, presumably, would be as disabling as to forget all. Total recall, moreover, would make the present narrative unnecessary and indeed impossible, for autobiography exists precisely because of the gaps in our memory, and because we struggle to recall.

Con-Versing with the Self: Dialogue and Dissent

Memory's 'otherness', as we have seen, is conveyed through its explicit address by the narrator, through the narrator's self-address, and through the split between *le négrillon* and the *je*. It is most evocatively suggested, however, by the textual fragments (undesignated inserts of verse in *Antan d'enfance*; the lyrical contributions of the *répondeurs* in *Chemin-d'école*; the reflective passages of *A Bout d'enfance*) which create fissures in the narrative flow of all three volumes. In *A Bout d'enfance* these fragments, although distinguished from their surrounding context by italics, are themselves in prose, and employ narrative tenses, notably the imperfect and the past historic. As such, and in contrast to the other volumes, they act less as an interruption than as a supplement, less as an enigma to be decoded than as an interpretative metacommentary, and convey a mature perspective which glosses and elaborates on the events of the diegesis. But in *Antan d'enfance* and *Chemin-d'école*, which will be the main focus of this section, short snatches of verse perforate the narrative.[18] These interventions are usually in the infinitive or, less frequently, the present tense – if indeed a verbal frame is used at all – and occur from unidentified or shifting subject positions. They are oblique, impressionistic and elusive, defying easy categorising and interpretation, and tend to be only tenuously attached to their surrounding narrative context. They convey the sense of an immediate blazing-up of consciousness, and allow the raw material of memory to infuse and reactivate the prose passages.[19] These textual kernels constitute a series of still images (in contrast to the 'moving images' conveyed by the narrative sequences in *A Bout d'enfance*) which, through a kind of affective return, carry particularly powerful – if not obviously 'significant' – moments of childhood memory.

These lyrical interruptions convey the fragmentary and immediate nature of early childhood memory, and most frequently explore the intensity of physical experience. Their first appearance in *Antan d'enfance* ('Bobo suintant sur chaque genou/c'est autant de galons', *AE*, p. 68) is suspended between the evocation of the ritual 'messe du punch' in which the father and his friends engage, and the declaration that the young boy feels excluded from the world of his older siblings. The fragment appears to have sprung from nowhere, a kind of unmanageable force which has burst through the narrative, as though beyond the narrator's control. The sense of exclusion from the adult domain is here crystallized in the memory of the battle scars of childhood; re-membering the body allows access, perhaps, to a more tangible, trustworthy and material sense of the past. Although excluded from the rituals of his elders, the child has earned his stripes, as it were, through the battles of childhood.[20] The next intervention is similar in its focus on the (pointedly unheroic) physicality of the child's body. It also interjects, spontaneously it seems, at a point at which he feels painfully excluded from the world of school with which his siblings seem so obsessed: 'Reniflée sur sept rythmes/La mèche à la narine mûrissait jusqu'au jaune...' (*AE*, p. 74). The body, again, becomes the privileged locus for the spontaneous re-enactment of memory, and this memory is less concerned with the 'momentous' event (pivotal occurrences, turning points, significant conversations) than with sensation and physical perception. Snotty noses, bruised thumbs and bandaged fingers (*AE*, p. 116), salivating over chocolate (*AE*, p. 78): such quintessential childhood experiences of physicality are implicitly set in contrast with the adult world, the world of law and order, in which the instincts and functions of the body must be controlled.

In the second section of *Antan d'enfance*, 'Sortir', memory is frequently distilled from the sense, or rather the sensuality, of taste. Over an extended section of the text, the poetic stanzas constitute a sensuous and effusive celebration of a variety of Martinican fruits – 'mangot vert' (p. 113), 'letchi' (p. 119), 'mandarine' (p. 121), 'quénette' (p. 127), 'pomme cannelle' (p. 136), 'corossol' (p. 152), 'icaque' (p. 161). Again, these inserts are set in opposition to the longed for – and deliberately resuscitated – 'mémoire volontaire' which constitutes the greater part of the text.[21] It will suffice to quote one of these lyrical interludes to give a flavour of the others:

> Le mangot vert
> torturé jusqu'à la crème fondante
> de son caca-pigeon
> si l'agape est sacrée le mangot l'est aussi
> et la saison sans même parler (p. 113)

Here, we see that food has a particularly powerful mnemonic value within childhood memory, something that has been true of autobiographies through the ages. As Rosemary Lloyd points out in a study of the nineteenth-century *récit d'enfance*:

> While it can be argued that ordinary recall is intricately bound up with language and intellect, involuntary memory, which frequently puts us more directly in contact with our childhood than does willed recall, more often bypasses articulate language altogether, perhaps because it is triggered most strongly, as Proust suggests, by those senses for which we have the fewest words, those of smell and taste.[22]

These stanzas do indeed bypass what Lloyd calls 'articulate language', in that their 'meaning' is less important than features such as sound and rhythm. In the challenge that they pose to interpretation they are strongly reminiscent of Proust's 'mémoire involontaire', emphasising the present-ness of psychological time, a private code of freely associated images triggered by the seemingly insignificant. The taste of food unleashes the spontaneous, euphoric and highly pleasurable moment of recall – a particularly powerful agent in terms of childhood memory.[23]

In *Chemin-d'école*, the poetic stanzas emanate from the enigmatic and ethereal textual presence (and absence) of the *répondeurs*, who converse with the narrator. Their first intervention, in a footnote ('On t'entend! On t'entend!', p. 20), replies to an exhortation by Man Ninotte to all her sons, and reads therefore like a communally voiced utterance from the family in general, in the call and response mode. A few pages later, the *répondeurs* intervene again, this time in the first person:

> *Répondeurs*:
> Les cloisons ont conservé
> le temps des pétroglyphs.
> Ô je les vois encore!
> je me vois encore... (*CE*, p. 27)

Here, the walls of the house have conserved the 'prehistoric' time of the *négrillon*,[24] and his childhood scribbles are figured as 'petroglyphs'.[25] But the tentatively established 'je', savouring a moment of self-recognition and nostalgia, is immediately displaced by the second person imperative voice, urgently cajoling the narrator (now addressed as a *marqueur*, as in the fiction) to continue his quest for the past:

> *Répondeurs*:
> Marquez, Marqueur!...
> Marquez sans démarquer!...
> Marquez! (*CE*, p. 27)

The following page contains the only clarification of the role of the *répondeurs* (however tentative and allusive), and takes the form of a highly elliptical meditation:

> ...hélées ténues... Ô sensations sédimentées... connaissances du monde qui ne font plus que sentiments... lots de larmes et d'alarmes... sculpteurs de chair et d'âme... vous qui dans du vif avez fait mémoire d'homme... voyez, il vous convoque, encore renversé, toujours démuni, à peine plus affermi devant vous qu'au temps du prime émoi... Voici l'ordre: *Répondez!*... (*CE*, p. 28, italics in original)

The *répondeurs* are here addressed, in the *vous* form, from an unidentified narrative position, in an explanation of how the 'il' of the narrative will proceed. In these two extracts, the tension between the desire to 'marquer', to write, and to 'répondre', to speak, is articulated through a kind of dialogue. If the writer or *marqueur* is, by definition, at a remove from the past, the *répondeurs* represent the elemental or primal ('chair'; 'âme'; 'vif') aspects of the self, and are therefore harbingers of an authentic, primordial and originary memory, untainted by the veneer of socialisation and of written language. The narrator, faltering and hesitant ('démuni'; 'renversé'), continually summons the *répondeurs*. Like a childhood security blanket, they are invoked to reassure, to guide and to authenticate. However, undermining the appearance of command suggested by his imperative voice, the contributions of the *répondeurs* are often impertinent asides, creating an ironic distance between past and present self. For example, they mock the *négrillon*'s smugness as he prepares for school ('Vu sénateur/WopWop/manieur d'éponge', *CE*, p. 25), undermine the narrator's authority ('Ce n'est pas dans le texte', *CE*, p. 138), and mischievously seek forgiveness from a powerful literary ancestor for a pastiche of Baudelaire's well-known poem, 'L'Albatros' ('Que Charles-Pierre me pardonne', *CE*, p. 137).

The *répondeurs* tend to desert the narrator at moments of tension and uneasiness, in which the fragile identity under construction is particularly besieged (for example, the departure of Man Ninotte on the child's first day at school, p. 36; the realisation of the increasing dominance of French over 'la petite langue créole', p. 188). Indeed, they consistently defy the control of the narrator, and are invoked unsuccessfully, and with increasing desperation, throughout *Chemin-d'école* ('Je demande les Répondeurs', p. 18; 'Répondez', p. 36; 'Où sont mes Répondeurs?', p. 59; 'Ô Répondeurs, enlevez-moi de là' p. 180; 'Répondeurs, je ne suis pas bien là', p. 188). When they do intervene, the *répondeurs* infiltrate the narrative in a seemingly spontaneous way, as though on their own initiative, inhabiting both the main body of the text and its footnotes. Neither their precise role nor their pronominal position is fixed or stable: they allow self-colloquy as well as direct address to other characters in the works (notably Man Ninotte). Their plural designation is undermined by the 'je' perspective from which they often speak. Thus, they at once correspond with, and to, the narrator, and the relationship established between prose and poetry, and between self and other(s), is a flexible and transmuting one. In many instances, indeed, they simply amplify particular moments in the narrative. In this sense, they are reminiscent of the

Greek chorus or, more appropriately, of the storyteller's audience, acting as a participatory and appreciative *destinataire* (such interjections as 'Rêve bel' (*CE*, p. 24), and the repeated '*Fer*' can be seen to function in this way).[26]

Thus, the *répondeurs* fulfil the three functions which Lejeune ascribes to the second voice in Sarraute's *Enfance*: *contrôle*, *écoute* and *collaboration*.[27] They frequently intervene in order to correct, to rephrase and to authenticate. They act as guarantors for the truth of the occasional detail ('J'ai dit "bille"/ En fait, on disait "mab"', *CE*, p. 130), as well as underwriting the veracity of the project more generally, entering into dialogue with the narrator in his struggle with memory. We are told, for example, that Man Ninotte punishes her son's lies only when they are devoid of imagination and creativity. The narrator, seeming to adopt her casual attitude to the truth,[28] asserts that 'on ne ment que quand on raconte mal', and concludes that 'J'ai cette tradition-là' (*CE*, p. 140). And yet, this endorsement of creativity and fictionality over accuracy threatens to undermine the validity of the entire autobiographical project. The *répondeurs* immediately intervene, in a rousing and pulsating vow, to refute this claim, and to pull the narrative back from out-and-out artifice:

> *Répondeurs*:
> Je ne fréquente
> Ni menteurs
> Ni malparlants
> Ni batteurs de gueule.
> Entre le mentir
> Et la piqûre d'os de gombos
> Je choisis la piqûre!... (*CE*, p. 140)

A few pages later, the narrative again threatens to slide into whimsy, when the narrator declares, 'sans mentir', that the torrents of milk discarded by the schoolchildren were so great as to hamper the progress of pirates. It is as though the narrator has gone too far, mischievously overstepping the limits of the (implicit) contract between reader and writer. The *répondeurs*, while not quibbling directly with this story, re-emerge as agents of caution, and assert once again the trustworthiness of the *récit*: 'Me casser/la cheville/sur un/os-fruit-à-pain/plutôt qu'un seul mentir' (*CE*, p. 144). In both examples, the seeming willingness to subject the body to pain serves to underline the sincerity of the oath. While the factual accuracy of the account is thus often undermined by hesitancy, self-doubt, alternative versions and blatant invention, the presence of the *répondeurs* consolidates authority while appearing to undermine it, so that the device acts as a guarantor of the 'authenticity' of the account.

But as I suggested above, the primary function of the *répondeurs*, whether they act as witness, interlocutor, devil's advocate, chorus or audience, is to infuse the written text with a sense of orality and rhythm.[29] It is the degree to which this oral quality is accentuated which distinguishes their role from that of the verse inserts of the first volume. For in this second text, the inserts have become more urgent and vocal, having acquired a cacophonous, contestatory and noisy tone, conveyed, for example, through onomatopœia, accelerated rhythms and pervasive exclamation marks. We have seen already that in *Antan d'enfance*, the stanzas evoke a range of traditional Martinican fruits, as well as local traditions of cooking and play. In *Chemin-d'école* the *répondeurs* act as a more marked repository for the *créolité* so threatened by the excesses of the education system. Answering back to the narrator, they re-invest the written form of autobiography with the rhythmic tones of the spoken word, dialoguing with the narrating subject. (The substitution of the Creole word *mab* for *bille*, quoted above, is a particularly obvious example of this.) Very often, the *répondeurs* and the *créolité* they articulate are effectively pushed to the margins, accommodated in footnotes which act as a space of exuberant overspill rather than of definition or clarification.[30] For example, when the young schoolboy Gros-Lombric discovers that he knows only his Creole name (that is, the name used orally, rather than the written name of the *état civil*), the *répondeurs* expand, in a footnote, upon the various guises of this unofficial, but more familiar, name: 'Non Bwa-mitan/Non Savann/Non neg-soubawou/Non Kongo!' (*CE*, p. 53). The use of the phonetic *non* rather than *nom* reveals a refusal of standard French orthography and a more immediate concern with orality. Moreover, the nicknames of the plantation acquire, through the negative, a resisting and subversive quality. Later, the *répondeurs* supply a list of Creole curses in footnote ('ils disaient aussi: *Patat siwo...*', *CE*, p. 127), appearing to delight in their sly litany. But they are not only confined to the margins, and their interventions circulate throughout the body of the text. Gros-Lombric's attempt to put a spell on the teacher prompts the *répondeurs* to embark on a gleeful enumeration of possible accidents ('Une glissade briseuse d'os?/Sur elle/Un malcadi?/Sur elle...', *CE*, p. 163), again reminiscent of the call-and-response mode of the story-teller's performance. Significantly, they are afforded the last word in both sections, and voice expressions from the repertoire of the Creole storyteller: 'Envie' closes with 'Amarre tes reins!', while 'Survie' ends, 'Conteurs, contez...!/ Ho, la place est belle!' (*CE*, p. 189). These closing lines underscore the performative quality of the narrative. Throughout all three autobiographical works, secure meanings and conclusive inter-pretations of the past have been contested. The ending of *Chemin-d'école*, much like that of *Chronique des sept misères*, suggests that just as every oral performance is tentative and open to revision in the next act of telling, so too the narrative which has now reached its end is only one possible version among many. If autobiography is above all about imposing order on that which is shapeless and inchoate, then the bubbling up of the poetic stanzas in both *Antan d'enfance* and *Chemin-d'école* challenges that order, and infuses the texts with a sense of improvisation and cacophony, as a multiplicity of voices jostle for position.

We have seen above that the *répondeurs* can be seen as avatars of *créolité*. They articulate the rhythms of polyphony and orality, breaking up the (already weak) linearity of the text. Unabsorbed into the stream of the narrative, they bear witness to the manner in which the text nurtures difference and welcomes alternative versions and non-hierar-chical modes of relation, and suggest that memory is an intense and unpredictable impulse which lurks where it is least expected. In a more general sense, they would seem to condense 'the otherness of memory', interrupting continuity and sequentiality, and withholding clear-cut meaning. Indeed, in their linguistic and generic 'otherness', and in their refusal to yield to the imperatives of transparency and teleology, they might be said to convey a sense of Glissantian opacity.[31] Through the very 'meaninglessness' of the interjections, at least in their unelaborated and highly elusive quality, they simultaneously reveal and conceal meaning. They thus respect the right of memory to be elsewhere, and create a protected lyrical zone suspended from the continuity of narra-tive, permitting memory to harbour its secrets rather than demanding that it surrender a clear-cut and transparent account.

The Shadow of History

I have already mentioned the marked turn towards autobiography among contemporary Antillean authors in the 1990s. In accounting for this phenomenon in the Antilles and in Algeria, Suzanne Crosta invokes the millennium as a turning point at which personal and collective memory intersect.[32] But, as I noted in the Introduction, in the specific context of the French Caribbean, the millennial high point of retrospection was underpinned – and overshadowed – by two further anniversaries with a very particular charge: the 500th anniversary of Columbus's 'discovery' of the New World in 1992, and the 150th anniversary of the abolition of slavery in 1998. A heightened attentiveness to history characterized the decade, and both anniversaries were subject to extensive media coverage, local conferences, festivals, publications and other commemorative practices. And yet, inevitably, what was underlined in these commemorations was precisely the dereliction of collective memory, and the irretrievability of the Caribbean past. In this context, the autobiographical turn seems to express a need to recover the individual past, in order perhaps to give access to the disturbed memory of the collective, but more commonly to compensate for the lacunæ in that very memory.[33] Suzette Henke has argued that for those writing out of situations of individual or collective historical trauma, autobiography is frequently a 'powerful form of scriptotherapy'.[34] Mary Gallagher, too, suggests that such works can 'function as a literature of recovery in two senses of the term: in organising an individual life into a narrative (recovery as recording), they could perhaps facilitate a recovery of the collective psyche (recovery as rehabilitation)'.[35] Although in these autobiographies narrative is frequently suspended (with apostrophes to memory, acknowledgements of the temptation of falsity, running commentaries on the project in hand), and although lacunæ and gaps are emphasized, the genre, in contrast to the historical project, allows at the very least the tantalizing possibility of a developmental, fully drawn account of a particular period. Moreover, childhood imagination can act as a powerful supplement, filling out the gaps in official authorized versions of history and, as Daniel Maximin suggests in *Tu, c'est l'enfance*, helping to 'comble[r] les oublis de l'histoire'.[36]

And yet, while such a compensatory function can be discerned in many contemporary texts, *Antan d'enfance* and *A Bout d'enfance* are notable, on the surface at least, for the relative scarcity of explicit historical signposting. They emphasize instead the inscape of memory, are manifestly concerned, as I mentioned above, with the *autos*, the self, as well as with *bios* (life) and *graphein* (writing), and privilege *histoire(s)* almost to the exclusion of *Histoire*. If, for example, it is a convention of the autobiographies of Confiant, Condé, Pineau and Ollivier that the story of slavery is directly addressed, frequently through a naïve and awkwardly fielded question to an adult,[37] Chamoiseau's autobiographies are noteworthy precisely for the absence of such a 'primal scene'. And while it is certainly true that stories of the community inflect these narratives, and that many of the rituals of life in Fort-de-France are evoked, these are resolutely small-scale and 'minor' events: the fear of the cyclone (*AE*, pp. 103–104), the daily arrival of fresh water (*AE*, p. 79), the installation of the first lifts and escalators (*BE*, pp. 121–23). The narrator also resurrects that which had already disappeared before his time, for example the communal kitchens (*AE*, p. 39), the now defunct skills of the *pacotilleuse* (a Caribbean pedlar), or the lost traditions of Creole medicine. In the impulse towards the reconstruction of the self, there is a desire to recover and to preserve aspects of the Creole past which have ceased to exist, or which pre-date the narrator's very existence. But in general, there is a very attenuated sense of historical momentum, or of a local political context in terms of scene-setting or explanation. History is either entirely absent, or marginalized so as to make no sense, as in the vague reference to the Christmas riots in Fort-de-France: 'un Noël de cendres, de sang, de feu, quelque levée incompréhensible' (*AE*, p. 63). To this extent, the use of the diminutive *le négrillon* also serves to cast the story in a minor mode, and to underplay the impact of history. Instead, the poetics and inner depths of an individual, self-observing childhood are privileged. It is the sense of a nostalgic self-reflexivity, and an ongoing attempt to fathom the operation of memory, as well as its results, that distinguishes Chamoiseau's autobiographies from those of many of his contemporaries.[38]

Conversely, however, *Chemin-d'école* reveals on closer examination an oblique undertow of reference to large-scale, upper-case History. The story of slavery, in particular, is indelibly present, albeit in an unassimilated and fragmentary form. It looms, for example, in the more frightening aspects of school life. In the *école maternelle* the threat of the dungeon exerts an exaggerated horror on the schoolchildren, as does the whip used by the schoolmaster. A further echo can be heard when, in a throw-back to one of the emblematic practices of slave resistance, the children in the playground 'ravalaient presque leur langue' (*CE*, p. 61).[39] Later, and perhaps in a reference to Joseph Zobel,[40] the master reiterates the platitude that education is the only escape from the slave past:

> Sinon c'étaient les champs-de-canne, les dalots balayés, les tambours-et-ti-
> bois, c'était charrier des sacs au bord-de-mer pour l'appétit des békés, racler

des coquillages sur la boue des Terres-Sainville, aller fouiller les canaux de La Levée ou pire, se retrouver à traîner dans les rues les chaînes de l'ignorance et de la bêtise. L'obscurité bestiale où on perdait à jamais de l'idée de l'Homme. (*CE*, p. 66)

The anachronistic invocation of the threat of slavery in the 1950s' classroom signals the powerful afterlife of the institution. And the 'chains of ignorance' referred to in the master's Enlightenment-inspired humanist monologue acquire a heightened ominousness in this post-plantation environment.

But the most significant example of the haunting presence-absence of slavery is in the encounter with the patronymic during the school roll call. The scene appears, at first sight, to stage a fairly classic psychoanalytic scenario. In Lacanian terms, subjectivity arises with the child's entry into the Symbolic (male) order, which entails the acquisition of language, a name, and social prohibitions. The progression which *Chemin-d'école* traces, from *école maternelle* to *collège*, has in many ways signified a transition from the sensuality and security of the private sphere, and identification with the mother, to the rigidity of the symbolic order, and the world of masculinity.[41] And in this new school, regimented and fiercely regulated, social prohibitions (enforced silence and stillness, the repression of Creole, even bladder control) feature heavily. When the *négrillon* hears his name read out from the register, he realizes in a moment of acute self-consciousness that 'Son nom était un machin compliqué rempli de noms d'animaux, de chat, de chameau, de volatiles et d'os' (*CE*, 51).[42] The patronymic, which the child can neither identify with nor even pronounce, splits apart at the semes, and it is further estranged or delegitimized by the association of its component parts with the animal world. Rather than shoring up a sense of identity, or encouraging self-definition and recognition, the official name of the *état civil* engenders alienation and shock, as well as the temptation of regression: in order to 'soften' the word the child tries to 'téter les syllabes les plus dures'.

But the episode cannot be read as a straightforward exploration of the Lacanian paradigm. I noted above the extent to which *Histoire* is subjugated to *histoire* in these works, and so it is highly significant that this episode occurs immediately after the only explicit reference to slavery in the text. For just a page earlier, the illegitimacy of the name in a postplantation society is highlighted, ironically and inadvertently, by the master himself. His enthusiasm for the cultural assimilation which the *état civil* represents ('disposer d'un nom se fête [...] carr figurez-vous qu'il n'y a pas si longtemps, esclaves, nous n'en disposions pas!', *CE*, p. 50) serves only to reinscribe the French provenance of the patronymic, and its belated arrival in the Caribbean. The strangeness of the phonemes articulated, with some difficulty, by the young boy, and the quintessentially French sound of the name and its component parts, means that this estrangement should be read within the context of the specific history of the Antilles, rather than in more general psychoanalytical terms. As Patrick Crowley argues, 'The name itself, *le nom*, would appear to be too substantive, too tightly linked to filial successions, too associated with colonial strategies advanced through the *état civil*'.[43] This episode, which is, moreover, the only moment in which Philippe Lejeune's autobiographical pact is explicitly sealed, vividly dramatizes the uneasy relationship between the Caribbean subject and a patronymic which, rather than fixing origins and identity, has contributed directly to their erasure.[44]

As the text progresses, the extent to which the experience of schooling – and particularly the encounter with the *état civil* – resonates with the collective memory of slavery is brought out more fully. In one of the most lyrical of the *répondeurs*' interventions, the violence of the *maîtres* of the past, the plantation slavers, becomes explicitly linked, through the name, to that inflicted by the present-day masters of the republican schoolroom:

> *Répondeurs*:
> Les Maîtres armés
> gravaient Etat civil
> en stigmates sur les jambes
> mémoire-peau
> registres de cicatrices
> ho douleurs fossiles
> les tibias osent des songes (*CE*, p. 92)

The verse ostensibly refers to the schoolmaster's use of the cane; we have been told just a page earlier that 'le maître était armé', and the line recurs on the page following this intervention. However, the registers of student names acquire a sinister association with the slave registers, the *registres de cicatrices*, and the name is figured as a scar, at once concealing and revealing the violence of the past. The play around the word 'os' (bone), a *signifiant* which does not actually appear, but which is phonetically and semantically activated in the sequence 'tibias osent' as well as 'fossiles' – and which, as we have seen, has been identified earlier in the name Chamoiseau – suggests that the body continues to bear witness to slavery. And if slavery now represents a 'douleur fossile' (a painful but deeply embedded or petrified memory), it nonetheless remains a scar on the subconscious, and inscribed on skin ('mémoire-peau') and bones. This is, moreover, despite the history lessons of the schoolroom, which would seek to marginalize it, for the insert occurs in the middle of a litany of historical names and traumatic events – Robespierre, La Guerre 14, Hiroshima – from which slavery figures as a noticeable absence.

The name 'Chamoiseau' is therefore an uneasy one for the narrator to relate (to), linked as it is to a past of colonial violence and, given the circumstances of its emergence, to a present of cultural domination. Conversely, the forename poses no such problem: so strong is the identification with it that the very young child fears that wiping it from a wall on which it has been scribbled will result in his annihilation (*CE*, p. 30). Elsewhere, and in addition to *le négrillon*, the narrator marshals a range of apparently pejorative soubriquets which poke fun at the child he once was. Many of these ('l'Attila des blattes rouges', *AE*, p. 15; 'conquistador'; 'bourreau'; 'Le futur Grand [qui] ruminait une colonisation du monde', *BE*, p. 20) would appear to carry very negative associations in the postcolonial context. And yet, in contrast to the (superficially more neutral) patronymic, these terms shed their violent and exploitative associations. They do not so much signal a sense of alienation or tortured self-estrangement (perhaps a tempting conclusion, but one which is reserved as we have seen for the patronymic), but permit rather a gentle irony and a mock-heroic grandeur, very much in keeping with the function of the traditional Creole nickname. In this affectionate and nostalgic renaming, which draws on both diminutive and grandiose forms, the narrator conveys a temporal and psychological distance from his past self, and invites the reader's sympathy. At such moments, the autobiographer can again be seen as a *conteur*, articulating the self-derision identified by Chamoiseau and Confiant as essential to the art.[45] Another range of self-designations – 'le Préhominien' (*CE*, p. 27), 'ce nouvel homo sapiens' (*CE*, p. 38), 'cet *erectus* en devenant *sapiens*' (*BE*, p. 29, italics in original) – figure childhood as a prehistoric age which, although complete with its own periodisations, remains mysterious and accessible largely through speculation. As these examples show (and indeed the reference to petroglyphs, discussed earlier, reinforces the point), autobiography permits a playful reappropriation of, and connection to, the deeper recesses of prehistory. This fascination with the prehistoric will gain an increasing prominence in Chamoiseau's work. Prehistory, in fact, seems to provide a more resonant resource for Antillean memory than what we call history. Like the Caribbean past, these ancient epochs can only be accessed through speculation and, at times, a certain imaginative effort, rather than via the documentary materials of more recent historiography. Moreover, if modernity is experienced as discontinuity and rupture for the Caribbean writer, these reconstructions contract and intensify prehistoric time, across a single life, suggesting a seamless and continuous evolutionary history from which, by virtue of its remoteness in time and its universality, even diasporic peoples cannot be excluded.

Assimilation, *Négritude, Créolité* and the Body (Politic)

Although, as I have argued above, all three autobiographical texts are primarily concerned with self-investigation, we have also seen how communal memory is explored, particularly in *Chemin-d'école*. Indeed this work explicitly claims a 'representative' status, in both senses of the word: in representing (telling the story of) a particular experience of the excesses of the republican school, the text also claims to represent (to speak on behalf of) the postcolonial community more generally. In a short insert, between epigraphs and text proper, the author dedicates the story to a litany of 'petites personnes', those 'qui avez dû affronter une école coloniale, oui vous qui aujourd'hui en d'autres manières l'affrontez encore'. Recalling Césaire's famous declaration that 'ma bouche sera la bouche des malheurs de ceux qui n'ont pas de bouche',[46] Chamoiseau (the initials PC can be read as a more reliable authorial signature than such fictional designations as 'Oiseau de Cham') identifies himself as *porte-parole*: 'Cette parole de rire amère […] est dite en votre nom' (*CE*, p. 13). The narrative, addressed to the 'semblable' and 'frère' who has participated in the Antillean school experience, thus claims the status of an exemplary account, as well as a personal one.

But this sense of representativity can be taken a step further. For in many respects, the *négrillon*'s experience metonymically corresponds to the cultural development of the Antilles more generally, or at least coincides with Chamoiseau's vision of this development as set out in the *Eloge de la créolité* and elsewhere. In a mirroring of individual and collectivity, the young boy is subjected in the schoolroom to the uncompromising promotion of two cultural models (French assimilation and then *négritude*), before rediscovering, and eventually rejoicing in, his own repressed sense of *créolité*. So the *négrillon*'s trajectory in *Chemin-d'école* conforms on one level to Fredric Jameson's notorious characterization of post-colonial writing as allegorical. In a much maligned passage, Jameson states that '[third] world texts, even those which are seemingly private and invested with a properly libidinal dynamic, necessarily project a political dimension in the form of a national allegory: the story of the private individual is always an allegory of the embattled situation of the public third-world culture and society'.[47] While Jameson has been criticized for the sweeping nature of his claim, it is difficult to read *Chemin-d'école* without viewing the *négrillon*'s experience as being a sort of allegory of the prevailing cultural tensions on the island, and to see particular episodes and figures as being radically overdetermined in terms of Martinican history.[48] Indeed, although as we saw above the designation 'le négrillon' is a way of facilitating access to the self the narrator once was, it also functions to generalize the experience described.[49] The story of this little black boy is in fact the story of a multitude. The Francophile excesses of 'le Maître' (an obviously loaded term in the context) which, as we have seen, are initially a source of intense alienation for the *négrillon* and his peers, are gradually internalized by the schoolboys, much as the Creole population more generally was to succumb to a gradual *francisation*. This is poignantly suggested in a reference to the 'hero' of the reading primers:

> Aux yeux de Gros-Lombric, le Petit-Pierre des lectures faisait figure d'extraterrestre. Mais pour lui, comme pour la plupart d'entre nous, à mesure des lectures sacralisées, c'est Petit-Pierre qui devenait normal. Ou sont mes répondeurs? (*CE*, p. 155)

This absorption of metropolitan norms is the condition of Martinican society beyond the school as well, and this allows Chamoiseau to criticize and to poke fun at the cultural mimetism of Martinican society in the wake of departmentalization. The elevation of French culture, to the detriment of its local version, is shown in all its absurdity, and the fetishized, hypercorrected pronunciation of the French 'r' is only the most obvious marker of the 'béatitude franco-universelle' which the master imposes on the children (*CE*, p. 141).

Celia Britton has shown how the discourse of assimilation has a corporeal, and in particular a digestive, aspect.[50] In *Chemin-d'école* this association is highlighted when the schoolchildren enthusiastically ingest the milk of the mother country, 'ce lait universel qui nous provenait de France en concentré-nestlé et en poudre moderne' (*CE*, p. 142). In a telling instance of metropolitan disregard for the particularities of *la plus grande France*, the milk is served hot in this tropical climate. It is clearly distinguished by its chemical aftertaste from the thick, creamy liquid which Man Ninotte buys from a local seller, and initially is all the more palatable for this artificiality. The children see the product as a symbol of advancement from 'la géhenne du local', and drinking it becomes a moment of privileged communion with the *mère-patrie*. The master, in particular, savours it 'avec autant de plaisir que s'il avait tété à l'une des mamelles civilisatrices du progrès' (p. 142). What is interesting, however, is that the children themselves begin to reject the milk, partly because they have heard that it is enriched with vitamins and other mysterious agents of civilisation and amelioration.[51] Rumours circulate about the milk being poisoned, and here, crucially, *créolité* is reasserted in a whole litany of imagined contaminations and curses. The milk 'se mua en réceptacle des épouvantes créoles: sueur-molocoye, poil-bambou, caca-z'oreille-de-mûlet-mâle, plumes de poules noires frisées' (*CE*, p. 142). Thus it becomes an object of suspicion, and in the end cannot be digested or kept down by the schoolchildren. This resistance – a direct counterpoint to the loving evocation of Martinican fruits in *Antan d'enfance* – clearly signifies a refusal to simply 'swallow' the values of France, and in particular conveys a rejection of the *mère-patrie*'s mission to improve and civilize.

But if such acerbic critiques of metropolitan domination and of enforced assimilation constitute something of a set piece in narratives of (post)colonial schooling, *Chemin-d'école* also accommodates a sharp rebuke to the extremes of *négritude*. When the francophile master falls ill (it remains unclear whether or not his illness is the result of schoolboy magic) he is replaced by a substitute teacher, known as the 'maître-indigène'. This teacher, significantly described as being 'en opposition', is an avid follower of Césaire and an enthusiastic proponent of *négritude*: 'Il chantait le nez large contre le nez pincé, le cheveu crépu contre le cheveu-fil, l'émotion contre la raison' (*CE*, p. 170). His harking back to Africa ('face à l'Europe il dressait l'Afrique', *CE*, p. 170) reveals the limitations of *négritude*, at least as they are perceived by the *créolité* writers. In literally substituting one set of racial stereotypes for another (stereotypes which emphasize the physical manifestations of race), and in thereby inverting the binary oppositions of his predecessor, he perpetuates the essentialism of racism itself. Indeed in the end, the children are struck by the similarity of two men whose cultural instincts ought to diametrically oppose them.

Chemin-d'école closes with the coming to writing of the *négrillon* who, closely watched by that avatar of *créolité* Gros-Lombric, vows to preserve a sense of Creole heritage, in the first instance in his own schoolboy notebook:

> Il lui aurait fallu [à Gros-Lombric] un vieux don de voyance pour deviner que – dans ce saccage de leur univers natal, dans cette ruine intérieure telle-ment invalidante – le négrillon, penché sur son cahier, encrait sans trop savoir une tracée de survie. (*CE*, p. 189)

Of course, this 'encrage' or writing can also be seen as an 'ancrage', a fixing or a setting down of an otherwise fragile story. Here, the future writer sets himself up as a cultural conservator. Turning his gaze away from both France and Africa, and by extension from both the indigenous and the assimilated master, he will articulate his own (and ideally, his country's) 'retour au pays natal'. In thus celebrating the Creole culture so harshly repressed, and yet so stubbornly present, he will provide a life-line, a 'tracée de survie' for the community more generally. To this extent, *Chemin-d'école* can be seen as a working out, in narrative, of the concerns of the *créolité* movement, as theorized in both the *Eloge de la créolité* and in *Lettres créoles*. In the manner described by Jameson, then, the schoolroom can be seen as a microcosm of many of the political tensions and cultural debates which were incipient in Martinican society in the period in which the story is set, and which would become full-blown polemics by the time the text was written. The ending posits a neat reso-lution, through which writing, however inadequate, is identified as the only way to ensure the perpetuation of Creole culture.

There remains, however, an uneasy irony in the presentation of Gros-Lombric, the personification of the link to the Creole past, who is at one point described as being 'toutes-mémoires' (*CE*, p. 169). In the course of this chapter, we have seen how the body functions as a repository for individual memory: autobiography is described as an inventory of scars (*BE*, p. 25), and adult hands 'se souviennent en cicatrices' (*BE*, p. 91). Moreover, collective memory – and particularly the memory of slavery – is figured in terms of its residual presence in the body. The body acts, too, as an intermittent guarantor of the veracity of the account. For example, the *répondeurs* in *Chemin-d'école* claim to prefer the physical pain of the broken ankle or the sting to the possibility of lying. And it is also, as we saw above, the vehicle through which French culture passes, and therefore, potentially, a conductor of cultural amnesia. In Gros-Lombric, however, the body's relationship to memory is instrumentalized in quite a different way. The character is clearly meant to represent the Creole shadow of both the collective (Martinique) and the individual (the narrator). He is the only other schoolchild individualized or even named, and he embodies a corporeal 'other' to the more cerebral narrator with whom he shares a bench. In a telling image, the teachers walk around the playground totally oblivious to Gros-Lombric 'en frissons dans leur ombre salvatrice' (*CE*, p. 60). So, in a rather neat typology, Gros-Lombric stands at one end of a cultural continuum, and Petit Pierre, the blue-eyed, blond-haired protagonist of the school reading primers, at the other, while the *négrillon* hovers ambivalently between the two. The use of diminutives and augmentatives is significant here; if Petit Pierre and *le négrillon* suggest smallness and vulnerability, Gros-Lombric's name emphasizes physical bulk, and conjures up, through derivatives such as *grossier*, notions of coarseness and vulgarity.[52] And throughout the text, Gros-Lombric is aligned with the corporeal and, more problematically still, the primitive and the animalistic. In some cases, this is an effect of free indirect speech, and therefore serves to articulate the prejudices and repressed memories of the educated elite. So, for example, when the master finally realizes the poverty in which the child lives, his shock is rendered in comic hyperbole:

> Le Maître, lui, en fut atterré. Son univers de fermes idylliques, de moulins, de bergers, de féeries d'automne auprès des mares musicales, achoppait ici-là. L'ancienne barbarie des champs de cannes-à-sucre... l'indigence des cases... la nuit de la négraille créole semblait avoir traversé le temps, et s'être amassée aux portes de l'En-ville. (*CE*, p. 155, ellipses in original)

But these associations are in play in the narrator's discourse as well. Gros-Lombric is repeatedly characterized with reference to his body (*CE*, p. 104, p. 107, p. 115, p. 180, p. 181), and indeed at one point is described as 'transpirant comme un cheval empoisonné' (*CE*, pp. 78–79). As the educational process progresses, this Manichean division becomes more entrenched: we learn that 'l'esprit du négrillon se mit à faire papillon' (*CE*, p. 100), while Gros-Lombric, on the other hand, 'avait besoin de ses mains, il triturait la table, se grattait les pieds, puis le nez, se tordait sur une fesse, puis sur une autre, comme si son corps contraint exigeait un toucher fourmillant pour entrer dans le monde' (*CE*, p. 101). In many ways, then, Gros-Lombric, in all of his restless, uncontrollable physicality, is portrayed as a kind of Caliban figure. He apprehends the world through the corporeal and the tangible. Indeed, Gros-Lombric's skill is in mental arithmetic; his inability to be 'taught language', as Caliban had

been by Prospero, makes the poetry of Shakespeare's character inaccessible. In his character, *créolité* and corporeality are intertwined in a
manner that participates in the unsatisfactory binaries of *négritude*, binaries which are themselves, ostensibly at least, being challenged in
Chemin-d'école. This contradiction or tension epitomizes the exclusionary logic that underwrites much of the discourse of *créolité* – a
discourse which would of course assert its distance from such oppositional and exclusionary thought – and will be explored in more detail in
the next chapter.

CHAPTER 3

Memory Re-collected: Witnesses and Words

The relationship with the past is one of the most fraught aspects in the negotiation of a postcolonial identity, and indeed history is frequently figured in postcolonial writing as a restraining or a restrictive force. For Joyce's Stephen Dedalus history, famously, is the nightmare from which he wants to awake, while Salman Rushdie's Saleem Sinai describes himself as being 'handcuffed to history' on the opening page of *Midnight's Children*. Such images of entrapment or restraint testify to the oppressive 'presentness' of the past in the postcolonial imaginary. As we have already seen, in the context of the Caribbean – where a historical consciousness has been even more radically disturbed by the traumas of genocide, transplantation and slavery – many writers have conceded the irrecoverable nature of history, and have attempted accordingly to recreate a sense of collective memory in their work. Dominique Chancé argues that while Glissant is the writer who has most systematically theorized the question of history, 'la plupart des romans antillais prennent sens dans une même quête du temps et d'une mémoire collective', a theme which gives contemporary literature much of its coherence.[1] But the prevalence of this generalized obsession with the past means that many contemporary writers simultaneously strain to escape what Derek Walcott calls the New World 'servitude to the muse of history'.[2] This double bind means that they can appear to be oppressed by the overwhelming presence of the past, while at the same time being haunted by its (apparent) dereliction.

It also means, in the case of Chamoiseau, that the processes of (re)collection are repeatedly foregrounded in fiction, often taking on a very literal and mundane meaning. Collective memory can no longer be taken for granted; rather, it now has to be actively resuscitated, salvaged, (re)collected and transmitted by the *marqueur de paroles*, a liminal and anxious figure who has taken over from the *maître de la parole*, the storyteller. Texts frequently claim to be the direct result of a dialogic exchange between a privileged source of collective memory and the narrator, thus – and despite the incredible nature of many of the events recounted – downplaying their fictional status. As a 'marker', rather than a maker, this figure returns again and again to scenes of utterance and iteration, and laments the waning of the oral tradition as a fundamental attenuation of the transmission of memory. Novels such as *Solibo Magnifique* and *Texaco*, on which we will concentrate in this chapter, reflect at length on the compromises and corruptions involved in transcribing the spoken word of authentic witness and unmediated presence, and foreground acts of transmission and relation. While the traditional writer is 'd'un autre monde, il rumine, élabore ou prospecte', the *marqueur* has a more mundane, less speculative task; he is someone who 'recueille et transmet' (*SM*, pp. 169–70), and is merely a 'dérisoire cueilleur de choses fuyantes' (*SM*, p. 225). At the end of *Texaco*, the *marqueur* states that he has patched up and numbered Marie-Sophie's notebooks, the source of his novel, before depositing them in the Bibliothèque Schoelcher. As Chancé observes, 'on ne peut pousser plus loin la modestie, dans la description de la littérature comme travail artisanal. Le symbole est clair: le narrateur n'est plus celui qui raconte, mais celui qui relie'.[3] Literature has (apparently) become a matter of *bricolage* and of semi-skilled labour or reportage, rather than the product of the unpredictable dictates of the creative imagination.

Such novels appear to privilege a Derridean 'metaphysics of presence', in their unabashed emphasis on the authenticity of the spoken word, delivered by one interlocutor to another. And yet literature is reluctantly acknowledged to be essential in the attempt to create and preserve this memory. The re-enactment of historical memory is now shown to be intimately, if problematically, intertwined with the literary project. For the division between the fields of history and fiction (enshrined in Western thought, despite a longstanding tradition of the 'historical novel'), establishes a spurious binary opposition between two coterminous discourses, an opposition undermined by the etymological proximity of the two words.[4] Indeed, given that Caribbean history cannot be totally accessible to historians, the *créolistes* argue that it is *primarily* to the creative artist that the task of inaugurating a historical consciousness must fall:

> Notre Chronique est dessous les dates, dessous les faits répertoriés. *Nous sommes Paroles sous l'écriture.* Seule la connaissance poétique, la connaissance romanesque, la connaissance littéraire, bref, la connaissance artistique, pourra [...] nous ramener évanescents aux réanimations de la conscience. (*Eloge*, pp. 37–38).[5]

Crucially, the residual presence of the past is emphasized; memory is a kind of undercurrent in that it runs *beneath* the dates and facts of what the *créolistes* term the shockwaves of history, a subterranean and often invisible substratum which sustains people and place. This is not, however, the settled, encrypted deposit which the psychoanalytic critics Nicolas Abraham and Maria Torok have described, in *L'Ecorce et le noyau*, as a preservative repression, a means by which memory is entombed in a safe place awaiting rediscovery.[6] Rather, memory is here figured as an organic, responsive and vulnerable faculty, generally possessed by community elders, and continually open to the tropisms of stimulation and revitalization: 'cette mémoire-sable voltigée dans le paysage, dans la terre, dans des fragments de cerveaux de vieux-nègres, tout en richesse émotionnelle, en sensations, en intuitions' (*Eloge*, p. 38).

Such theoretical observations, which are extensively played out in fiction, depend on a perhaps rather too categorical opposition of surface and depth. So, in *Texaco*, for example, Esternome resolves not to 'refaire l'Histoire, mais le vieux nègre de la Doum révèle *dessous* l'Histoire, des histoires dont aucun livre ne parle, et qui pour nous comprendre sont les plus essentielles' (p. 45, my italics). These unwritten stories, obliquely evoking Africa and its customs, are the most essential of all. Later in the same novel, Esternome evokes the 'histoires que nous eûmes *dessous* l'Histoire des gouverneurs, des impératrices, des békés, et finalement des mulâtres' (p. 136, my italics).[7] This distinction strongly resonates with the arguments advanced by Pierre Nora in *Les Lieux de mémoire*. History, Nora argues, emerges where an organic and 'deep' connection to the past has been lost, and can only ever be an incomplete and problematic reconstruction, an observation which chimes, as we shall see, with Chamoiseau's view of the relationship of the written and the spoken word. Both writers privilege what they problematically term 'la mémoire vraie',[8] and have been accused of promoting a nostalgic or romantic attachment to an authentic and idealized past. A sense of this dichotomy between history and memory, as well as the unapologetic privileging of the latter, is written into the very structure of novels such as *Solibo Magnifique*, *Texaco* and *Biblique des derniers gestes*. Typically, the opening pages stage a confrontation between the processes and procedures of history-making (archives, chronologies, written documents), and a fragile but resilient collective memory. In *Solibo Magnifique*, while the tortuously detailed police report which opens the novel cannot explain the storyteller's death, the 'vieux-nègre' Congo instantly and accurately diagnoses the 'égorgette de la parole' which has felled the storyteller. The chronology which precedes *Texaco* glosses five thousand years of history in a single sentence, 'Galibis, Arawaks, Caraïbes occupent les îles antillaises'. Yet underlying this blunt account is the fact that right into the late nineteenth century, Esternome's building techniques remain informed by the practices of these indigenous people; he comments at one stage, 'métier c'est belle mémoire' (*Texaco*, p. 53). *Biblique des derniers gestes* is divided into two sections which reinscribe the opposition between surface and depth: the 'livre de la conscience du pays officiel', dominated by imported American television and by heavily mediatized visits from French ministers, and the much more lengthy 'livre de l'agonie', which explores the 'pays enterré', again mobilizing very literally the notion of depth. In all of these cases, there is a sense in which a nebulous but resilient memory has taken hold in the interstices of official discourse, counteracting its homogenizing moves, and providing an alternative and consolatory sense of continuity for the ex-slave population.

Nora identifies a fundamental opposition in terms of the operation of collective memory: the *milieu de mémoire* signifies life, and is 'toujours portée par des groupes vivants'.[9] The *lieu de mémoire* – museum, archive, holiday, 'invented tradition' – emerges when cultural memory is about to disappear. It can function to block the work of forgetting, but is ultimately an empty and disconnected signifier. Many of these novels take place at the precise interval in which, as Nora suggests, the *milieu de mémoire* is being overtaken by the *lieu de mémoire*, moments in which 'la conscience de la rupture avec le passé' are unmistakably heightened.[10] In *Solibo Magnifique*, *Texaco* and *Biblique*, the situation described in the present is freighted with a sense of impending and irrevocable loss and degeneration. The keepers of memory (Marie-Sophie, Bibidji) have died or are close to death, and their arts and skills have become obsolete. Solibo's charcoal piles up in the absence of buyers. Congo is the last maker of manioc graters, as the newly popular 'made-in-france' (sic) equivalents 'défirent le manioc des habitudes, et même des mémoires' (*SM*, p. 204). Again, and in a manner typical of the *milieu de mémoire*, memory is located in the quotidian and the local, and is undone by the imported, the imposed, the mass-produced. More generally, the novels deal less with the production society from which they have emerged (the plantation, and the Creole culture engendered by it), than with its decline, and highlight in particular what Fredric Jameson calls 'the processes of reproduction', including 'movie cameras, video, tape recorders, the whole technology of the production and the reproduction of the simulacrum'.[11]

References to the reproduction of information are indeed so frequent, and so insistently is our attention drawn to the *lieu de mémoire*, that the island could be seen on one level to be experiencing a surfeit of memory, and to be driven by an obsessive need to commemorate – and indeed to commodify – its past. Statues of Desnambuc, Joséphine, and war memorials are major features of the island's geography. In *Solibo Magnifique*, Pilon can take his pick from a whole range of contradictory *lieux de mémoire*, celebrating Césaire's poetry while remaining in complete ignorance of it, and commemorating the 'libération des esclaves par eux-mêmes', while at the same time quivering in excitement 'aux messes schoelchériennes du dieu libérateur' (*SM*, pp. 118–19). The narrator stresses that the storyteller-hero has resisted recuperation by the commodifying forces of official memory-making: he operates outside the decrees of the 'autorité folklorique' and the 'action culturelle' (*SM*, p. 26). Near the end of his life, the authorities had solicited his participation at cultural festivals, 'mais Solibo, craignant cette sorte de mise en conservation où l'on quittait la vie pour un cadre d'artifice, avait prétexté de mystérieuses obligations. Seule l'igname sotte, disait-il, fournit la corde qui l'étrangle' (*SM*, pp. 222–23). In other words, and again in a manner reminiscent of Nora, the life-blood of memory is threatened by the dead hand of history. The storyteller maintains his status as bearer of 'authentic' witness, while simultaneously seeming to anticipate his own eventual demise. Although he has remained uncontaminated by these official attempts at recuperation, he has been brought down by a society that is increasingly indifferent to him. The attempt to conserve memory artificially is imagined as a (self-induced) strangling, a motif which haunts Chamoiseau's work – signifying as it does the elimination of breath and of the voice – and which inflects this novel in particular.[12]

This distinction between 'good' and 'bad' memory – a kind of rhetorical signature which underlies the work of Chamoiseau, like that of Nora and Jameson – is reinscribed in *Biblique*. The celebrations of Césaire's eightieth birthday amount to a bland revisiting of the already overly familiar cardinal points of the poet-statesman's life, and pointedly reinforce his affiliation with the metropolis: 'nous relisions pour la dix-millième fois le récit de son arrivée dans le cénacle de la Sorbonne' (*BDG*, p. 17). Moreover, the institutionalization of memory has once again been counter-productive:

> Nous suivions avec délices ce documentaire du Centre régional de documentation pédagogique, où de pédagogiques personnes, drapées de noir, charroyeuses de flambeaux, hallucinées de haute concentration, récitaient ses poèmes. Nous avions donc là (en théâtre, films, articles, rétrospectives, diaporamas financés par nos instances locales...) de quoi nous passionner d'une réussite *qui semblait être la nôtre*. (*BDG*, pp. 17–18, my italics)

The emptiness and awkwardness of the *lieu de mémoire* is intimated by the stilted syntax of 'de pédagogiques personnes', as well as in the telling 'sembler' of the last clause. Césaire's story appears superficially to have resonance for the Martinican people, but in this novel, as throughout Chamoiseau's work, his achievements mean little to the local population, and have never really been incorporated into collective memory. And, more damagingly still, this anniversary is one of the events that over-shadow the death of the old warrior, a 'true' avatar of memory.

Inevitably, these explicit references to the production and corruption of memory cannot fail to raise questions around Chamoiseau's own implication in the very practices which he is critiquing. After all, the charge of nostalgia and of folkloristic regression has been one of the most persistent criticisms of his writing, which, as we saw earlier, has been said to celebrate 'a museumified Martinique, a diorama'd Martinique, a picturesque and "pastified" Martinique that promotes a 'feel-good' nostalgia for people who are otherwise busy adjusting to the complexi-ties of a rapidly modernizing lifestyle'.[13] Similarly, Roy Caldwell argues that 'if the true Martinican identity sought by Chamoiseau can only be found in a past of resistance and suffering, how can this identity be sustained today in a comfortable world of social security checks and tele-vised football?'[14] If such reservations are frequently expressed by critics from the 'outside', as it were,[15] it is perhaps local Caribbean writers them-selves who are most frustrated by this presentation of their islands. Maryse Condé wonders, 'are we condemned *ad vitam æternam* to speak of vegetable markets, storytellers, "dorlis", "koutem"...? Are we condemned to explore to saturation the resources of our narrow land? We live in a world where, already, such frontiers have ceased to exist.'[16] Meanwhile the Martinican writer René Ménil – who is cited (ironically?) in *Solibo Magnifique* as a 'philosophe d'ici-là' (p. 28) – makes his point more forcefully still:

> Qu'un romancier, qui est censé faire un roman, c'est-à-dire un récit où à travers des personnages imaginaires, il doit être question de révéler des aspects inconnus de notre angoisse de vivre et de notre destin final – que ce romancier tienne à m'apprendre comment on prépare le 'touffé requin', les fureurs du carnaval antillais, la ferveur de la Toussaint – tout y passe, dans une manière d'aventure ethnologique tantôt culinaire tantôt agricole et jardinière, tantôt zoologique avec des colibris et des papillons – alors le langage littéraire nécessairement déchoit et tombe dans une pédagogie à l'usage des touristes ou bien dans des meilleurs cas, une défense politique de notre identité culturelle.[17]

Although Chamoiseau is not mentioned by name, he is clearly implicated in this description. His standard response to such criticisms, meanwhile, is that literary modernity has nothing to do with the chronological or geographical setting of a text, and that the choice of subject matter is distinct from the 'problématique' being explored.[18] Such a defence deflects the ideological charge of self-exoticism underlying these criticisms. He thus does not confront directly the uncomfortable sense that such postmodern idealizations of the rural and of the regional can too closely resemble celebrations of poverty.

But the charge is addressed more playfully, perhaps, in the opening of *Biblique*, which sees a local journalist in desperate pursuit of one of the 'grandes dames de la chanson créole' (*BDG*, p. 18). On one level, this is a paradigmatic Chamoiseau scenario. The journalist could be seen as an authorial alter ego, given the centrality of such metafictional figures elsewhere, and the object of his enquiry is, on the surface at least, *precisely* the kind of heroine that has been privileged in other novels. And yet the singer's credentials are somewhat undermined by the fact that she was last seen singing the Marseillaise on the 14 July, and that she regrets having spent her life in 'ce petit pays' while 'en Métropole une carrière de diva s'était offerte à elle' (*BDG*, p. 18). The dossier, meanwhile, eventually appears in the television supplement of *France-Antilles*, and sells out instantly. Local history is never so popular, it seems, as when it is accommodated among the glossy listings of imported American series. Indeed so great is the demand for the piece – an instant collector's item – that it is first photocopied in bulk, and then scanned into a website. No better example could be found of Fredric Jameson's characterization of postmodern culture as simulacra of originals that never in fact existed. But the episode could also be read as a satirical retort from Chamoiseau to his critics. By highlighting the fetishization of an entirely phoney memory by the Martinican people (who simultaneously ignore the old independence fighter), as well as the canny manipulation of this memory by the singer and the journalist, Chamoiseau by implication bolsters the projects of more 'authentic' recovery that have been at the heart of his previous novels. These grotesque doubles of author and source reveal a writer who is well aware of the temptations of a spurious nostalgia, and yet who is resolutely turned towards the past as a way of understanding the present.

Nicola King argues that Pierre Nora's work expresses 'not only a nostalgia for a particular version of the past, but also a nostalgia for a certain kind of memory, one which would enable an unmediated access to the past and the restoration of lost continuities'.[19] Chamoiseau's novels, too, undeniably express a longing precisely for such lost continuities, while acknowledging that these have irrefutably disappeared. Most emanate from testimonial scenes, and obsessively highlight their status as documents of direct experience: the tributes around Solibo's corpse, and later the depositions in the police station by the witnesses-turned-suspects; the multiple transmissions of the stories of *Texaco*; Balthazar's wake in *Biblique*. In these texts the acts of (re)generation, transmission and inheritance are inscribed within a familial imaginary which can be seen to compensate for historical rupture. So despite the constant valorizing of the principles of the 'courbe' and the 'détour', as ways of deviating from the logic of causality and teleology, there is a contrary logic simultaneously at work, which emphasizes inter-generational transmission and the sense of an authentic 'line' of transmission. Both Solibo and Balthazar act as father figures for Oiseau de Cham; the narrator calls Solibo 'Papa', while the latter frequently addresses him in affectionate diminutives (*SM*, p. 63, p. 76, p. 82). Similarly, Esternome passes on his story to his daughter, who in turn transmits it to the young town planner (a student addressed by her as 'petit bonhomme', and described as a 'garçon bien elevé', *Texaco*, pp. 37–38), and then eventually to 'ti-Cham'. The role of the *marqueur*, meanwhile, in *Texaco* and *Solibo* has ostensibly been one of simple transcription of the spoken word. And yet the multiple frames which surround the texts, their fragmented, piecemeal lay-out on the page, their wealth of intertextual reference (including frequent allusions to other Chamoiseau works), as well as the constant foregrounding of the circumstances of their own production, simultaneously draw attention to their highly mediated, inescapably secondary quality as written artefacts. All is self-consciously relayed through the act of narration itself, as though no pre-existent, chronological or coherent truths can be distinguished. Before it can be understood or passed on, the past has first to be constructed, and the site of this construction is the present. It is precisely these 'construction sites' which I now want to explore, with particular reference to *Solibo* and *Texaco*.

Archiving Orality: *Solibo Magnifique*

At the start of *Solibo Magnifique*, the eponymous hero is found dead on the Savannah in Fort-de-France, his corpse located with reference to two contrasting symbols of memory: a tamarind tree and a war memorial. He is entangled in the roots of the tree, but lies to one side of the monument, suggesting an alternative, indigenous means of remembering, oppositional to the official 'lieux de mémoire' of the French state. Throughout the novel Solibo is associated with the tree, and by extension with the practice of *marronnage* (pp. 46; 187; 196). But while the runaway slaves aspired to the heroic heights of the *mornes*, Solibo – whose name, we learn, signifies 'nègre tombé au dernier cran' (p. 78) – occupies the fallen land of the Savannah, and his story takes place after the '"fall" of departmentalization'.[20] Solibo is an expert in the techniques of everyday survival, techniques specifically linked to the oral tradition.[21] In addition, he is the source of the narrative roots (albeit belated, post-plantation roots) of the community, filling in gaps and providing explanations for the collectivity. He speaks from and of memory, explaining the origins of the market to the narrator, and talking 'de charbon, d'ignames, d'amour, de chansons oubliées et de mémoire, de mémoire' (p. 45). Significantly, too, he explains the narrator's patronymic, linking it to *the* paradigmatic story of origins ('pour eux, tu étais descendant (donc oiseau du) Cham de la Bible, celui qui avait la peau noire', p. 57). Moreover, the entourage attracted by Solibo's tales – 'antiques Syriens'; 'vieilles immortelles' and most notably Congo, 'l'Antique' (p. 107), 'débiteur de quatre siècles' (p. 37), whose antiquated accent is no longer understood even by his peers (p. 41) – themselves embody a certain ancestral memory, clearly connecting present-day Martinique to its past.

Kirby Farrell notes that 'all detective stories are post-traumatic because they presuppose some violation'.[22] In this detective story without a crime, the violation is of an insidious and silent nature. Solibo's body assumes a metonymic status, an identification encouraged by the half-rhyme Magnifique–Martinique. The island, like the novel's hero, is being strangled from within by the inexorable progress of French culture. Solibo's appearances on the Savannah have become less frequent and more sparsely attended, and the struggle between memory and oblivion is repeatedly figured through metaphors of loss and degeneration, most obviously symbolized in the decaying corpse at the centre of the story. In a manner that recalls Walter Benjamin's essay 'The Storyteller',[23] the demise of the age of the orally transmitted folktale signals the passing of the values of wisdom, of collectivity, and of art that has a social use-value, while the age of the novel – ambivalently heralded in this text – can be seen as the age of information. And information alone, as the *procès-verbal* shows, is an entirely inadequate means of apprehending Martinican reality.

The novel proceeds along two separate lines of enquiry: the official police procedure, an inevitably wrong-footed investigation into a non-existent crime, and the attempts by Oiseau de Cham and his co-accused to conjure up the (true) nature of Solibo's life. Their testimonies occur initially around Solibo's corpse, in a kind of impromptu wake, and later in the police station, as people again bear witness to Solibo's life and death. As the poles of this distinction might suggest, the approach to memory is a hierarchical one, valorizing the aural over the visual, the unofficial over the official. Indeed, the novel offers a sustained critique of the reliance on empirical and positivistic truth, and particularly under-mines the validity of archival evidence, the touchstone of both the detective and the historian. Like *Texaco*, it opens with a paratextual insert which appears to tether the story to objective facts. The 'procès-verbal', however, in its pedantic attention to the verifiable details of the death, is hopelessly inadequate to explain the mysterious 'égorgette de la parole' which kills the storyteller. The police report is based exclusively on what can be seen and, more tellingly, what cannot, for the scene of the (non-)crime is littered with red herrings and with meaningless clues.

> Il [le corps] ne présente aucun *signe* de putréfaction. Aucune écorchure, égratignure ou contusion *ne se voit* sur le visage [...]. Aucun traumatisme n'est *visible* sur la poitrine [...]. Le crâne ne porte aucune blessure *apparente*. L'endroit *semble* avoir été piétiné. Aucune trace de pas n'est nettement *visible*. (*SM*, p. 19, my italics)

The accumulation of negatives around these expressions of seeing under-scores the irrelevance of evidence (etymologically, that which can be seen).

Ironically, however, the investigation is characterized by an exag-gerated recourse to one of the historian's key resources, photography, typified in the excesses of the police photographer: 'Il photographie d'abord [...] il photographie ceci, il photographie cela [...] quand il a fini de photographier, eh bien mes amis, preuve qu'il ne paye pas la pellicule, il photographie encore' (*SM*, pp. 130–31). As in *Chronique* the photo-graph, rather than vouchsafing authenticity, is a highly unreliable guarantor of reality. Photos, for example, absurdly testify to the bril-liance and efficiency of the two inept police officers of the novel. The 'éventuelle gloire d'une photo en journal' motivates Bouaffesse (p. 104), and his wish is fulfilled a few pages later when a reporter from *France-Antilles* 'photographi[e] le brigadier-chef et ses zouaves en pose avantageuse devant le cadavre' (p. 113). Meanwhile, carnival has become a spectacle for metropolitan police officers who have come to fill up their 'albums de souvenirs' (p. 165), while tourists wrongly assume that Congo is dressed up for the occasion, and have him pose for photographs with their children (p. 205). The most meaningful photo is the one which has not been taken; the narrator wonders 'où est la photo-kodak qui n'a pas été faite de sa vie verticale, du temps où sa parole enveloppait les cadavres veillés, terrassant l'angoisse des nuits mortuaires' (p. 42). Inevitably, the text suggests, such a photo could never be realized; the still image is an ossified record which betrays the true sense of an ephemeral reality.

Writing, too, is figured as a distorting, impoverishing and untrustworthy medium. Significantly, our first introduction to the *marqueur de paroles* is as a suspect in the murder investigation, and writing is frequently aligned with death in these novels. Oiseau de Cham is a pathetic creature before his encounter with Solibo, his tape recorder failing, his asthma playing up and even his memory waning (*SM*, pp. 43–45). In a passage which has become something of a set piece, Solibo advises the narrator that 'On n'écrit jamais la parole, mais des mots, tu aurais dû parler. Ecrire, c'est comme sortir le lambi de la mer pour dire: voici le lambi! La parole répond: où est la mer?' (*SM*, p. 53). At the end of *Biblique*, the island is compared to a polished shell, 'dont on a tué la chair et que l'on a verni' (p. 698). These images strongly echo Nora's description of the *lieu de mémoire* as a sterile and lifeless environment: 'comme ces coquilles sur le rivage quand se retire la mer de la mémoire vivante'.[24] Like the memorial practices Nora describes, writing cuts off the spontaneous spoken word from its natural habitat, depriving it of the nurturing context on which it depends for survival.

If Creole orality is (rather too unproblematically) associated with plenitude, immediacy and memory, then the official world of records and archives is where this memory is most threatened. Indeed, the real violence of *Solibo Magnifique* is only unleashed once the witnesses encounter the police, and enter the domain of official procedure. As the narrator ominously comments, 'de simples écoutants de contes-cricraks devenaient des *témoins*' (*SM*, p. 29, italics in original). These are manifestly reluctant witnesses, forced to cross the line between orality and the written, a process which will eventually entail two further deaths. As this section of the narrative progresses, the violence of the officers – described as 'des prédateurs à l'envol pour un sang' (p. 200) – assumes an increasingly excessive tone. The *brigadier-chef* Bouaffesse is 'plus excité qu'un chasseur sous un vol de sarcelles' (p. 169), and regrets the absence of 'un petit bout de cervelle qui traîne, et que j'aurais pu mettre dans un sachet' (p. 87). The terror of the suspects is epitomized by Didon, who soils himself in his panic. In the station, witnesses are stripped, tortured and eventually killed, and the objects of the archive – registers, directories, notebooks, typewriters – are transformed into torture weapons, used to threaten and to beat suspects in order to force their testimony. Bouaffesse's pathological tendencies, and his brutal treatment of witnesses and archives in the relatively peaceful surroundings of Martinique, take on a particularly sinister character given his frequently mentioned but very murky stint in the Algerian War.

In his influential essay *Mal d'archive*, Derrida's etymological starting point is the notion of *origin* (the term refers to the Greek word *arkhe*, which means commencement), and he links the word also to the principle of authority. The archive, then, is the place of co-existence of origin and law, of *commencement* and of *commandement*, a particularly resonant duality in terms of a crime novel (whose generic thrust is to identify origins and originality) set largely in a police station. The archival project, Derrida argues, is an act of intrinsic violence, a consignation 'qui tend à coordonner un seul corpus, en un système ou une synchronie dans laquelle tous les éléments articulent l'unité d'une configuration idéale',[25] precisely the aim of the police procedure.[26] There is, Derrida suggests, no preservation without destruction, 'la nécessité invincible' of the archive.[27] Working against itself, the archive works against the perpetuation of memory, and towards forgetting. While forensic evidence proliferates absurdly in this novel, the actual facts of the case become more and more difficult to identify. The police archivist's dossier on Solibo, complete with 'fiches', 'photos anthropométriques', 'relevé topographique', 'numérotation', 'empreintes digitales' (p. 167), serves only to obscure the case further, just as the dossier on Congo which he 'exhumes' is irrelevant to the current case. Meanwhile, as the archive hypertrophies ('dossiers épars, le téléphone, les gros cahiers, les vêtements de Congo et de Sucette', p. 173), the brutality involved in the collection of evidence increases. In the last paragraph of the main narrative of *Solibo*, the *marqueur* returns to the station to hand his manuscript over to the policemen:

> Quand, devant moi, ils eurent agrafé leurs procès-verbaux, leurs rapports, leurs photos qui ne représentaient rien, qu'ils eurent noué leur gros dossier de merde pour le descendre aux archives, signifiant ainsi qu'une enquête inutile venait de s'achever, ils avaient découvert que cet homme était la vibration d'un monde finissant, pleine de douleur, qui n'aura pour réceptacle que les vents et les mémoires indifférentes, et dont tout cela n'avait bordé que la simple onde du souffle ultime. (*SM*, p. 227)

In this nostalgic lament for a 'monde finissant', memory is figured variously as wind, wave or breath, emphasizing the natural, the spontaneous and the ephemeral, in contrast with the meaningless permanence of the archive, or the degraded and sullied quality of the 'dossier de merde'.

Declan Kiberd, writing on Joyce's *Ulysses*, also discusses the relationship between voice and written word. He argues that this novel, which Chamoiseau cites as a key influence,[28]

> is a prolonged farewell to written literature, and a rejection of its attempts to colonize speech and thought. Its mockery of the hyper-literary Stephen, of the writerly talk of librarians, of the excremental nature of printed magazines, is a preparation for its restoration of the human voice in Molly Bloom; and, in a book in which each chapter is named for a bodily organ, the restoration of her voice becomes a synecdoche to the recovery into art of the whole human body [...]. A restored body becomes an image of the recovered community, since the protection of a body from outside contact has often been the mark of a repressive society.[29]

If, then, Joyce's epic can be read as the site of a recovery from literature, through the reintegration of the body, *Solibo Magnifique* works to a quite different conclusion.[30] As Glissant reminds us, 'le conteur antillais ne dit jamais "moi"; il dit presque toujours "mon corps"'.[31] In *Solibo Magnifique*, the age of the storyteller is repeatedly figured through the body: the *quimboiseur* states that '[le] souffle est la force, la force est l'idée du corps sur la vie' (*SM*, p. 219), while Solibo's heyday is described as 'une époque de mémoire en bouche' (p. 223) for which contemporary society 'n'en avait plus l'oreille' (p. 222). This period of face-to-face communication is resolutely corporeal, and memory is a kind of body language which is inscribed on and conveyed through limbs and organs. And indeed while Solibo is alive, the integration of the storyteller's body, and its direct link to the voice, is affirmed: when he bleeds Man Gnam's pig, for example, 'sa voix vibrait dans son front, dans ses joues, habitait ses yeux, sa poitrine et son ventre' (p. 81). Once dead, however, this body can no longer signify any kind of unity, and the community's response gestures towards *dis*membering rather than remembering, and towards fragmentation, dissection and severance. As he falls to the ground, for example, the gaze of the crowd inexplicably zeroes in on his legs. Later, the frantic attempts to revive him are less than holistic, separating out the various parts of his body for individual attention: he is slapped on the face, his shoes are removed, his ears are rubbed, his chest is thumped and mouth-to-mouth resuscitation is attempted, a process which is replicated with Doudou Ménar (p. 135). Moreover, we are told several times, in great detail, of Solibo's autopsy – the dismemberment of corporeal parts into little fragments, the insistence of the refrain 'on a découpé' (pp. 25–26; p. 214) – to the extent that even his last meal, a traditional Martinican recipe, *touffé-requin*, is symbolically cut out of his stomach.

Chamoiseau's subsequent novel, *Texaco*, also deals with many of these issues – notably, the conversion of the oral testimony into a written form – and gives sustained attention to the relationship between history and reality, and their construction through language. But *Texaco* deconstructs and complicates some of the binary oppositions of this earlier novel, a binary already implicit, perhaps, in the duality of the Solibo–Oiseau relationship. Through a whole series of *mises en abîme* of the literary process,[32] the later novel features a number of writer-figures whose varying styles of, and attitudes towards, writing show that literature itself cannot be viewed as a homogeneous or unified activity, in unproblematic opposition to orality. As such, to return to Kiberd's insights, there is plenty of scope for mockery of the 'writerly' or the 'hyper-literary', and each chapter is ironically named not for the body, but for the Book (Annunciation; Sermon; Resurrection). Moreover, I mentioned above the association of Solibo with the tree. While this parallel on one level evokes the dynamic and kinetic impulses of *marronnage*, it more frequently emphasizes a static and rooted position. For example, Solibo chides the narrator: 'Z'Oiseau, tu dis: La tradition, la tradition, la tradition…, tu mets pleurer par terre sur le pied-bois qui perd ses feuilles, comme si la feuille était la racine!… Laisse la tradition, et surveille la racine' (*SM*, p. 63). *Texaco*, on the other hand, rejects the foundationalism of trees and roots, and moves towards a more rhizomatic and relational model of history and tradition, based on the multiple rather than the unitary, and on the *interweaving* of multiple roots into a 'tresse d'histoires'. The narrative of *Texaco* has become more self-reflexive still, dwelling at length on history and historiography, as well as on memory, and is profoundly aware of the institutional processes which it criticizes, but from which it cannot escape. For example, the first words of the narrative-proper of the story (as opposed to the frames which surround it) are in the form of an epigraph from Ti-Cirique, the Haitian writer, deriding the 'nègreries' of the narrator's *créolité* (*Texaco*, p. 19). Right from the outset, then, the novel voices an awareness of the sociological and theoretical debates of which it is itself a part. And while *Solibo* deals in lurid detail with the dissection of the hero's body, a metaphor for the disintegration of memory, *Texaco* closes on a scene of reintegration and stitching up, as the *marqueur* repairs the tattered notebooks in which Marie-Sophie has transcribed her father's words. However problematic the gesture is, it suggests a more ambivalent, more relational and less polarized view of the orality–literature dynamic than that explored in *Solibo*, and one which marks *Texaco* out as a more recognizably postmodern text.

Postmodern Approaches: *Texaco*

> Oh Sophie ma doudoune, tu dis 'l'Histoire' mais ça ne veut rien
> dire, il y a tellement de vies et tellement de destins, tellement de
> tracées pour faire notre seul chemin. Toi tu dis l'Histoire, moi je
> dis *les histoires*. Celle que tu crois tige-maîtresse de notre manioc
> n'est qu'une tige parmi d'autres...
> Esternome in *Texaco*, p. 102, italics in original

Texaco's postmodern credentials are everywhere in evidence, from its pervasive and ironic intertextuality to its metafictional reflections on the circumstances of its own production. Like *Chronique des sept misères*, it opens with an appeal to linearity: Marie-Sophie exhorts, 'mais ne perdons pas le fil, et reprenons l'affaire maille par maille, avec si possible une maille avant l'autre' (*Texaco*, p. 21). And, as in *Chronique*, this apparent commitment to linearity, causality and textuality[33] is immediately undermined as a series of flashback sequences project back through three different versions of the town planner's arrival.[34] Marie-Sophie's repeated resolution to avoid detours ('le détour serait risqué', p. 24) serves only to open the narrative up to digression, permitting her to smuggle in from the margins the 'illegitimate' and the irrelevant, in other words the very stories which she claims to want to repress. Thus, she continually loses the thread of her own story, just as the three sections of *Texaco* ('Annonciation', 'Sermon de Marie-Sophie' and 'Résurrection') do not accommodate a neat beginning, middle and end. Rather, they give way to a disjointed narration which begins in 1985 with Marie-Sophie's meeting with the town planner, then reverts to 1823, and her paternal grandfather's story, and finally moves forward, beyond the starting point of the novel, to the 'present day' narrative of the *marqueur* (1986). Events tend to surge quickly forward and then fall back into obscurity at her whim, or according to the meanders of her own and her father's recollections, and the thread of her narrative is interrupted not only by extracts from her *cahiers* and those of the town planner, but also by extended digressions (the 'Noutéka des mornes'; the 'Paroles du vieux nègre de la Doum'; the 'Songeries d'Idoménée en petit aperçu').

The narrative structure ensures that the reader is positioned at a series of removes from the events recounted, and access to the 'true' story – which is, of course, shown to be in itself a fiction – is continually deferred. The novel, for all its claims to tell it like it was, is in fact a rather dubious chain of oral transmissions yoked together in a heavily constructed text. Patrick Chamoiseau authors the narrative of his fictional alter-ego, 'Oiseau de Cham'/*le marqueur de paroles*, who has recorded and edited the oral testimony of Marie-Sophie Laborieux (a testimony already given to the town planner, and which has been responsible for the salvation of Texaco), who has in her turn transcribed and translated (from Creole to French) her father's memoirs in the *cahiers*. Like a Chinese whisper, then, any given version is second-, third- or fourth-hand, thus marked by the deformations of multiple transmissions and retransmissions. Both Esternome and his daughter are unreliable narrators, due to old age, forgetfulness, wilful distortion or indeed an alcohol-induced haziness. This, it is suggested, does not detract in any way from the validity of their open-ended and often dubious stories. Although Marie-Sophie is christened 'L'Informatrice' by Oiseau de Cham – that is, someone who possesses and transmits knowledge – the authority which she claims for herself is continually called into question. She cannot remember her own age (p. 35), and in this first section of the novel, she provides him with three different versions of the arrival of the 'Christ', undercutting each one by the declaration 'Et si c'est pas comme ça, ça n'a pas d'importance' (p. 38). At the end of the novel, the *marqueur de paroles* states that '[il] lui arrivait, bien qu'elle me le cachât, d'avoir des trous de mémoire, et de se répéter, ou de se contredire' (p. 423). So while the 'Informatrice' is the sole source of the *histoires* of *Texaco*, neither the narrator nor the reader can take her entirely at her word, but are reminded instead of the provisionality and inherently constructed nature of her version of the past.

But it is without doubt in its reflections on history and historiography that *Texaco*, perhaps more than any other Chamoiseau novel, can be considered a postmodern work. In the postcolonial context, as the editor of a recent collection explains, postmodernism has a 'double relationship' with history, indicating 'both a break with colonial pasts and an ongoing engagement with their legacies and renewals',[35] and this double relationship is at the very centre of *Texaco*. I noted in the Introduction the extent to which the discourses of contemporary Caribbean writers resonate with, or indeed have anticipated, the observations of postmodern thinkers, particularly in the approach to history. In its most basic formulation, postmodernism famously posits a distrust of the 'méta-récit' at the centre of its project,[36] and, in its more commonly accepted strain at least, has been centrally concerned not just with history, but with the means of its transmission.[37] The shift in emphasis thus ushered in has been described by one critic as 'the collapse of the upper case',[38] a reorientation which also nicely describes Glissant's preference for *histoires*, in the plural and in the lower case, as a more suitable vector of the Caribbean past than their upper-case and singular homonym *Histoire*. This distinction, as the epigraph suggests, is adopted and frequently deployed by Chamoiseau. More generally, an emphasis on hybridity, opacity and multiplicity, as well as on the inadequacy of definitive interpretations, is an emphasis that the postcolonial – and in particular the Antillean – writer frequently shares with the postmodern theorist. Meanwhile, writers such as Hayden White have argued that history is subject to the same rules of 'emplotment' and rhetorical organisation as fiction; it is only by being assigned to story*lines* that the disparate facts of the past can be apprehended in any meaningful way, a notion implicit in, and yet deconstructed by, Esternome's assertion in my epigraph.[39]

In one of the best-known studies of postmodern narrative, *The Poetics of Postmodernism* (1988),[40] Linda Hutcheon proposed the now classic model of 'historiographic metafiction'. From our current, early-twenty-first-century perspective, some of Hutcheon's observations are so familiar as to have acquired the status of critical orthodoxy: many of the key concepts she repeatedly (over?)stresses, such as multiplicity and indeterminacy, were already very familiar from the work of White and others. None the less, this seminal study anticipates many of the principles extolled in the *Eloge*, which was to appear a year later, and it echoes to a remarkable extent the reflections contained in *Texaco*. The usefulness of Hutcheon's theory for the present discussion lies in the fact that she privileges the epistemological and the hermeneutic over the ontological, a particularly fertile approach in a context in which the 'what' of the past can never be known. Her approach is also of interest because it will help us see the transition in Chamoiseau's work from textuality – the keynote of her analysis – to an æsthetics of materiality, which will be explored in the next chapter.

Historiographic metafiction, Hutcheon argues, is composed of '[t]hose well known and popular novels which are both intensively self-reflexive and yet paradoxically also lay claim to historical events and personages'.[41] In their theoretical self-awareness of history and fiction as human constructs, and in their explicit concern with the local, the regional and the peripheral, 'these novels become the grounds for rethinking and reworking the past'.[42] Thus, Hutcheon resolutely defends the 'historical' nature of postmodernism, arguing that, in historiographic metafiction, history is not made obsolete but rather is being rethought as a human construct.[43] For all their playful and highly self-conscious strategies, novels such as *Solibo* and *Texaco* remain located in a historically referential frame, suggesting not a transcending of history, but a 'problematized inscribing of subjectivity into history'.[44] The importance of this referential framework is most obviously reflected in the 'Repères chronologiques de nos élans pour conquérir la ville' with which *Texaco* opens. This chronology mimics the conventions of the history textbook, but its five 'ages' (for example, 'Temps de paille', 'Temps de carbet') are organized according to the materials used in house-building, a clear attempt to domesticate time and to ground history in local, rather than (supposedly) universal, materials. Within the chronology, Glissant's 'absurde catalogue de l'histoire officielle'[45] – the arrival of Columbus; details of the French war effort – is supplemented with the 'significant' dates of Martinican history, such as the eruption of Mount Pelée or the election of Césaire as mayor of Fort-de-France. Into this master narrative are insinuated the *histoires* of Marie-Sophie's family, so that, for example, the installation of the petrol company, Texaco, on the ground to which it will give its name, carries as much weight as the event which succeeds it: 'La France déclare la guerre à l'Allemagne'. These lower-order events are distinguished typographically by the use of italics – conferring a disruptive and urgent impression as they filter through the familiar fixed points of official History – and they eventually displace the master narrative completely.[46] In this way, the conventions of historiography are at once installed and subverted.

Hutcheon argues that one of the defining characteristics of historiographic metafiction is its focus on the 'the ex-centrics, the marginalized, the peripheral figures of fictional history'.[47] Similarly, an explicit aim of the *créolité* movement is 'de donner à voir les héros insignifiants, les héros anonymes, les oubliés de la Chronique coloniale' (*Eloge*, p. 40). The powerful *békés*, the upwardly mobile mulatto class, and even the maroon slave celebrated by Glissant as the only authentic Antillean hero, are noticeable by their absence in Chamoiseau's early novels. His protagonists are the archetypal marginals of society, those deemed too insignificant to warrant attention in traditional historical analyses, such as the all but redundant *djobeurs* of the market or the unemployed underclass of *Solibo Magnifique*. If the eponymous storyteller of that novel is a more 'traditional' hero, it is also significant that he is already dead at the start of the narrative, and that the novel's cast is composed of the motley crew outlined in the list of suspects. Texaco too is situated in a peripheral, borderline zone outside the centre of Fort-de-France – a position which mirrors the precarious condition of its inhabitants – and its heroine, as an elderly, childless, black woman, is marginalized on several grounds. Moreover, many of the characters are literally 'eccentrics' and misfits, and indeed characters such as Ti-Cirique, the intellectual, or Basile, the fanatical sportsman, are somehow set apart by virtue of their obsessive commitment to a particular, and often fanciful, cause.

History, then, is figured as an exclusive and forbidding domain for the characters of Chamoiseau's novels. Occasionally, they fulfil 'bit parts', stepping briefly onto centre stage for random interventions, but they are generally bemused by – and excluded from – its processes. In *Texaco*, particularly, one has the impression that history is rumbling away somewhere in the background of the text, and indeed it is frequently figured as a rumour or a murmur. Esternome's detachment from the canonical events of the past is a source of continual frustration to his daughter; quite frequently in his narrative, he brushes up against history in the making, only to be diverted by the meanderings of his love life. For example, when Schoelcher's proposals concerning abolition are first mentioned by his politicized colleague, he can think only of Ninon. Marie-Sophie comments acerbically: 'Vivre une période comme celle-là en ne songeant qu'au matériel d'une négresclave relève pour moi d'une ruine cervicale due aux rhums trop sucés près des violons grinçants' (*Texaco*, p. 101). Likewise, while discussions about the forthcoming emancipation of slaves engulf Fort-de-France, he spends his time fighting a rival for Ninon's affections. The turbulent post-emancipation era is similarly defined by the details of Esternome's physical relationship with this lover.[48] And, as the newly liberated population make for the town of Saint-Pierre, Ninon and Esternome happily remain on the sidelines, in a rare moment of sexual and emotional fulfilment: '[ils] restaient comme ça, hors du monde, gardant sur l'Histoire en passage l'œil des bœufs en savane' (p. 124). The vicissitudes of 'peripheral' events are placed right at the core of the narrative, and they demand a new, fluid and wide-ranging narrative form. Through Esternome's rambling, seemingly trivial and often contradictory memories, Marie-Sophie uncovers alternative, non-identical histories which challenge and disrupt the narrative of hegemonic History, and which ultimately prove a more useful resource in her mission to lead her people to a new place.

The foregrounding of marginal characters is accompanied by the marginalization of 'central' historical events and figures in *Texaco*. World War I, described vaguely as 'une la-guerre', is not understood by

Esternome, who finds himself even more marginalized by History than before:

> Depuis Saint-Pierre, il était comme décroché du monde. Ejecté de l'Histoire, il vivait ses histoires sans décoder les événements ainsi qu'il l'avait fait en son temps de jeunesse. Nous avions perdu pied, Marie-Sophie... comment te dire? Combattre les chaînes nous dressait dans le monde, affronter la liberté aussi. Mais après, il n'y eut rien à affronter sinon qu'à se glisser dans l'aveuglage d'En-ville. (*Texaco*, p. 209)

The collapse of the plantation system causes the ex-slave population to lose their footing; while it endured, they had a clear place in the order of things, and in *Histoire*, whether as victims or as rebels. The disappearance of the plantation as a socio-economic model brings about the collapse of yet another metanarrative, and the disorientation experienced by the people, who feel that they have nothing left to confront, undermines the comfortable certainties of progressive History. Mary Gallagher has noted that in many Caribbean novels, the fractured relationship with the past means that 'sequential time is interrupted, spatialized and displaced',[49] and yet here the experience of having been banished from the heavenly Saint-Pierre by the volcano of 1902 is conveyed as an expulsion from History. In other words, space is here afforded a certain temporal quality, so that physical eviction signifies a loss of time and of history. This attachment to space, and yearning for place, will be discussed in the next chapter. Meanwhile Marie-Sophie's summary judgement of the war – 'départ-en-fanfare et retour-queue-coupée' – does not seek to diminish the importance of the catastrophe, but rather voices the limited understanding and the disillusionment of the Martinican soldiers, who returned to the country physically and emotionally scarred.

Not only is history sidelined in historiographic metafiction but, as Hutcheon explains, 'historical personages take on a different, particularized and ex-centric status'.[50] The figures of upper-case, canonical History feature in most Chamoiseau novels, but their role tends to be a cameo one, only vaguely understood (or sometimes comically misunderstood) by the population at large. In Chapter 1, I alluded to the delight caused by de Gaulle's radio address to the island ('Un 24 du mois de juin il s'adressa à nous, à nous oui! À nous directement', *CSM*, p. 56). In a text in which temporal markers are generally absent, this date, at once precise and vague, suggests the *illusion* of participation created by the people's new-found importance to the French war effort. For what they fail to see is that de Gaulle's intervention is a self-serving gesture motivated solely by the need to find soldiers to fight in France's war, and that his 'direct' address issues in fact from a distance of thousands of kilometres. In *Texaco*, the pathetically grateful attitude of the war veterans, crippled in the cause of an indifferent metropolis, underlines the abusiveness of the colonial relationship: 'Un vieux-nègre charroyait ses chaussures de 14 comme preuve de son amour (il y avait perdu quatre de ses orteils). Un autre, poussé dans une brouette, venait rappeler ses jambes offertes à la Patrie et redire à de Gaulle qu'il restait disponible pour son prochain appel' (p. 361). De Gaulle's infamous visit to Martinique in 1963 is also revealed to be an empty performance. His words are conveyed from afar, and indeed distorted, by loudspeakers, and although Marie-Sophie follows him on his walkabout through Fort-de-France, 'à chaque fois, il était ailleurs' (*Texaco*, p. 363). Like her father, and by implication like her fellow islanders, she is excluded from the so-called momentous historical events of Martinique, pushed to the margins – at one point she falls into the sea – both literally and metaphorically. De Gaulle's distance from his people is again underlined, notably in the apparent confusion as to whether he commends the islanders for being 'français' or 'foncés'. The contact with 'History' has been so highly mediated that the truth becomes undecipherable.[51]

In another of his many reflections on the construction of history, Esternome displays a characteristic suspicion of the linear and the teleological, urging Marie-Sophie to 'pense[r] aux courbes':

> Sophie, c'était quitter leurs histoires, pour baille-descendre dans notre histoire. Mais leurs histoires à eux continuaient, et notre part prenait comme ça une autre courbe. Pense aux courbes. Les caraïbes vivaient une courbe. Les mulâtres avaient une courbe à eux, et les békés appuyaient sur une autre, et le tout frémissait de l'Histoire que les bateaux de France jour après jour débarquaient à Saint-Pierre. (*Texaco*, pp. 138–39)

The distinction established here is revealing: upper-case History is conceived of as a product shipped in from France and imposed on the island. In other words, even the ruling white elite on the island, the *békés*, are not seen to be in possession of that particular privilege. Esternome conceptualizes the histories of the Martinican population as a series of distinct and mutually complicating 'courbes', rather than as a directional or linear progression. This trope, like Glissant's concept of the 'détour', is particularly valuable for the ex-slave population. For the *courbe* represents a deviant way to sidestep or to out-manœuvre the master(s), to 'quitter leurs histoires'. The attainment of the *mornes* by the ex-slave population, evoked in this quotation, represents one such historical detour, a sidestepping of the controlling impulses of the master (narrative), an attempt to carve out a space beyond the master's control, both literally ('les békés n'avaient pièce griffe en terre') and discursively (this event is absent from 'official' history).

More to the point, history is consistently shown to be neither neutral nor innocent, but is clearly seen to be constituted *through* language. While, for example, history seeks to fill in the blanks of the past and to eradicate uncertainty and doubt, Esternome claims a quite different relationship to the past, declaring that '[il] ne faut pas répondre à toutes les questions' (*Texaco*, p. 64). Hence, he refuses to answer Marie-Sophie's childhood questions about slavery (p. 44), and similarly eschews any description of the *béké* master of the house into which he was born a slave (p. 58). Slavery is a notable silence, beyond language, a present-absent which is all the more powerfully suggested for being only minimally described. On the other hand, taking ownership of the word itself is an assertion of agency by the slaves, allowing a sidestepping of the master's authority:

> Ils disaient avec leurs mots: l'esclavage. Pour nous c'était entendre l'estravaille. Quand ils le surent et dirent à leur tour l'estravaille pour nous parler en proximité, nous avions déjà raccourci l'affaire sur l'idée de travail... hi hi hi, la parole sillonnait, Sophie, la parole sillonnait comme une arme...
> (*Texaco*, p. 58)

In subverting the language of the master, the slaves become active agents in their own history, seizing the power to name. The spoken word 'sillonne' cuts through the unified and unitary narrative of 'esclavage', opening up furrows and fissures, and providing a productive and subversive 'détour' within which the slave population can maintain a sense of opacity. Again, the value of the non-linear, or the *courbe*, is underlined. Later, Esternome explains to his daughter, 'Marie-phie, mon sucre d'orge, en créole on sait nommer l'esclavage, ou les chaînes, ou le fouet, mais aucun de nos mots ou pièce de nos titimes ne dit l'abolition' (p. 116). If, according to Wittgenstein's dictum, the limits of one's language are the limits of one's world, then the obverse is also true. The highly charged signifier 'Abolition', so crucial to the linear, progressive history of Martinique, means literally nothing to the slave population, who find themselves just as exploited as before; Esternome comments wryly, 'La sueur, Marie-Sophie, avait le même vieux goût' (p. 129). The non-existence of the word for 'abolition' in the Creole lexicon thus does not reveal a deficiency in the language itself, but suggests rather its unnecessary status for the black population. Of more relevance for the slaves is the wresting of liberty by the people themselves:

> Sophie, je ne sais pas ce que tu cries 'Révolution', mais tu peux fêter ce jour de mai. On possède ce souvenir-là, alors qu'un lot d'autres souvenirs ont été effacés, des charges de nos colères n'ont pas gardé une trace! [...] Et puis

> Sophie, crie-le comme tu veux et fais avec ce que tu veux. L'Histoire n'en
> vaut pas plus. (*Texaco*, p. 117)

The word 'révolution', a catchphrase of the historian with its connotations of definitive turning points and of absolute beginnings and endings, is not one that Esternome recognizes. Beyond these rhetorical implications, the revolutionary narrative stresses the generosity of France, and emphasizes the centrality of the French abolitionist Victor Schoelcher. The May date preferred by Esternome commemorates a spontaneous uprising by the slaves themselves, which pre-empted by ten days the official ratification of the revolution led by Schoelcher on 27 April.[52] This collective memory, which sees the agency of the slaves overtake the indulgence of the master, is crucially figured as a memory that is owned by the slaves ('on possède ce souvenir-là'). In true postmodern style, the novel has us explore the strategic investment of particular groups or political ideologies in these specific formations of memory.

In the imitation of the outward features of reliable historiography, *Texaco* participates in the postmodern project, 'the challenging of certainty, the asking of questions, the revealing of fiction-making where we might once have accepted the existence of some absolute "truth"'.[53] While the apparatuses of 'official history' are undermined, an imaginative and creative approach to the past is positively endorsed. If Marie-Sophie tends to lose the thread of her own story, her father is even further removed from Cartesian rationality, choosing to 'spin yarns' rather than to respect the monolithic and exclusionary ideal of truth. She remembers him 'recréant le pays au gré de sa mémoire et de ce qu'il savait (ou imaginait) des histoires que nous eûmes dessous l'Histoire des gouverneurs, des impératrices, des békés, et finalement des mulâtres' (p. 136). He thus delves underneath the 'sliding scale' of historically important figures, a hierarchy from which the slave population is excluded. What he imagines acquires as much currency as what he empirically 'knows', because Esternome's story, like that of his ancestors, is accessible only through an effort of the imagination:

> Mon Esternome [...] me disait tout puis le contraire de tout. L'envers valait
> l'endroit, et l'endroit le plus souvent était des deux côtés. Et quand il s'y
> perdait il murmurait confus: Aveuglage, embrouillage, petite Sophie, rien
> n'était clair en ce temps-là. (*Texaco*, p. 83)

No fixed guarantee of meaning is possible, but multiple alternatives are offered. Thus, conventional notions of a unified, monolithic and objective truth are disregarded in favour of a more fluid and imaginative evocation of the past. Indeed, the elasticity of the term *histoires* would seem not only to admit the oral, the fictional and the imagined, but also accommodates the blatantly fabricated or the outlandish; 'raconter des histoires' means to tell a fib, to make something up. And indeed, deliberate fabrication is endorsed by Esternome (using again the image of an interlacing of *courbes*) as a means to a more authentic 'retrieval' of the past:

> Dans ce que je te dis là, il y a le presque-vrai, et le parfois-vrai, et le vrai à moitié. Dire une vie c'est ça, natter tout ça comme on tresse les courbes du bois-côtelettes pour lever une case. Et le vrai-vrai naît de cette tresse. Et puis, Sophie, *il ne faut pas avoir peur de mentir si tu veux tout savoir...* (p. 139, my italics)

In novels such as *Solibo Magnifique* and *Texaco*, history loses any pretensions to unity or teleology, and becomes instead a negotiation between the objective fact and the imagined event, between the written document and the orally transmitted story, between the momentous and the trivial. The novelist is not a figure isolated from history; rather, fiction provides a privileged means of recovering the past, not through re-telling, but through an imaginative act of re-creation. Thus, the notion of a unitary and singular History is supplanted by a heterogeneous and endlessly proliferating one, one that privileges those lower-case stories which have been edited out of the dominant narrative. While the 'tige-maîtresse' referred to in the opening epigraph, like the root, is predicated upon stable origins and unified progression, Esternome endorses instead a rhizomatic model (a model typically grounded in the local soil and its manioc), and envisages history as a tangled and inclusive narrative. He suggests that the fact that a single version of the past (the 'tige-maîtresse') has gained precedence over all others is the arbitrary result of the unequal power relations on the island, rather than deriving from any inherent sense of 'value' or importance. History, then, is a relative rather than an absolute narrative. It is only in the knitting together of all the separate strands of the island history – strands which each group has conceptualized in their own fashion – that a properly collective history becomes viable.

Texaco uses 'the paratextual apparatus of historiography [...] to both inscribe and undermine the authority and objectivity of historical sources and explanations'.[54] And it is particularly in *Texaco* that narrators seek to legitimize an authority that they themselves have compromised. While Oiseau de Cham cannot count on his tape recorder, it did at least serve to 'compenser les trous de [s]on attention' (p. 423). Given, however, that these lapses of attention are exacerbated by Marie-Sophie's frequent 'trous de mémoire', the narrator's reliability is simultaneously bolstered and undermined. On the closing page of the novel, the *authorial* voice – rather than the by now familiar narratorial voice of 'Oiseau de Cham'/*le marqueur* – intrudes, naming and thanking the real inhabitants of Texaco (among them Serge Letchimy, architect and, since 2001, mayor of Fort-de-France). Chamoiseau thus invokes the tone of documentary realism or of ethnography – a frequently invoked discipline – to reinforce the authenticity of the novel, and to suggest its status as a social chronicle. In recognizably postmodern fashion, the narrative uses and abuses, instals and then destabilizes convention, self-consciously pointing to its own inherent paradoxes and provisionality. The transition from *Solibo Magnifique* to *Texaco* could be read as a progression from a lament for the past towards a narrative in which 'the past as "referent" finds itself gradually bracketed, and then effaced altogether, leaving us with nothing but texts'.[55] This privileging of textuality will, however, be counteracted by an increasing investment in the physical relics and traces of the past, a kind of materialization of memory, which will be the subject of the next chapter.

CHAPTER 4

Memory Materialized:
Traces of the Past

Memory is at once an innate capacity, and an intangible 'store' of past experiences, sensations, abilities and events. But as recent studies of memory have repeatedly underlined, it is mediated through and stimulated by *things*: sites, monuments or archives in the public domain, and paraphernalia, possessions or souvenirs in the personal sphere. In his highly critical study of the prevalence of memory as an explicit theme in recent writing, Kerwin Klein argues that contemporary memory is frequently vested in 'a dramatically imperfect piece of material culture, and such fragments are best if imbued with pathos'. These memorial tropes, he argues, have emerged as one of the common features of our new cultural history, in which, time and again, 'readers confront the abject object; photographs are torn, mementos faded, toys broken'.[1] Whatever the validity of Klein's polemical analysis – and I have discussed some of its limitations in the Introduction – it is undeniable that the items of material culture which he discusses are remarkable for their absence in Chamoiseau's work, which is largely devoid of the 'stuff' of life: furniture, toys, presents, objects, clothes.[2] This absence cannot be seen, moreover, as a simple reflection of the non-Western, non-materialistic culture which his works describe; indeed, such a description of Martinican society is in any case questionable. Even in an early plantation novel such as Zobel's *La Rue Cases-nègres*, the narrator is repeatedly drawn to precisely such 'abject objects' – the sugar box, the 'planche' on which Médouze sleeps, and, most poignantly, the bowl so valued by Man Tine – if only to suggest their scarcity and preciousness, and by extension to reinforce the poverty of the setting.[3] In Chamoiseau's writing, however, with the possible exception of *Biblique*, the *objet (re)trouvé* provides no stimulus to memory, no metaphorical portal into the past, and indeed is only very rarely evoked. Rather, as we saw in the previous chapter, it is the spoken word, in all of its ephemeral and intangible mystery, which stimulates and conveys the connection to the past, and which is repeatedly placed at the centre of the novelistic quest.

Despite the general paucity of reference to physical objects, however, a sense of longing for a material or tangible connection to the past becomes increasingly prominent as Chamoiseau's work progresses. This yearning, which already inflects *Texaco* and *Guyane: traces-mémoires du bagne* becomes more pronounced in later works (*Ecrire en pays dominé*; *L'Esclave vieil homme*; *Cases en pays-mêlés*). Such a material connection is not to be found, however, in the monuments which are such a recurrent feature of the postcolonial topography. *Guyane* opens with the statement that 'Nos Monuments demeurent comme des douleurs. Ils témoignent de douleurs. Ils conservent des douleurs' (p. 13). The capital M – the upper case is always to be treated with some suspicion in Chamoiseau's work – suggests that we are in the realm of large-scale and exclusionary History, precisely the mode from which, as we saw in Chapter 3, painful slave experiences are absent; or, if they are present, they are unrecognizably distorted. While History commemorates its chosen individuals and events in a highly visible and self-confident way, Chamoiseau is more concerned to recover the overlooked and contingent traces of the past. The *trace*, or *trace-mémoires*, a privileged term in both fiction and theory, functions as a link to the collective past, a usually physical relic or artefact, providing unintended collateral against the attrition of forgetting. In one of his many, evolving definitions of the term,[4] Chamoiseau explains that

> La *Trace* est marque concrète: tambour, arbre, bateau, panier, un quartier, une chanson, un sentier qui s'en va... Les *mémoires* irradient dans la Trace, elles *l'habitent* d'une présence-sans-matière offerte à l'émotion. Leurs associations, *Traces-mémoires*, ne font pas monuments, ni ne cristallisent une mémoire unique: elles sont le jeu des mémoires qui se sont emmêlées. [...] Leurs significations demeurent évolutives, non figées-univoques comme celles du monument. (*EPD*, p. 120, italics in original)

Unlike the monument – whose monolithic aspirations, Chamoiseau implies, impose a unitary signification and seek to determine interpretation – the trace's meaning is unfixed and multivalent, registering collective endeavour rather than celebrating individual achievement, and open to continual reinterpretation. The trace is valued precisely for its direct, spontaneous and contingent relationship with collective memory, an immediacy which stands in stark contrast to the distortions of both memorialization (monuments and statues) and mechanical reproduction – tape recorders, computers, cameras, the written word itself. While the archive, the text and the monument succeed the event, and have an unmistakably secondary quality, the trace is a kind of raw material which would appear to guarantee an æsthetics of authenticity and immediacy, and in which the potentially corrupting processes of interpretation and interference are minimized. The term as Chamoiseau uses it resonates strongly with Paul Ricœur's notion of the trace, as outlined in *Temps et récit III*. In this volume, Ricœur argues that history – the writing of narratives – is responsible for instituting a sense of historical time, through such 'reflective instruments' as the calendar, generational succession, documents and archives, and the trace.[5] Most of these have been decisively revealed as inadequate vectors of temporality in the Caribbean. But Ricœur's final term, the *trace*, corresponds closely to Chamoiseau's deployment of the same word. Both writers are concerned with vestiges, material entities, remainders and sign-effects, and seek to show how physical objects shape – and are shaped by – collective memory. For it is precisely what Ricœur calls the 'caractère chosique' of the trace which lends it significance.[6] This chapter will examine two very different instances of the trace as represented in Chamoiseau's work. First, memory is frequently vested in the Creole house, a construction that signifies more fully by its material make-up than by its interior or its contents. We will then discuss the stones and bones which haunt Chamoiseau's writing, and which become increasingly prominent in later works.

La Case Créole

A whole history remains to be written of *spaces* – which would at the same time be the history of *powers* [...] from the great strategies of geopolitics to the little tactics of the habitat.[7]
Michel Foucault

Historically, African-American people believed that the construction of a homeplace, however fragile and tenuous (the slave hut, the wooden shack) had a radical political dimension.[8]
bell hooks

Guyane: traces-mémoires du bagne opens with the acknowledgement that the statues and marble plaques which punctuate postcolonial space celebrate only the colonists and their exploits. However, the text goes on to acknowledge a whole range of less ostentatious, more concealed edifices (forts, churches, chapels, mills, dungeons, buildings and plantation out-houses) which harbour the long-repressed memory of the slave population. These places have a peculiarly spectral and uncanny quality in Chamoiseau's work, at once familiar and unfamiliar, representing what Freud would describe as that which 'ought to remain hidden but which has come to light'.[9] As storehouses of the slave experience, they are frequently shown to be haunted and in need of purification, not because of their direct implication in acts of brutality and torture, but rather because the population in the present has forgotten or repressed such atrocities. We will return to this idea in more detail in Chapter 5.

On the other hand, one of the most positive, least *unheimlich* (unhomely) sites in Chamoiseau's work is that of the house, known in Creole as *la case*, which occupies a central position in the Creole landscape of memory and identity. In *Texaco*, the house acquires a fully drawn metaphorical dimension, while more recently Chamoiseau has authored the text for a collaborative publication, *Cases en pays-mêlés*, in which a narrative celebrating the *case créole* is accompanied by photographs of traditional houses in a number of Caribbean islands. One reason for the importance afforded to the house is its apparent independence from the plantation structure. The houses which most interest Chamoiseau are those built (and constantly rebuilt) by the newly liberated slaves and their descendants after the abolition of slavery and beyond. These fragile edifices, because they exemplify a tentative claiming of space and an affirmation of settlement, represent one of the emblematic examples of Creole culture, creativity and improvisation.

The house fulfils quite a different symbolic function, then, to that with which it is associated in the traditional European context. In *La Poétique de l'espace*, for example, Gaston Bachelard analyses the centrality of the house in identity formation, celebrating 'la plénitude première de l'être de la maison', and wondering whether the material solidity of the building permits an 'essence intime et concrète' to emerge.[10] Alain Robbe-Grillet similarly points to this correspondence of self and home in his critique of the classic novel, *Pour un nouveau roman*:

> Le grand roman du XIXe siècle en particulier, Balzac en tête, regorge de maisons, de mobiliers, de costumes, longuement, minutieusement décrits [...]. Il s'agissait le plus souvent de planter un décor, de définir un cadre de l'action, de présenter l'apparence physique de ses protagonistes. Le poids des choses ainsi posées de façon précise constituait un univers stable et sûr, auquel on pouvait ensuite se référer.[11]

Robbe-Grillet suggests that in the traditional nineteenth-century novel, the house is at the heart of a wider representational nexus, and serves in its solidity and antiquity to underwrite the certainties of a whole fictional universe. Writing in 1976, however, Edward Brathwaite declares that one of the greatest problems facing the West Indian writer is precisely how to write about houses: 'A house suggests clearly defined boundaries: physical, emotional, traditional. The traditional English/European novel is a "house" and is usually, in one way or another, about houses'.[12] For the Antillean writer, Brathwaite suggests, the space of the home is far from being one of plenitude, generational continuity or ontological security, far from the 'intimité protégée' of Bachelard or from the 'univers stable et sûr' which Robbe-Grillet discerns in Balzac.[13] And indeed in Chamoiseau's work, the house is rarely seen as a sanctuary or as a place of protective retreat. It is precisely the permeability of its boundaries (its doors, windows and locks) that is emphasized, and very little of significance happens *intra muros*. While Bachelard argues that personal space provides a means of asserting an individual identity and of bolstering a sense of selfhood distinct from the other (outside), Glissant would counter, as we have seen, that the Antillean artist is concerned not so much with the 'être intime' as with the fact that 'cet intime est inséparable du devenir de la communauté'.[14] This privileging of the community over the individual psyche is clearly exemplified in Chamoiseau's work.[15] Immersion in the domestic space is imbued with primarily negative undertones; it is a way of cutting oneself off from the community, and is usually associated with painful and traumatic experiences.[16]

If, then, domestic scenes of *inhabiting* space are relatively rare, *Texaco* focuses on the building process in the aftermath of abolition, and pays particular attention to the materials employed. The material construction and maintenance of the house is a fundamental and urgent matter, given the total absence of any such pre-existing structures. The building process is complicated by the climatic reality of an island under constant threat of cyclones, and which has been substantially marked by one of the worst volcanic disasters in history. Moreover, the house is shown to be under continual threat of human assault (eviction, looting and burning, and all manner of physical attack on its structure). Just as the word 'En-ville', created by Chamoiseau, emphasizes the notion of a dynamic process, a trajectory towards the city rather than an accomplished reality, so the depiction of the house turns on the acquisition and attainment of a precarious and ever-evolving space (the 'en-case', so to speak), rather than on the enjoyment of this space as an intimate retreat. The 'Noutéka des mornes', a crucial section which outlines the struggle for space in the hills, puts the house at the centre of the project: 'Calcule sur l'endroit de ta case. Le restant va bonnement' (p. 147). The novel's characters include builders, carpenters, masons and a town planner, and details of interior space as a traditional décor are entirely subsumed by the elaboration of the material structure of the house (its foundations, its framework, its beams and its roof). The construction – or perhaps more appropriately the fabrication – of the domestic space is imbued with a highly symbolic charge, and the multiple materials appropriated and deployed by the people are lovingly listed as so many strands in an ever-evolving identity. Creating a 'house of one's own' signals an attempt to take possession of space, an initiative which is metonymically associated with the radical need to claim, or rather to construct, an identity.

Born into the plantation (significantly, in French, the *habitation*), Esternome is the son of a domestic slave rather than a *nègre-de-terre*. He admits to his daughter in his later years that he had been 'un vrai nègre de Grand-case', looking down on the slaves who worked outside, throwing himself into the gossip and intrigue of the house, and scheming to ingratiate himself with the master's family. The very fact of being *inside* the 'Big House', and hence confronted in an intimate manner with the lives of the white family, means that the internalization of its structures and practices is almost inevitable; indeed, on acquiring his liberty, Esternome is reluctant to depart.[17] But it is this attachment to the *Grand-case* which provides the inspiration for his career as a builder, and has a key role in shaping a story whose plot is, in fact, driven by the basic need to claim a plot of land on which to settle. For the young boy, the fascination engendered by the house has less to do with the more obvious markers of opulence (furnishings, food or clothing, for example) than with the skeleton of the house, the materials used in its construction, and the fortification with which it is surrounded:

> C'était une longue bâtisse de bois immortelle, environnée d'épineux pieds-citrons, de glycérias et d'orchidées. [...]. Une magie diffuse naissait, lui sembla-t-il, de l'amarre des poteaux et des planches. Il se demandait quelle qualité de force avait pu élever cela, associer ces essences, domestiquer ces vents, ces ombres mœlleuses et ces lumières. Cette admiration atteignit un sommet dans l'oublié grenier où une géométrie de poutrelles nouait l'ensemble de la Grand-case. Cette vue de la charpente détermina sans doute les tracées de sa vie, de son destin et finalement du mien. (*Texaco*, p. 54)

Most impressive, then, is the planter's apparent success in mastering his environment and in erecting a seemingly invincible habitat. The key words (*longue, immortelle, force, domestiquer*) lay the emphasis on duration, indestructibility and exclusion, while the mystery and magic of the building mean that it is frequently compared to a cathedral. Physically set apart from its surroundings, the master's house is a forbidding and intimidating structure:

> La Grand-case s'élevait au centre des dépendances, des bâtiments et des pail-lotes. A partir d'elle, rayonnaient les champs, les jardins, les emblavures de café escaladant la pente des arbres au bois précieux. Elle dominait le tout, semblait tout aspirer. Le harassement des bœufs, le désarroi des nègres, les belletés de la canne, le chuintement des moulins, cette boue, ces odeurs, ce

pourri de bagasse existaient afin de nourrir ses beaux-airs de puissance. (*Texaco*, p. 55)

Everything, it seems, is designed to feed the illusion of omnipotence that the master's house represents. Of course, this exaggerated and ostentatious dominance of space can be seen in itself to derive from a lack of security. As Homi Bhabha reminds us, the power of the colonizer is always under threat; surveillance is therefore both a necessity and a pleasure.[18] Here the house, in its privileged panoptical position, presents an ideal vantage point, literally at the centre of things. Moreover, in addition to fulfilling the master's scopic drive, the house must also be seen by the slaves, in order to reinforce their sense of subjugation. They cannot escape the view of the house, 'l'apercevant des partout du travail, en gard[ant] l'œil furtif que nous aurions plus tard sur la face des En-villes ou de leur cathédrale' (p. 55). In its rigid verticality and its impenetrable dimensions, the house proves more awe-inspiring than the *béké* himself. Indeed, the master's sense of power and control depends on the house, whose solidity and permanence project a compensatory image of power which he is, somewhat pathetically, unable to fulfil:

> Le géreur et les chefs enoblissaient leurs pas à l'approche de ses marches, leur gorge canaille se trouvait une huile douce, et dessous la galerie ils ôtaient leur chapeau. La personne du Béké n'obtenait point semblable respect. Dans les champs, découpée sur la lointaine façade, sa silhouette à cheval semblait frêle ou débile – mais de près, sur le pas de sa demeure, elle était invincible. (*Texaco*, p. 55)

But if excess is commonly acknowledged as a strategy to mask lack, then the show of command exhibited by the white man in the Caribbean served to compensate for a profound sense of insecurity and disentitlement. For the seeming permanence of the *Grand-case* proves to be as illusory as the principles on which the *habitation* was founded, and the buildings collapse with the first cyclone. The illusory nature of such apparent invincibility is definitively underlined in the wake of abolition, when the destitution of the Big House is variously conveyed through its being 'ouverte aux quatre vents' (p. 119), or indeed, conversely, in its being 'fermée dure comme avec des clous' (p. 108).[19]

If the master had neither an ancestral home in the Caribbean, nor a repertoire of appropriate construction techniques, handed down over generations, at his disposal, so too the African populations came as strangers to the islands. But the projects of construction on which the ex-slaves eventually embark, like the 'little tactics of the habitat' identified by Foucault,[20] diverge significantly from those of the colonizer. While both are concerned with the attempt to claim space, the project initiated by Esternome, for example, proceeds in fits and starts and, in its own detours and setbacks, can be seen to evolve as an organic and dynamic process, rather than being imposed with a false sense of certainty from the outset. The Normandy carpenter Théodorus Koco-doux, brought in to oversee the repair of the plantation in the aftermath of a devastating cyclone, acts in this respect as a kind of mentor to Esternome. Crucially, Koco-doux's art is a composite *bricolage*, drawing on metropolitan, African and aboriginal Caribbean techniques, so that 'A mesure-en mesure, *sa science des constructions devint particulière, accordée aux manières du vent et de la terre dans ce pays de nouveautés*' (p. 69, my italics). The 'temps de carbet et d'ajoupas', in other words the period of Amerindian civilization spanning almost 5000 years, is missing from the diegetic space of the novel itself, which opens with the 'temps de paille'. This absence starkly reflects the obliteration of the native Carib and Arawak people from the island space, and from the representation of the island's history. Crucially, however, Esternome assimilates aspects of their techniques and materials: 'Des Caraïbes, j'ai retenu la technique du couvert en profitant des matériaux du paysage. Roseaux. Lataniers. Palmistes' (*Texaco*, p. 53). Rather than being mapped on from the outside, then, this is a poetics of space which has evolved naturally and organically out of the remarkable hybridity of this particular island context. In a section entitled 'docteur-cases' Esternome's burgeoning talent in construction is described as an experimental and ever-evolving one. His first house was built from bamboo, but 'au gré de ses humeurs mon Esternome leva d'autres qualités de cases [...] un koudmen à telle heure, une faveur s'il te plaît. Si bien qu'ils ne manquèrent de rien, ni plants pour le jardin, ni feuille pour la médecine' (*Texaco*, pp. 150–51). If the houses are founded on the basis of this spontaneous 'koudmen' (*coup de main*), which marshals various talents and skills in a mutual project of *entr'aide*, they are maintained by virtue of their protean and adaptable nature. Unlike the *Grand-case*, which in its vertical rigidity, hardness and closure runs the risk of absolute and irreparable destruction, it is the potential of the little houses to be dismantled, renovated or extended at will – in a sense their very precariousness and pliability – which ironically guarantees their survival:

> De terrasses en terrasses, mon docteur construisit pour les autres des cases de crécré, des cases de bois-ravine, des cases de bois-murette, de canéfices et bien sûr de campêches. Il construisit des cases faciles à déplacer si la terre changeait trop, et des cases cramponnées à des têtes de falaises. Quand le bois n'était pas abondant, il complétait la tresse avec une terre grasse mêlée de petites feuilles et pétries au talon sous cadence de tambours. En d'autres

lieux, il plaquait aux parois un crépi de son cru (chaux-coquillages-sable et caca-bœuf). (*Texaco*, p. 151)

Here, the volume of composite nouns, conjoined by one or several hyphens, reflects Esternome's ingenious and opportunistic techniques, based on an audacious combination of *métissage* and recycling. Later, his daughter adopts a similarly enterprising approach in her endeavours to found the novel's eponymous quarter: 'Désormais tout pouvait me servir, un bout de ficelle, la grâce d'un clou, une caisse abandonnée... toute qualité était bonne qualité' (p. 329). Such an approach would seem to enact Bourdieu's notion of the 'habitus', a notion which mobilizes the notion (temporal, and even temperamental) of the habit, and celebrates 'the durably installed generative principle of regulated improvisations'.[21] The principles on which the *Grand-case* is founded appear to ignore the specificities of place, and to treat it rather as a blank canvas to be appropriated and settled. In stark contrast, father and daughter would seem to view place, much as Bourdieu would advocate, as a practice rather than a geographic or topographic location, the site of a series of repetitive but evolving transactions, resolutely grounded in local material conditions.

Esternome's identity is tightly intertwined with his vocation as a builder, to the extent that his very vocabulary is determined by this *métier*. He is incapable of describing his sexual experiences with Osélia because he 'ne disposait dans sa calebasse que des méthodes de charpenterie et rien des cinquante-douze pages de dictionnaire utiles' (*Texaco*, p. 78), while his love for Ninon is evoked in images that emphasize solidity ('l'enlacement des charpentes'; 'le prise d'une maçonnerie', p. 99). Moreover, access to the first person pronoun, in other words subjectivity itself, is directly enabled by this project of construction, so that space and subjectivity are shown to be deeply, reciprocally, imbricated. In an extended passage of almost three pages, which immediately succeeds the 'Noutéka des mornes', Esternome outlines the progressive fortification of these houses, intersplicing this text with the refrain 'je, je, je':

> Mon Esternome battait-bouche dans le *Je*. Je ceci. Je cela. J'ai construit des cases avec un bois-amer qui décourage la dent des termites affamées. Pour les poteaux, je prenais l'acajou, Marie-Sophie, ou le simarouba qui étonne les oiseaux, ou encore l'acoma, le balat, l'angelin, les longues fougères, le bois-lézarde ou bien le courbaril [...]. Moi je sais. Je. Je. Je. (*Texaco*, p. 157)

The progression from *Noutéka* ('nous étions') to *je* should not be seen as a triumphant statement of sovereign individualism, however. Self-assertion parallels rather than precedes the establishment of a community, and Esternome's resounding adoption of the 'je' is not the automatic entitlement of liberation but, crucially, is *earned* through his newly acquired knowledge of his environment ('Moi je sais'). These Creole houses, in their progressive construction, mirror – and directly contribute to – the diminishing sense of dislocation and exile experienced by Esternome and his peers. The 'enracinement' of the people, however, is neither proprietorial nor rigid in its attachment to place. Rather, it is an affirmation of liberty and of freedom of manœuvre, exploding restrictive definitions of home, and opening the structure up to any number of versatile materials and compositions. Esternome's loving litanies of materials are statements of abundance, variety and resourcefulness, signifying a profuse and unrestricted deployment of sources, liberally structured into a habitat beyond conventions, fixed points or stereotypes.

The reappropriation of these multiple and proliferating materials can be seen to mirror the art of the novelist himself. If, as Brathwaite suggested, every novel is a house, then the spatial organization of *Texaco* reflects the heterogeneous and audacious practices of the Creole people. Just as lexical materials are re-combined into startling configurations, so major canonical intertexts – the Bible, Greek myth, Césaire – are sampled, reduced to scraps, and then (seemingly) randomly adopted, adapted, reworked and discarded. In other words, intertextual counterpoints most frequently remain unabsorbed and unassimilated into the text under construction, and tend rather to draw attention to their own 'otherness' from it. The novel is itself jerry-built from fragments drawn from disparate fictional sources – the *cahiers* in which are transcribed Esternome's words, letters, inserts such as the 'Noutéka' or the 'Songeries d'Idoménée', the notes exchanged between *marqueur* and *urbaniste*, the transcription of the *informatrice*'s words – and felicitously re-assembled, so that bits and pieces of narrative eventually form into a montage of interconnected lives. It is hardly surprising that the discourse used to describe the ideal home coincides largely with that used in the *Eloge de la créolité*, for example, which uses the mosaic as a metaphor of Creole identity. So too in *Texaco*, Marie-Sophie describes 'Nos cases (reconstruites trente-douze fois) semblaient de délirantes mosaïques: des bouts de toutes qualités s'ajoutaient à des éclats de toutes espèces' (p. 367). In a sense the text becomes itself a sort of building site, drawing attention to its multiple materials rather than to any sense of cohesion or coherence. It is the disparate and interweaving threads binding the text(ile)/*Texaco* together which are privileged over any sense of seamlessness, just as it is through the agency of the community that the quarter, however uncomfortably, is able to gel together. The houses of Texaco, which are said to form a community which pre-dates the human community (p. 304), are 'soudées par le malheur', and they are 'détruites bien souvent ensemble' (p. 364).

The town planner who comes to demolish the eponymous slum, at the chronological end-point but the diegetic opening of the novel, finally discerns in it a poetics of space that counters Bachelard: 'cette poétique de cases vouée au désir de vivre' (*Texaco*, p. 269). Survival itself is the objective which undergirds the construction and maintenance of the houses of the *petit peuple* and the 'poetics of space' which defines them is what Régis Antoine has called an 'esthétique des bribes',[22] an expression which recalls Foucault's 'little tactics of the habitat', cited in the epigraph. In other words, the solid, regimented and hierarchical disposition of the house in the nineteenth-century bourgeois novel suggests a secure view of self and world, and indeed of one's sense of one's proper place in the world. Similarly, it is precisely in the Creole people's scavenging and makeshift response to construction, destruction and reconstruction, and their ability to glean, to recycle and make something new out of the randomly assorted detritus which is available, that the metonymic association between self and space can be seen to be carried through.

The 'Repères chronologiques de nos élans pour conquérir la ville' with which *Texaco* opens anchor the text in a neat chronological framework based on the actual framework of the Creole house. Serving themselves as a kind of threshold, they announce a progression from the 'temps de carbet et d'ajoupas' to the 'temps béton', through various key materials used in the building process, in a manner reminiscent of the fable of the three little pigs.[23] The progressive fixing of the Creole people in time and space, their trajectory from the relative insecurity of straw and crate wood, to the finality of concrete, would seem to be a satisfactory conclusion to the novel, a compensatory response to Jacques André's evocation of the Antillean condition as one of a '*vacillement* des repères' (my italics).[24] And yet this conclusion remains problematic, and the desirability of the outcome is undermined at several points. The finality of the age of concrete is flagged up in the paratext through an onomatopœic effect; the preposition 'de', which harnesses the 'temps' to its associated material in the other periods, and thus in a sense 'ærates' the typographical organization ('temps de carbet et d'ajoupas'; 'temps de fibrociment' etc.), is noticeably missing from the 'temps béton'. The phonetic result of this absence is a dull, leaden assonance (a sound not improved by its proximity to 'embêtant'), while on a semantic level the effect is to reinforce fixity and definitiveness. Construction ceases to be a dynamic, organic and reversible process, and becomes, rather, a final and accomplished state. To compensate for André's 'vacillement des repères' with an over-rigid fixing of these *repères* in concrete is certainly seen as a victory, but perhaps a flawed one. As Marie-Sophie points out, this new order provokes not only delight in its permanence and solidity, but also the vague fear of the next police raid, 'car le béton était plus cher, plus lourd, plus encombrant. Détruit c'était une catastrophe dont on ne pouvait se relever à l'aise' (*Texaco*, p. 399). The progression from the hybrid, jerry-built hut to the permanence of the concrete house makes any makeshift, spontaneous approach to summary relocation and rebuilding impossible. The new order, moreover, inevitably raises expectations in terms of quality of life and material wealth; the investment in concrete leads in fact to a new materialism, which 'demandait des certitudes et exigeait d'autres conforts dont l'absence se faisait bizarrement insoutenable' (p. 400).

This material(istic) progression, from straw to concrete, has a metafictional corollary in the transition from the tumultuous orality of the spoken word to the massive solidity of the printed book. Entry into the two symbolic orders of writing and concrete, which guarantee the survival, respectively, of the Creole word and the Creole house, has its own cost. Pragmatically desirable, in that they guarantee a sense of posterity, both concrete and writing are discursively associated with death.[25] For Marie-Sophie, writing and death become consubstantial: in a section entitled 'Ecrire-mourir', near the start of the 'temps béton', she declares that 'vers cette époque oui je commençai à écrire, c'est-à-dire: un peu mourir', and describes her sense of having killed her father through transcribing his words, commenting that 'chaque phrase formolait un peu de lui' (p. 353). Equally, the 'temps béton' is for her a 'temps d'asphyxie. Le ciment de Texaco se figeait dans mon corps' (p. 393). Like the projects of renovation which have literally plastered over the cracks of Texaco, thus stifling its mosaic-like fissures and its vital idiosyncrasies, the formaldehyde of writing holds the living word in a false state of suspension. This inexorable progression is paralleled by the fact that the spoken word of her illiterate father ends up being translated and housed in the Bibliothèque Schoelcher at the end of the novel.

The interventions from Esternome, which become less frequent as the text progresses, are entirely absent from the age of concrete, and this section of the novel is accordingly denser and more monolithic. While a number of excerpts extraneous to the diegesis are accommodated, it is significant that most of these refer to other *texts* (the *marqueur* on Glissant, p. 354; Ti-Cirique on Jacques Roumain and Césaire, as well as Cervantes and Joyce, pp. 357–58), while the highly learned (and often specifically literary) interactions between town planner and *marqueur* account for the rest. These interventions between the *urbaniste* (a representative of institutional authority) and the *marqueur* (another authorial double, implicated, however reluctantly, in the symbolic order) reveal both to be well-meaning but ultimately misguided figures. While the latter is painfully aware of the inadequacy of his attempts to inscribe the word, the former remains convinced that his efforts have ensured the quarter's survival as a living *lieu de mémoire*, a term he specifically uses. Ironically, as Chris Bongie argues, 'the town planner's presence on this site of resistance to cultural oblivion is the sign of its contamination by history'.[26] The traditional Creole home requires no institutional support, but is an organic, living construction. However, like the oral tradition which is also mourned in *Texaco*, this house has been collapsed into a static order of definition and sameness, a state which metonymically gestures to the condition of the assimilated island more generally.

An even more pronounced sense of nostalgia (quite literally, home sickness) inflects the tale which Chamoiseau contributes to the phototext *Cases en pays-mêlés* (2000). This collaboration with Jean-Luc de Laguarigue, the bulk of which is made up of images of Caribbean houses, celebrates traditional Creole architecture as a uniquely appropriate metaphor for – and actual repository of – popular memory. The story opens with the news that a traditional straw house has been destroyed by fire. The family who had lived there are instantly consoled by the promise of a 'nouvelle case en bonnes planches et clous de France'. The community, concurring that the original material used 'n'avait aucun sens' (*CPM*, p. 10), views the house's obliteration as a welcome event. It is only the intervention of the *conteur*, M. Isomère Calypso, which troubles this consensus, and suggests the loss and impoverishment inherent in the disappearance of this 'vrac de mémoires'. The positioning of the storyteller as a uniquely sensitive cultural commentator reinscribes the association between a fragile orality and the improvised and disappearing Creole house, a parallel implicit throughout *Texaco*. Isomère later states that 'le conte est dans la case. La case est dans le conte' (p. 12), not least because both are associated with the dead of night ('le jour appartient au travail; la nuit appartient à la case', p. 13), and the litany of building materials, already familiar to readers of *Texaco*, reinforces the extent to which the house is directly linked to a particularly local memory. It is for this reason, the storyteller states, that one must mourn every house that disappears, 'Car ce n'est pas un abri qui s'en va. C'est un souvenir. C'est une histoire. C'est une manière de prendre la vie et d'organiser ce que l'on sait du monde' (p. 11). Once again, Bourdieu's *habitus*, the sense that place has to be created out of practice, habit and improvisation, is implicitly in play.

Pliability and fragility remain the qualities which, ironically, give the house the strength to withstand assault:

> Si le vent souffle, si l'eau déborde, la pluie fracasse, la case peut se défaire mais se refait facile. Si la vie bouge, l'usine s'éloigne, le champ recule, si la bonne terre se trouve plus loin, que la vie change, alors la case peut se soulever et s'emporter plus loin. (p. 15)

Because of its evolution over generations, the house is a kind of palimpsest, overwritten with layers of techniques and materials. Not only is it a site of memory, but it is in fact shown to be actively endowed with the capacity to remember, a rare quality among even the human characters in Chamoiseau's work. Although the memory of Africans and Caribs is emphasized (the indigenous inhabitants of the Caribbean are imprinted in the structures of the *case*: 'Ils construisaient tout cela d'une manière dont la case se souvient. C'est pourquoi toute case parle caraïbe pour qui sait l'écouter', p. 16), the house also remembers the 'mains trop claires' of the Europeans. Interestingly, then, in this later work, the *Grand-case* is presented as a less oppositional space than in *Texaco* or *L'Esclave vieil homme et le molosse*. While Esternome's techniques were initially inspired by the imposing structure of the *béké*'s house, this building and the *case créole* are generally presented in a context of polarization. Here, however, perhaps in keeping with the values of hybridity and interconnection signalled in the title (this is, after all, a 'pays mêlé'), the two structures are presented as complicit and inextricably intertwined; the narrator comments that 'Toute Grand-case provient donc des carbets caraïbes et des souvenirs perdus, souvenirs d'Europe, souvenirs d'Afrique. Et toute Grande-case est case dans son esprit' (p. 14). In other words, the master's and the slave's house both emerge from the context of the plantation. More to the point, the *Grand-case* was usually built by slaves or, later, by the labouring population made up of ex-slaves. This suggests that the two constructions share certain foundational elements, and that they cannot be seen as hermetically sealed one from the other.

The disintegration of the straw house, it is suggested in *Cases en pays-mêlés*, is not entirely accidental. It is linked, rather, to the broader cultural forces at work on the island, forces which it seems have encouraged the house to bring about its own destruction: 'Parfois, à force de ne plus comprendre, elle prend feu toute seule' (*CPM*, p. 17). In this personification the house, like one of the many aged protagonists in Chamoiseau's work, finds itself disorientated, out of time, and unable to endure. This notion of a self-destructive, suicidal *case* also inflects the second edition of the re-packaged *Antan d'enfance*, *Une enfance créole I* (1993; 1996), in which an additional paratext, signed 'Patrick Chamoiseau' and dated 'January 1996', has been inserted. 'L'Incendie de la vieille maison' is an account of the author's witnessing the devastation of his childhood home by fire, a threatened loss which in many ways eerily haunted both *Antan d'enfance* and *Chemin-d'école*. Describing the devastation caused by the fire, Chamoiseau comments, 'Je la soupçonne d'avoir voulu finir-avec-ça, comme disent les vieux nègres' (*Une enfance créole* I, p. 11), again suggesting that the fire results from a willed determination to escape the reality of contemporary Martinique.

Time and again in both autobiographies, the house's potential for (self-)destruction is intimated, and in the last two paragraphs of *Antan d'enfance* there is already a sense of impending doom: while in the past the house signified a 'noblesse diffuse', and its once vital are energies underlined ('vie', 'saisons' and 'sève ancienne'), the final two paragraphs seem to prefigure the house's demise. The last paragraph reveals that Man Ninotte is the only mother remaining in the otherwise deserted communal building, and figures the house as dying in its own dust. The emphasis is on vulnerability and frailty, as the house stands as a 'notaire fragile' to the memories which it has witnessed. As the narrator laments his 'enfance charbonnée', childhood and space become consubstantial, and he suggests that the destruction of the house in some way brings to an end any possibility of his rewriting this period:

> *Antan d'enfance* et *Chemin-d'école*: ces textes s'achèvent donc par un raide incendie. [...]. Le feu les a figés désormais. La présence de la vieille maison les autorisait à bouger, à couler, à vieillir, à se voir transformés par de nouveaux détails. Là, maintenant, dans la lueur de forge qui nimbe ma dernière vision d'elle, tout s'est raidi au grand jamais. Raidi et déraidi. Je ne pourrai plus y ajouter une ligne qui ne soit de nostalgie et de regret profond... – donc, qui ne soit étrangère à mon enfance créole. (pp. 12–13)

While the house endured, it seems, it held open for the writer the possibility of revisiting – therefore of rewriting – the story of childhood. Its destruction fixes forever its memory, and closes the door on this period of his life. As throughout Chamoiseau's work, place is an essential and active agent in, rather than a backdrop to, the construction of memory, and the destruction of a highly symbolic space such as the Creole house is shown to be an irredeemable loss which also has repercussions of an æsthetic nature. Once more, it is the house's status as *trace* (in other words, its physical connection to the past, rather than its symbolic nature) which is implicitly emphasized. This notion of the *trace* becomes increasingly significant within Chamoiseau's poetics, and will be explored in more detail below.

Primordial Materials: Stones and Bones

At the centre of the quest described in *Texaco* is the Creole house, a fragile structure set in opposition to the encroachment of concrete, an encroachment which is most obviously manifest in the increasing dominance of built-up apartment blocks and hotel chains. Improvisation, permeability and pliability are the qualities which are particularly celebrated in this chaotic and composite structure. Yet it is precisely these attributes which ensure the increasing marginalization of the traditional *case créole* in the contemporary Martinican landscape, and which explain the elegiac and nostalgic tone of *Cases en pays-mêlés*.

Throughout the 'temps-béton' in which *Texaco* culminates, concrete is discursively linked to inertia, petrification and, ultimately, oblivion. But elsewhere, naturally occurring stone is presented in a diametrical opposition to these negative qualities. The large standing stones and rocks found in forest land, ravines and clearings throughout the Caribbean gain an increasing prominence in Chamoiseau's work, and tend to symbolize a kind of primal connection to the pre-historic past. If marble and monuments – in other words worked, crafted or sculpted stone – are inadequate or distorting manifestations of the processes of collective memory, these ancient stones, apparently formed by primordial energies, emerge as a kind of ideal material. They stand as precious markers of temporal duration, permanence and continuity, markers which are otherwise unavailable in landscape and architecture. In a useful analysis of the trope of duration in Caribbean writing, Mary Gallagher cites Bachelard's observation that duration cannot be remembered as such; 'its density or extension', she notes, 'are captured, however – that is, materialized or spatialized – in the sedimented trace'. Gallagher goes on to observe that 'in French, the word for duration, "durée", has the same etymology as "dur" (hard or unyielding)'.[27] If the desire for a sense of duration is a stated aim of the *créolité* movement – it claims that literature should 'nous restitue[r] à la durée, à l'espace-temps continu' (*Eloge*,

p. 38) – then these stones provide a privileged realization of *dureté*, of duration and of endurance. For example, in *Guyane: traces-mémoires du bagne*, the opening epigraph from Segalen celebrates the immemorial qualities of the stones (immovability, unyieldingness, permanence), as well their memorial potential: 'Seules immobiles contre le défilé, voici les Pierres mémoriales que nul ordre de marche ne peut toucher ni ébranler' (p. 11). These ancient formations are at once outside time and deeply imbricated in it; they suggest a connection to a time beyond memory, while they simultaneously – by virtue of their very age and physical scale – encourage reflection on the past. It is through their timelessness, indeed, that they can be made to speak to every time.

Just as the construction techniques of the Caribs and the Arawaks are continually valorized in *Texaco* and *Cases en pays-mêlés*, so it is the stones' connection to the original Amerindian inhabitants of the island which gives them particular significance. As such, they represent a time before the brutal fractures of colonialism and slavery. In other words, counteracting the sense of belatedness that attends the Caribbean subject, these stones project a sense of temporal depth, and represent what Roger Caillois would describe as 'archives de la Genèse'.[28] Their position in forest space, moreover, among the 'Grands-bois' which, similarly, 'connaissaient l'Avant', and which 'recelaient l'hostie d'une innocence passée' (*EVH*, pp. 96–97), contributes to a sense of pre-lapsarian, Edenic bliss.[29] If, then, as Isomère comments, 'la case connaît le temps' (*CPM*, p. 14), suggesting that the house has evolved from the successive and brutal overlay of different historical periods, it could be countered, to quote Caillois once more, that stone is 'd'avant l'histoire, d'immémoriales seigneuries'.[30]

More to the point, the stones are the repositories of the first art produced on the islands; as such, they signify both historical and cultural origins. Over fifty pages of artists' images of the Caribbean – ranging from Gauguin to Wilfredo Lam to the work of contemporary Antillean sculptors – precede the literary history which constitutes the main part of *Lettres créoles*. The first image we see, however, is a photograph of an Amerindian rock engraving, depicting Kallinago, 'chef qui partit à la conquête des îles du Vent Monolithe' (*LC*, p. i); a footnote tells us that the Kalinagos [sic] were later renamed Caribs by the colonizers (p. 16), showing how completely the colonial mission has shaped even the history which predates it. Moreover, Chamoiseau and Confiant devote the first chapter of *Lettres créoles* to 'La roche écrite'. The appeal of such prehistoric art is of course not unique to the New World. In a recent article

Douglas Smith explores the literary response to the discovery of the Lascaux cave drawings in France in 1940, and notes that the event was used by writers such as Char and Malraux, writing in a wartime context, and later confronted with the real possibility of nuclear war, to put into question the whole notion of origins.[31] But in the Antillean context, the engravings have quite a different meaning. In the petroglyphics and engravings described, Chamoiseau and Confiant detect the hand of the first writers of the islands, who had 'tracé des cercles, des zigzags, des pointillés, des hachures'. The drawings which embellish the rocks suggest a 'parole fondatrice' and a 'récit des origines' (*LC*, p. 19); indeed, one of the myths of origins inspired by the engravings is related here, and has a highly biblical tone, beginning significantly with the words 'au commencement'. The chapter concludes with the acknowledgement that this silent literature continues to inform contemporary culture, with 'ces paroles brisées, éparses, partielles, qui remontent la tracée infinie de notre absence de Genèse' (p. 20).

Crucially, these drawings serve not only to compensate for this absent Genesis, but they provide powerful evidence of an æsthetic tradition divorced from the obligations of hunting and gathering. Again, as Smith shows, this was one of the most appealing aspects of the Lascaux discovery, and Bataille for one believed that '[h]uman beings do not fully become human beings until *homo faber*, the tool-maker whose values are governed by utility, becomes *homo ludens*, the playful artist who is no longer constrained by the limits of the materially useful'.[32] Such an apparently superfluous activity, expressing ludic, non-utilitarian values, carries an unimaginably stronger resonance – and is therefore to be all the more celebrated – in a culture whose entire *raison d'être*, in the modern period at least, has until relatively recently been exclusively based on the enforcement of labour for the pursuit of profit. The rock engraver therefore figures as a particularly inspiring ancestor in a culture which frequently proclaims the scarcity of such figures.[33] Chamoiseau and Confiant go on to suggest that with the appearance of the French *corsaires*, and the onset of colonial struggle, the *graveur*'s once crucial art becomes suddenly irrelevant ('Hélas! le métier de graveur n'avait plus tellement cours!', pp. 19–20). In his sudden and regrettable redundancy, then, the *graveur* can be seen as the benighted precursor of both the *conteur* and, thereafter, the *marqueur*.

In *Ecrire en pays dominé* – whose third section, 'Anabiose', has the subtitle 'Sur la pierre monde' – the stone is examined in a more sustained manner, so as to bring out a whole nexus of associations with the tombstone, the philosopher's stone and the memorial stone or *stèle*. Early in the text, the narrator summons the Amerindians, now only to be found in the mystical 'chant perdu des pierres perdus' (p. 24), and their voice, like the stones and rocks with which they are linked, resonates throughout the work. The narrator moves imaginatively through various subject positions ('moi-Colons'; 'moi-Chinois'), and eventually he takes on the voice of these indigenous peoples:

> Ce moi-Amérindiens me fit *quêter l'absence* [...]. J'ai remonté ainsi les anses tranquilles de la côte caraïbe, où le sable momifie des mémoires. Remonter la plage sombre qui souligne la ville morte, et aller pour rejoindre la Montagne, jusqu'à cette falaise qu'une légende institue Tombeau-des-Caraïbes. La présence-absence amérindienne est là, peuplant le sol en statuettes brisées, en haches, en herminettes, en disques de céramique, en restes de jaspe ou d'andésite, en pierres à trois pointes que les archéologues étiquettent comme énigmes. (*EPD*, p. 118, italics in original)

The coast – whose sand is described as 'mummifying' memories, conjuring up notions of retention, preservation and antiquity – harbours a whole range of material vestiges which will be progressively exhumed in the imagination. On reaching the legendary burial ground of the Caribs, the narrator discovers tools, utensils, fossils and mineral traces (andesite and jasper), as well as the enigmatic three-pointed stones. More significantly, this is also the site of human remains:

> De temps à autre des travaux publics exhument des miettes humaines devenues minérales. Au fond d'une anse, une pelle mécanique soulève tantôt ce que les archéologues appellent 'matériel anthropique': tessons de céramique, coquillages, ossements d'hommes et de femmes [...] comme si la nature concrétisait à sa manière *une présence-absence*. (*EPD*, p. 119, my italics)

This process is very much in keeping with Ricœur's notion of the trace, which is at once a signifier of presence and of absence, a 'marquage' (another word which resonates with a lexeme privileged by Chamoiseau) of anteriority, endurance and presence. This *marquage*, Ricœur argues,

> suggère d'abord l'idée d'un support plus dur, plus durable que l'activité transitoire des hommes: c'est en particulier parce que les hommes ont œuvré, commis leur ouvrage à la pierre, à l'os, aux tablettes d'argile cuite, au papyrus, au papier, à la bande magnétique, à la mémoire de l'ordinateur, que leurs œuvres survivent à leur ouvrage.[34]

Once again, the *dureté* and endurance of the trace are linked, and are set in opposition to the transience of human endeavour. Here, Ricœur suggests a comparison between the primitive technologies of sculpting on stone or engraving papyrus and the technologies of the present. It is a jarring juxtaposition, but one which finds a quite literal echo in

Chamoiseau's description of the imaginary dig, from which the narrator brings back fragments of Amerindian pottery: 'Morceaux épars. Formes brisées. Soupçons de modelages ou de sculpture. Je les ai disposés [...] près de l'ordinateur. J'écris en leur présence' (*EPD*, p. 119). For Chamoiseau as for Ricœur, the physicality of the written trace – however technologized – provides, through its potential for endurance, some resistance to the attrition of oblivion.

But it is without doubt in *L'Esclave vieil homme et le molosse*, the sister-text to *Ecrire en pays dominé*,[35] that the stone plays the most determining role. This hallucinatory, oneiric and deeply poetic novel tells the story of an old slave's flight from the plantation, pursued by the master and his dog. The *marronnage* through watery magma and forest space (with overt connotations of rebirth) ends when his way is blocked by an enormous volcanic rock. The story, ostensibly about physical displacement, is in fact much more concerned with a mental journey, a kind of imaginative odyssey in which the old man comes to identify in turn with the master and his dog, and in which his narrative is taken over by the voice of both. The seven chapter titles – the number is, of course, much favoured by Chamoiseau – suggest an elemental, primitive and unadorned fictional world: 'Matière'; 'Vivant'; 'Eaux'; 'Lunaire'; 'Solaire'; 'La Pierre'; 'Les Os'. The use of the definite article in the last two of these, however, appears to tether their meaning to a more concrete, more tangible reality, and stone (and, to a lesser extent, bone) are shown to have particular significance in the novel. Right from the beginning of the text, indeed, there is something in the description of the old man that suggests an immemorial quality, like that of the rock. His lack of a navel, for example, gestures towards a lack of ancestry, and confers on him a peculiarly timeless quality. He is described as 'un minéral de patiences immobiles' (p. 17), then as a 'pierre brûlante' (p. 45), and in the intercalated *entre-dire* by Glissant, which resonates obliquely with the main narrative, the first intervention describing an (other) old man announces 'il dure' (p. 16). The nexus of associations around *dureté-durée* comes to the fore once more in the *entre-dire* which precedes the chapter 'La Pierre'. Here, the Glissant text begins '*Cette pierre est une roche. [...] elle nous a fait trembler du tremblement de nos terres rouges, et c'est vrai, elle a enfanté le chien*' (*EVH*, p. 110, italics in original). This strange statement suggests, then, that the dog, too, has come from the rock, and the section goes on to mention the LaRoche/Laroche family, the *béké* family who are such an enduring presence in Glissant's novels. Such networks of echoes and vaguely intimated but ultimately enigmatic associations are typical of this novel, which like the rock itself is hard, opaque and resistant, reluctant to yield its meanings, and sedimented with an dense overlay of intertextual reference.

On being confronted by the rock, which he does not immediately recognize as such, the old slave is immediately struck by its immensity and by its hardness ('La chose est tassée, compacte, pleine d'elle-même', p. 115). But rather than being an impediment, the rock proves to be an animate and vital formation, a 'pierre vivante' whose numinous qualities induce a visionary response in the hero:

> Ma peau épouse la mousse ancienne et sent vivre le bloc immémorial. Sa densité. Insondables épaisseurs. [...]. Je la touche. Froide. Tiède. Vibrante au lointain de son cœur. Les âges l'ont couverte d'une vraie peau à frissons dessous mes doigts fiévreux. [...]. Je la tâte, ma paume effrite les matières, la pierre se réchauffe, fendille la coque d'une solitude de cimetière. La pierre est amicale. J'ouvre les bras pour la serrer contre moi, ou m'accrocher à elle laminée laminaire, et je ferme les yeux. (pp. 115–16)[36]

The tactile, sensory onrush, as man communes with the stone, and abandons himself to it, unleashes a remarkable surge of myth and memory, bringing to the surface a range of silenced practices from the times of slavery and before. Notably, the tribes of the indigenous populations, often subsumed under the term Carib, are listed: 'Guapoïdes. Saladoïdes. Calviny. Cayo. Suazey. Galibis. Toutes les époques s'y bousculant' (p. 131).[37] If the very physical contact with the material of the stone has precipitated this state of heightened consciousness, memory is equally, in turn, crystallized in specific materials, through which vast swathes of time are recalled: 'petites lamelles d'or [...] vases blancs tracassés par une rouille intime. Pierres à trois pointes instruites des trois derniers mystères. Conques de lambi sculptées, disposées en gardiennes. Des jarres scellées sur de pensifs squelettes' (p. 116). In every case the materials, and the practices associated with them (rituals, ceremonies and superstitions), connote a vital wisdom which stands against human weakness and transience. The vision in turn recalls, in a mysterious and mythical style, the key points of the Antillean past: 'une noueé de mers, de savanes, de Grandes-terres et d'îles, d'attentats et de guerres, de cales sombres et d'errances migrantes sur cent mille fois mille ans' (p. 117).

It is precisely at this point that the old slave notices the engravings which entirely cover the rock, and which supply a narrative sorely lacking in post-colonization Martinique. These signs convey a poetics of continuity and diversity, a resolutely pluralized 'ouélélé de mythes et de Genèses', as one people succeeded another, each leaving their distinctive mark. The old man, who admits to having long ignored the remaining members of the Carib population, now sees that the stone is a precious trace of their memory: 'La Pierre est des peuples. Des peuples dont il ne reste qu'elle. Leur seule mémoire, enveloppe de mille mémoires [...]. L'ultime matière de ces existences'. Through this contact, and the reverie it induces, the stone salves and soothes: 'j'embrasse la pierre comme un être-refuge. Je la presse contre moi. Je veux m'y dissoudre et ne rien laisser subsister de mes chairs'. Moreover, it represents a kind of time before time; in other words by pre-dating the shock of colonialism, it somehow transcends it. And finally, it is the power of the old slave's interaction with the rock, and the myriad of peoples which are made present in this mystical episode, which encourages the normally vicious hound to pass on, licking the old man playfully rather than devouring him. The inspirational and awe-inducing powers of the stone are thus emphasized, and it is directly responsible for the old man's survival.

In addition to the *entre-dire* from Glissant, which appears on the page facing each new chapter, all seven sections of *L'Esclave vieil homme et le molosse* are preceded by an epigraph, a short snatch of verse drawn from an enigmatic source whose title, 'Toucher', mobilizes once more notions of the tactile and the palpable. Each of these epigraphs is specifically concerned with bones. And in the novel's final chapter, 'Les os', the present-day *marqueur de paroles*, describing himself as a guardian of the past, takes up the narrative. The narrator's aged informant (the *vieux-nègre-bois*) embarks on a dig around the stone, looking it seems for some of the legendary buried treasure which had so obsessed Pipi in *Chronique des sept misères*. The *vieux-nègre-bois* returns from the site with only a sample of human bones. These bones, whose provenance is of course uncertain, provide, we are told, the inspiration for the novel we are now reading. But the fluidity and indeterminacy of the tale of *marronnage* is carried over into the present-day narrative. The conflicting versions presented (the *marqueur* either refused to go to see the stone, or he accepted but the old man was unable to find it; or one of his brothers went in his place; or else nobody saw it at all, 'à moins que ce ne fût mon frère', p. 130), along with conditional and subjunctive framing, and the frequent markers of uncertainty ('sans doute'; 'semble-t-il'), ensure that it is never clear whether the *marqueur* actually visited the stone, or whether he simply imagined that he did. In any case, when he is presented with the material, corporeal evidence of the bones, which he is able to handle and touch, he is filled with a mixture of pleasure and guilt. He acknowledges that the power of the bones derives precisely from their materiality: 'Nous avons si peu de mémoires intactes. Elles se sont usées, emmêlées en dérive, et n'ont jamais été répertoriées; il y avait là raison pour que ces os me troublent' (p. 132). In his dreams, he becomes captivated by the bones, listing femur, clavicles, vertebræ and in particular, the broken tibia. However, he is tormented by the sacrilege of having touched the bones (described as a 'relique' and as a 'garde-corps') and repeats obsessively that he ought not to have done so.

This final section of *L'Esclave vieil home et le molosse* has a deeply uncanny quality. This is partly a function of the doubling dynamic which underlies the entire text, breaking down the distinction between master and slave, slave and dog, *marron* and *marqueur*. It is exacerbated by the dream-like atmosphere, particularly heightened in this chapter, in which it becomes difficult to separate out diegetic 'fact' from reverie. For as Freud reminds us, the uncanny effect is often produced by 'erasing the distinction between imagination and reality'.[38] But the uncanniness is more than a matter of narrative indeterminacy, and is also connected with the function of the bones in the overall economy of the novel. Freud defines as uncanny 'that class of the terrifying that leads back to what is known of old and long familiar', and links the uncanny specifically to that which has been repressed. Dead bodies, he claims, have a particular place within the phenomenon of the uncanny. The bones of *L'Esclave vieil homme et le molosse*, buried under the large stone, are very literal manifestations of both death and repression. They can also be seen to represent what Freud, quoting the philosopher Schelling, describes as one of the key qualities of the uncanny, in that they conjure up by their very presence that which 'ought to have remained secret and hidden, but has come to light'.[39] Not only does the *vieux-nègre-bois* disturb the remains by taking away a relic, but the narrator is particularly ashamed that he has touched them. In the dreams which succeed his discovery of the bones, he obsessively returns to the scene in a kind of involuntary repetition, describing himself as 'victime d'une obsession, la plus éprouvante et *la plus familière*' (p. 132, my italics). The sense of horror residing in the familiar, of the simultaneously strange and familiar, is of course endemic to the dream-like uncanny realm. And this notion of the co-existence of the familiar and the strange brings us back, in these closing paragraphs, to the opening of the novel, and suggests that this dread familiarity should be read in collective, historical terms. It is after all significant that the *marqueur* chooses to connect the bones to the imaginary runaway slave, and therefore to produce a novel based on the maroon's story. As he admits himself, they could have been the remains of an individual from any one of the peoples (Békés, Blacks, Chinese, Amerindians) who have inhabited the island. This privileging of the slave narrative is all the more significant given the strange and seemingly contradictory opening to the novel, in which the narrator declares that 'les histoires d'esclavage ne nous passionnent guère. Peu de littérature se tient à ce propos', a statement immediately followed by the conflicting acknowledgement that 'nous nous sentons submergés par ce nœud de mémoires qui nous âcre d'oublis et de présences hurlantes' (*EVH*, p. 17). In this juxtaposition, Chamoiseau nicely points to the uncanny force of slavery in contemporary Martinique. If the uncanny is an old, long-familiar experience that has been repressed, and which then emerges in the present as a transformed anxiety, then the story of slavery – at once an overly familiar and terrifyingly present narrative, and yet the least familiar story of them all – is a particularly powerful example of the unhomely condition.

Confronted by the horror of these familiar-unfamiliar bones, the narrator declares that 'l'unique sortie s'effectue par l'Écrire. Ecrire. Je sus ainsi qu'un jour j'écrirais une histoire' (p. 132). This repeated and urgent appeal to writing, unusually assertive in an *œuvre* which generally proclaims its distance from the literary, is of particular interest here. Writing is shown to provide the only salvation from the horror of the past, and the episode resonates with Susan Stewart's important analysis of the relationship between orality and textuality:

> Speech leaves no mark in space; like gesture, it exists in its immediate context and can reappear only in another's voice [...]. But writing contaminates; writing leaves its trace, a trace beyond the life of the body. Thus, while speech gains authenticity, writing promises immortality, or at least the immortality of the material world in contrast to the mortality of the body. Our terror of the unmarked grave is a terror of the insignificance of a world without writing. The metaphor of the unmarked grave is one which joins the mute and the ambivalent; without the mark there is no boundary, no mark at which to begin the repetition.[40]

If the petroglyphs testify, in a rather reassuring manner, to ancient civilizations and to their æsthetic and cultural production, mediated through the trace, the buried bones, in their anonymity and their corporeality, provide a stark and uncanny synecdoche for a whole swathe of silenced, hidden, and forever inaccessible histories. The shame experienced by the *marqueur* is precisely that of not having respected the sacred boundaries of the body. But the bones function as both a curse and a gift, in that the guilt inspired by having touched them is what in turn provides the motivation for the novel. In this sense, the terror is redeemed through literature, which provides perhaps a unique defence against the uncanny, and a necessary corrective to amnesia. As the narrator comments in the closing of the novel,

> Le vieil esclave m'avait laissé ses os, c'est dire: charroi de mémoires et de temps rassemblés [...]. Très souvent, au rêve de cette pierre, songer de ce tibia, je m'affranchis des militantes urgences. Je prends mesure de la matière des os. [...] Frère, je n'aurais pas dû, mais j'ai touché aux os. (p. 134)

But there is also, finally, a sense in which this emphasis on *écriture* gestures towards a guilt of a meta-literary, self-reflexive nature. In this final chapter, it is as though the *marqueur*, always a thinly disguised Patrick Chamoiseau, is atoning for the invisibility in his writing of the runaway slave, a figure central to Glissant's writing, but whose marginalization has been one of the signatures of the *créolité* movement. In the opening of the novel, the narrator notes the apparent lack of interest in slavery in these 'terres amères des sucres' (p. 17). The final chapter begins with a typically ironic self-portrayal by the *marqueur*, who describes himself as a 'bailleur de nostalgies des âges et des époques, des certitudes et des identités' (p. 129). The complicity in this description of nostalgia, certainty and identity points to a literary project steeped in conservatism, and suggests a reliance on comfortable, familiar or clichéd subject matter. Meanwhile the *vieux-nègre-bois* congratulates the author-narrator for books that he has not read and, ironically, 'pour cet antan restitué du pays'. It is as the *marqueur* describes his latest endeavour, the 'pauvre épopée', *Texaco*, that the old man, 'sans doute pour dissiper l'ennui' (p. 130), begins to talk about the stone and bones. This interaction, between the tedious and misguided young writer and the older mentor, who finally initiates the narrator into a more vital and urgent past than the more recent one with which he has been until now concerned, might be seen as a *mise en abîme* of the relationship between Chamoiseau and that other *vieux-nègre-bois*, Glissant himself. For although Glissant, as we have seen, is a constant presence in Chamoiseau's work, he is of course given a particularly privileged position in the 'entre-dire' of *L'Esclave vieil homme et le molosse*, the intercalated, fragmentary text which itself treats of marooning. And this novel, like the one that succeeds it, *Biblique des derniers gestes*, repositions slavery and *marronnage* at the centre of the Caribbean experience.

This thematic shift has repercussions on a stylistic level, too. In the closing pages, the *marqueur* signals his commitment to a new kind of literary language, one that will attempt to combine the 'langage de conte' with the 'souffle de course', in other words, a medium which will inscribe the rhythms and gestures of the body in a written form. This language will be sufficiently open to take account of paradox, contradiction and opacity: 'Un langage qui dirait sa parole en le signalant muet. [...]. Un langage sans haut ni bas, total en son vouloir, ouvert en son principe'. It will be able, moreover, to communicate 'le pas-comprenable de la Pierre et des os' (p. 133), while expressing the hypnotic, hallucinatory rhythms of the runaway slave. This commitment to a new language and, by implication, to a revitalized poetics, deriving from and reflecting the slave experience, refers in the first instance to the present novel. But I would argue that it also heralds a new phase of Chamoiseau's work, one that asserts some distance from the *créolismes* and word-play so pervasive in earlier writing, and which also moves away from a generally referential perspective (albeit a perspective which has a frequently *magic* realist quality). The new phase instituted in this novel and continued in the next, as will be seen in the final chapter, is characterized by an outlandish, extravagant and unrealistic geography and history, by a more fluid sense of subjectivity and by a highly experimental approach to characterization. On the stylistic level, it will give rise to an even more linguistically ambitious and opaque idiom, based around contradiction, paradox and recalcitrance, glorying in the very notion of 'being difficult', and unapologetically cultivating ambiguity and indeterminacy.

CHAPTER 5

Flesh Made Word: Traumatic Memory in *Biblique des derniers gestes*

This study began with a reading of Chamoiseau's first novel, *Chronique des sept misères*, and reaches its end with his most recent, and most ambitious, to date, *Biblique des derniers gestes* (2002).[1] The striking similarity in the very titles of the two texts gestures towards a continuity of thematic preoccupation, and indeed of structure, across the *œuvre* as a whole. This coherence can be seen for example in the fact that *Biblique*, like *Texaco* and *Solibo*, opens in the debased contemporary present, and then projects back in time, uncovering a more vital, if painful, Creole past. The novel's hero, Balthazar Bodule-Jules (known also as Bibidji), is typical: he is a childless visionary, 'anormalement stérile' (p. 43), much like Marie-Sophie in *Texaco*, or the eponymous but anonymous hero of *L'Esclave vieil homme et le molosse*. The familiar personnel (elderly protagonist, hesitant and self-critical *marqueur de paroles*, Césaire himself) all figure as so many indicators of an instantly recognizable literary mode. And, like Marie-Sophie in *Texaco*, Bibidji is himself a writer, whose reflections on literature and on the writing process appear in 'feuillets', rather than the 'cahiers' of the earlier novel; this common occupation lends both novels a highly metafictional quality.[2]

Moreover, like all Chamoiseau's previous works, which can be read though an optic of loss and lament (from the autobiographies which mourn the disappearance of the magical apprehension of the child's world, to the individual novels which register the demise of local customs and traditions), the very title of *Biblique des derniers gestes* connotes a sense of nostalgia. While *Solibo* centred on the wake of the eponymous storyteller, this novel presents itself as the testimony of the old warrior in the 33 days of his prolonged final agony. The by now well-established rhetorical signature (good past, bad present) is even more acutely in evidence in *Biblique*, and the sense of a passing era underlies the text, from the 'derniers gestes' of the title, to the last *rhum agricole* served to the journalist by Bibidji. The novel is accordingly divided into two distinct sections. The first, 'Annonciation', is subtitled 'Livre de la conscience du pays officiel', and describes a superficial and image-obsessed Martinique. The second, much longer, book, the 'Livre de l'agonie', in addition to a meandering narrative of anti-colonial struggle and sexual conquest (which I shall call, for the purposes of brevity, the 'love and war' story), explores what one of its subsections describes as the 'pays enterré', the buried world of slave memory. As I argued in Chapter 3, Pierre Nora's opposition between living and organic memory and artificial history-making is apparently played out, in an equally oppositional manner, in the incompatibility between the two books which make up the novel.

As well as seeing here a continuation of familiar Chamoiseau themes, however, it is difficult not to read the novel as being in some way a culmination and a departure. The 'derniers gestes' of the title could in this sense have a self-reflexive dimension, and indeed the departure is evidenced quite literally in the fact that this is the only Chamoiseau novel in which much of the action takes place beyond Martinique. Hence, in addition to the almost obligatory cameo by Césaire, Bibidji rubs shoulders with figures such as Che Guevara and Patrice Lumumba. On a stylistic level too, the novel marks a transition. *Biblique* is written under the sign of excess and hyperbole, as the epigraph from Glissant announces: 'Nous pouvons aussi concevoir pour l'expression artistique une démesure de la démesure'.[3] This 'démesure' makes itself felt in the very dimensions of a novel that, at 789 pages, is the longest in the Caribbean tradition. But a sense of excessiveness also permeates language, characterization and plot. So if the opening section is clearly anchored in a referential and realistic fictional world, such moorings are cut away immediately the novel progresses to the 'Livre de l'agonie', a fantastical and exuberant picaresque which is composed of four sections or 'Incertitudes'.

The *marqueur de paroles* has in this novel ceased to be the gatherer and organizer of first-hand information. Rather, the literary project has become an openly creative and imaginative one, less the (supposedly) unmediated transcription of the protagonist's memories than a blatantly fictitious recreation which proceeds by approximation, guesswork and invention. Bibidji, in marked distinction to other Chamoiseau heroes, is an entirely silent witness, so that the novel presents itself as an extended extrapolation from his gestures, rather than the drama of the transmission of his words. As Lorna Milne remarks, 'maintenant, donc, c'est le narrateur qui fournit la parole, loin d'être soupçonné de l'avoir assassinée' (p. 185).[4] The narrator describes himself, significantly, as a 'témoin-créateur' (p. 290), suggesting that observation goes hand in hand with invention. The painstaking processes of listening and recording which had lain at the heart of the literary exercise in *Solibo* and *Texaco* are superseded by observation and imagination – Oiseau de Cham comments that 'il ne me restait qu'à le guetter, le surprendre, et tout imaginer' (p. 51) – and the whole project can therefore be seen as an attempt to write the body, rather than to transcribe the voice. In this 'bodytalk', we see a new focus on the materiality of the body, to the extent that the spoken word, already sidelined in *L'Esclave vieil homme et le molosse*, is for the first time explicitly devalued as a source of authenticity:

> Il [Bibidji] donnait tant de précisions qu'on eût pu le croire né pour de bon à cette époque maudite que les gens du pays essayaient d'oublier. Mais il n'y avait là que le folklore verbal des résistances réelles ou poétiques que nos romanciers, en mal de héros, avaient scribouillé à loisir. Son corps n'avait gardé pièce traces de ces histoires et aucun de ces muscles n'articulait un geste venu de ces époques que sa parole détaillait goulûment. (p. 67).

Here, the 'parole' – usually a privileged source of authenticity in Chamoiseau's work – is linked instead to the fictionalizing impulses of folklore, while the body is upheld as the only guarantor of truth.[5] Thus the novel continues the transition I discussed in the previous chapter, reflecting the shift from a concern with the interplay of the oral and the written (in *Solibo* and *Texaco*) to a pronounced focus on a more materialized, tangible and here embodied memory. As in *L'Esclave vieil homme* and *Chemin-d'école*, so in *Biblique* bones will have a privileged function in testifying to a long-buried slave past. But here it is primarily in the living, palpitating body that memory is shown to originate. Oiseau de Cham is insistently drawn to Bibidji's body, commenting that the old man 's'était toujours conservé une écoute de ses organes les plus insignifiants, comme s'il y avait eu là une mémoire particulière' (p. 55). Memory, then, is first and foremost a kind of carnal knowledge, as is evidenced continually throughout the novel:

> Les cellules de sa chair fonctionnaient comme de petites pierres ponces où se gravaient des souvenirs d'une précision hallucinée. C'est pourquoi son agonie s'était transformée en éveil de sa chair, en excédent de vie vibrante, car chaque miette de son corps exprimait sans attendre (et en vrac) toute la mémoire de ce qu'il avait été et que j'avais du mal à recueillir dans mes lentes écritures. (p. 246)

The body is here described as being engraved, and bears a direct indexical relationship to the past that neither the spoken nor the written word can attain, so that even its cells are shown to perform a mnemonic function.

The novel is thus the most extended and explicit ode to memory in all of Chamoiseau's *œuvre*. The quest for the past has become a more urgent and explicit aim, an idea voiced repeatedly by the narrator, the hero and his mentor, Man L'Oubliée, whose very name gestures towards a lost world of slave memory. Statements which emphasize the importance of memory stud the text; for example, Man L'Oubliée proclaims, '*En perdant la mémoire on perd le monde [...] et quand on perd le monde, on perd le fil même de sa vie*' (p. 471, italics in original). Moreover, she sees that Martinique is sick from its own oblivion, and breathes into her young charge 'la mémoire première [...] qui tient la matrice de la santé parfaite' (p. 147). Forgetting, meanwhile, has become a dangerous and a self-perpetuating activity: 'cet oubli générait un malheur incroyable qui lui-même renforçait cet oubli' (p. 471).

The Book of (Official) Memory

Biblique moves outwards, in both time and space, from Chamoiseau's more usual setting of twentieth-century Martinique, so that the protagonist experiences the Middle Passage, slavery, and even witnesses the beginnings of the universe itself, as well as venturing into a succession of anti-colonial struggles in countries such as Bolivia and Algeria. Although it encompasses an extravagant range of historical experience, then, *Biblique* begins in the most recent and recognizable present of all the novels; the references to Césaire's eightieth birthday allow us to date this opening section of the novel, with a precision unusual in Chamoiseau's work, to 1993. The 'Livre de la conscience du pays officiel' is shot through with references to contemporary phenomena: technology, cars, media, and perhaps most pointedly, and for the first time, to the plethora of humanitarian organizations and NGOs which appear to have acquired a stranglehold on the island. While it is a convention of many Chamoiseau novels that the opening pages stage a clash or a stand-off between the forces of 'official' culture, manifest in the ubiquitous *autorités* – town planners, social workers, policemen, administrators at the town hall – what is striking in *Biblique* is the very lack of any such conflict. If *Chronique*, *Solibo* and *Texaco* explored the movement *towards* passivity and dependency, this novel takes such abject dependency as a given, and this is most forcibly evoked in the response to the flood which coincides with Césaire's birthday celebrations. This flood is shown to be the direct result of the environmental ravages of 'Progress', a concept always linked in Chamoiseau's work to the disappearance of traditional wisdom. The forests which provided a buffer against the wind and water have been stripped away to make room for concrete hotels, and the rivers are now clogged up with cast-off BMWs, white goods and traditional furniture, sacrificed to imports from French chain stores.

The repetitive, almost hypnotic rhythms which are such a feature of the novel, and which will be discussed in greater detail later, are already in evidence in this opening section, mirroring the convulsive cycles of consumption, destruction and dependence which characterize the island. For example, the minister for Overseas Regions, who follows hot on the heels of the minister for human rights, is caught up in the 'immuable circuit des ruines spectaculaires', while just a few lines later the people 'suiv[ent] sur le circuit de nos ruines le Président du Conseil régional' (p. 21). Even disaster has become a commodity to be exhibited, marketed and exported. With the encouragement of the *métropole*, insurance companies are inundated with claims, and humanitarian organizations, as well as a plethora of other bodies – 'Lions, Kiwanis, Rotary, les francs-maçons, les rosicruciens...' (p. 23) – are cynically targeted. The glut of useless aid which this performance produces is ridiculed in the 730,000 cots, the 'Himalaya' of bottles of mineral water, and the rotting Icelandic seal meat which the town hall can neither distribute nor dispose of. Meanwhile television companies, hungry for sensational images of suffering and despair, 'filmèrent et refilmèrent la fange barbare', while a few lines later this point is reiterated: 'chacun fut filmé par trois ou quatre fois et sous des angles divers' (p. 19). The omnipresent television screens provide yet another surface for the projection of a hollow, but highly constructed, image. Ironic axioms ('Mère patrie est lointaine mes enfants, mais elle n'est pas ingrate', p. 20) and caricatural descriptions of metro-politan concern (the minister for human rights arrives in a 'hélicoptère angoissé', p. 19), reinforce the sense of dependency, so that a crippling sense of abandonment is experienced when the French ministers leave the island.

It is not only the *petit peuple* who are mocked for their superficiality and greed, however. The artists of the island, too, are implicated, because of their opportunistic exploitation of both the current 'disaster' and the historical traumas of the Antilles. Their exhibitionism, and their inability to represent or to communicate with those whose memory they claim to transmit, is ridiculed in their clichéd or needlessly obscure projects:

> Les artistes-plasticiens et les artisans-d'art mirent aux enchères tout ce qu'ils n'avaient su vendre durant leur existence. Nous dûmes acheter (dans une ivresse de bonne conscience) des formes en bois d'inspiration négriste, des poteries qui mélangeaient le souvenir d'Afrique aux désespoirs amérindiens, et un lot de tableaux difficiles à décrire tellement leurs harmonies relevaient d'une visée identitaire profonde. (pp. 24–25)

Like everything else on the island, art has become a product to be bought, although this commodity permits a smug afterglow of 'bonne consience' among its consumers.

And yet, perhaps because of this artistic vacuum, Martinique is simultaneously engaged in a frenzy of recording and commemoration, leading to a relentless, and ultimately meaningless, consumption of its own past, as well as a cunning manipulation of its present. Throughout this opening section, the narrative proceeds by litany, enumeration and hyperbole to suggest these excessive attempts to register and record. For example, to commemorate Césaire's birthday, 'nous relisions pour la dix millième fois le récit de son arrivée dans le cénacle de la Sorbonne'. Equally, 'nous relisions sa belle adresse contre Staline [...] ou cette diatribe terrible contre le colonialisme' (p. 17). But rather like the endlessly repeating circuit of ruins through which the French ministers move, these literary 'set pieces' represent a mechanical and superficial engagement with the ideas of the past. Every reading is already a re-reading, characterized by irrelevant detail and by habitual, futile quests, exemplified in the fact that people continue to torment themselves with the origins of the word *négritude*. Meanwhile, the plethora of *lieux de mémoire* (poetry recitals, plays, films, articles, retrospectives, slide shows) recall Ricœur's description of contemporary times: 'le trop de mémoire ici, le trop d'oubli ailleurs'.[6]

If the commemorative events marking Césaire's birthday are inadequate, so too is the excitement generated by the discovery of the 'grande dame de la chanson créole' by a local journalist. The singer, as noted in Chapter 3, might well have been the heroine of another Chamoiseau novel, just as the journalist might have been an authorial alter ego. Here, however, both characters are shown to be engaged in a process of commodification. The old woman tells her story in the television supplement of *France-Antilles*, indulges in crowd-pleasing recollections and regrets having stayed in the 'petit pays' when she could have had a career as a diva in France. The compulsive consumption of the old singer's story mirrors that of Césaire's birthday, so that 'nous lisions et relisions ce supplément télé qui très vite s'épuisa' (p. 18). Meanwhile, the qualities of authenticity, age and duration which she appears to embody are fetishistically sought in relatively recent documents. For example, the journalist figure is motivated to search for the old singer because he is attracted by the yellowing photograph of her performance on 14 July (a highly ironic date, given that it marks the French national holiday, as noted in Chapter 3). Moreover, her apparent beauty is enhanced by the 'encre ancienne' of the archived article, further testifying to the generalized quest for temporal depth, endurance and antiquity.

Both Césaire and the old songstress act as ironic doubles, then, to the hero of the novel, Balthazar Bodule-Jules, and the celebration and commemoration of both figures threatens to overshadow the final agony of the old warrior. In a pointed parallel, for example, we learn that Césaire had '*lui aussi* consacré son existence [...] à lutter sur un banc d'Assemblée contre le colonialisme' (p. 17, my italics); the juxtaposition serves only to highlight the sedentary, Paris-centred struggle in which Césaire was engaged. A stark binary is thus established between the showy celebrations of the poet-statesman's birthday, and the overshadowed 'authentic' memory of the elderly protagonist:

> La nouvelle de son agonie circula dans le pays enterré [...] en dehors des médias [...] où ne parvenaient ni l'eau ni l'électricité ni les journaux ni les antennes télé. Dessous l'indifférence officielle, il y eut des conques de lambi qui résonnèrent toutes seules. (p. 46)

Once again, memory is what lurks *beneath* official indifference. Television ærials, in their passive reception of highly mediated signals, contrast with the submarine materiality of the conch shells. For not only, as writers from Walcott to Brathwaite to Glissant remind us, is the sea a primary site of Caribbean history, but the shell's association with orality lends it a particularly charged connection to the past. And significantly, Bibidji displays no empty, nostalgic investment in the clichés of memory-making. In contrast to the 'vieille encre' which the journalist mistakes for authenticity, the old man's writing cannot be dated by the police, due to the fact that 'les Bic sèchent bien vite et se pétrifient trop' (p. 41). While Bibidji's story seems initially to inspire only the familiar cycles of unthinking consumption – 'Nous la lisions, la relisions, en un acte machinal enrayé sur sa répétition' – it finally begins to 'résonner dans le vide de nos rêves, à traverser les artifices de nos tourments et à nous obséder en creux telle une présence-absence' (p. 28). The reaction suggests that memory returns after a period of latency, functioning as a present-absent which is at once known and unknown.[7] Here, though, because of the particular atmosphere of this novel, the expression recalls both Freud's theorizations of the uncanny, and the unhomely as elaborated by Bhabha. I shall return to these theoretical counterpoints later in this chapter.

Memory Embodied

Bibidji stands in opposition to the oblivious or misguided characters of
the 'pays officiel', and in some respects has similarities with other
Chamoiseau hero(ine)s, such as Marie-Sophie and Pipi. His skill in
growing herbs and vegetables derives from a 'rapport ancestral à la
tourbe nourricière', and in his garden he deploys a number of horticul-
tural theories 'dont l'usage s'était gommé de la mémoire d'ici' (p. 37).
But Bibidji is unique in Chamoiseau's work in his attachment to memorial objects, objects which both trigger and retain memory. These items
carry an unusually strong affective charge, underwriting his legitimacy
and filiation, and providing a material connection to a chain of ancestors. For example, the enamel bowl inherited from his grandmother,
which he initially instals as a kind of familial souvenir, comes to represent a 'symbole de ces liens qu'il voulait maintenir avec les gens de sa
lignée' (p. 35). Other artefacts include the wardrobe inherited from an
ancestor, which is packed with photos, papers and objects 'chargés de
tant de souvenirs' (p. 756), an old oil lamp, and the *vieille mappemonde*
which has accompanied him through his journeys. But it is books in
particular which seem to be imbued with raw memory and which, as the
most precious mnemonic traces, provide a particularly emotive connection to the past. Significantly, this memorial connection is described in
corporeal terms: 'les ouvrages portaient les stigmates d'une éternité de
corps à corps, les pliures-cicatrices des lectures suspendues [...] ils
portaient les flétrissures de circonstances terribles' (p. 39). And just as
the body, the ultimate guarantor of memory, is figured in terms of inscription, so the book's corporeal qualities are highlighted in the references
to wounds, scars and stigmata. In their ragged physicality, these volumes
testify to a life of adventure.

But Bibidji is primarily a vector of *collective* memory. This is not a
memory that has been passed down intergenerationally, however, as in
the case of Marie-Sophie in *Texaco*. Rather, collective memory is insistently presented as an imaginative engagement with a distant and
irretrievable past. The narrator specifically advocates a Glissantian
vision prophétique du passé (italics in original), and aims to produce a
'témoignage visionnaire d'une mémoire collective' (p. 70), while the hero
urges the youth of Martinique to invent for themselves 'cette mémoire
fondatrice' (p. 254). This foundational memory goes beyond the claims
of Hirsch's postmemory, then, embracing events which have not been
passed down, which cannot possibly have been remembered, or which

have been so successfully repressed as to require significant memory work.

The obsessive interest in beginnings which was discussed in Chapter 1 finds its most far-reaching realization in an early section of the novel, 'Incertitudes d'un commencement au cœur ému du pays enterré'. The section stands in stark distinction to the meandering and repetitive nature of much of the text, and notably jars with the 'love and war' narrative, with its serial female lovers and its odyssey of anti-colonial struggle. For this section includes a short and densely packed sequence in which Bibidji is shown to witness some of the primal scenes of the slave past: transportation, suicide, infanticide, *marronage*. While these events are directly described in a very short section of the book, I shall argue in the course of this chapter that their intensity is such that they reverberate throughout the rest of the text. This brief sequence, indeed, constitutes the structural and thematic core of the entire novel, releasing a cluster of part-echoes, images, apparent doublings, circularities and uncanny effects, prefiguring and giving meaning to the weird, fantastical and frequently gruesome physical symptoms explored throughout the text. A closer examination of three important scenes from this key sequence, in which boundaries are transgressed and life and death are conjoined, will reveal the sense of traumatic memory which is in play, and will set the context for the following discussion of the uncanniness that underlies the book as a whole.

While, according to the *marqueur de paroles*, Bibidji is born in the early twentieth century,[8] two further mythified versions of his genesis are relayed by the protagonist himself. In the first account, Bibidji claims to have been born fifteen billion years ago, at the time of the 'Big Bang', while in the second variant he was born aboard a slave ship. The text draws an explicit parallel between these two imagined events, thereby establishing the Middle Passage as the foundational moment in Caribbean history. The journey from Africa, like the Big Bang, recreated the world anew, hurling matter in all directions, and rendering continuous memory impossible.[9] So just as the cosmological theory of origins posits a complete and explosive rupture with what had gone before, rather than an infinite or progressive temporal continuum, so too the Middle Passage must be seen as a decisive break in the experience of time and space. Indeed, the amnesia induced by the journey is set in motion even before Bibidji leaves Africa: 'Son corps, captif dans cette cale, se souvenait à peine de sa terre africaine. Ses frères (complices des négriers) l'avaient forcé à tournoyer sept fois autour du grand arbre de l'oubli' (p.

59). Significantly, too, it is the body which is described as no longer being able to remember the lost continent. Memory (and, more to the point, forgetting) is once more shown to be a corporeal activity. The body is the site not only of the physical hardships of transportation, but also of amnesia and repression.

For Bibidji, the slave ship is at once the crucible of a new collective Antillean identity, and the locus of a horrific loss of self. The hold is described as a tomb, but also as a terrifying cradle (p. 59), in which the cargo of slaves is surrounded not by amniotic fluid, but by sea water and salt tears. The stomach of the 'navire mangeur d'hommes' (p. 57) is an all-devouring rather than (pro)creative organ, which consumes, digests and expels its own endlessly decomposing contents:

> Ses chairs et son esprit s'étaient dissous dans un noir stomacal qui les digérait de seconde en seconde. [...] l'angoisse et l'incompréhension s'étaient muées en un ferment gastrique qui décomposait chaque atome de son être. Ce corps eut conscience de lui-même comme d'un chyme de chair et d'os... (p. 59)

In this interpenetration of bodies, flesh eats into flesh and the body overflows its limits through excretions and nausea: hands, feet and chains 'se nouaient et se renouaient dans les convulsions du navire, la chaleur, l'asphyxie, les vomissures, les excréments' (p. 60). The boiled vinegar sprinkled over the slaves is insufficient to kill the fevers which eat away at lungs, throats and brains, all organs which become liquefied into 'matières indescriptibles' (p. 61). In a nightmarish interaction, the slave chained to Bibidji dies, so that his living body intermingles with dead flesh:

> La chair glacée voulait lui aspirer son restant de chaleur, tentait d'entrer en lui, de l'avaler entier. Il avait voulu bondir pour briser ce contact. Le croc des fers fixés à son cou, ses poignets, ses chevilles, l'avaient crucifié dans l'espace minuscule où il devait survivre. La chair morte était demurée en ventouse contre lui, glaciale comme un abîme [...]. Il avait basculé en elle [la chair], elle s'était introduite en lui, et l'avait dispersé dans les chairs défaites tout au long de la cale. (pp. 59–60)

The ship, then, is the site of an obscene, intolerable corporeality; within its hold the human body breaks down, offering no discrete or continuous protective entity, so that life and death become unbearably coterminous. And just as the limits of the body are transgressed in the slave ship – terms such as 'explosion' and 'dilation' emphasize corporeal fragmentation, openness and vulnerability – so the limitlessness of the Caribbean's foundational trauma is also emphasized by the old man: 'L'horreur étant engagée [...] elle n'avait plus de limites. C'est ce qui caractérise la Traite des nègres et l'esclavage aux Amériques: son absence de limites' (p. 57).

Two further episodes of trauma are explored in this section. Both are primal scenes which haunt the slave imaginary, and both explore situations in which Bibidji is a helpless witness to the destruction of others. And both position the maternal slave body at the very heart of traumatic experience. In the first Bibidji, while aboard the ship, encounters one of the haunting set pieces of New World memory, slave suicide. A mother, who is mourning the death of her baby, throws herself overboard. Bibidji hears her fall into the ocean and, although helpless to save her, talks to her for as long as possible while she clings to the outside of the vessel. In a second incident, on the plantation, he witnesses another haunting scene of the slave past: infanticide. He comes across a slave in the process of giving birth and, in a confusion of self and other, imagines that it is he himself who is being born, describing the woman as his own mother. Then, suddenly, the life-giving gesture is transformed into a death-giving one, as the mother tightens her hold on the child: 'Elle semblait vouloir le faire rentrer dans sa poitrine' (p. 68). As in the hold of the ship, the boundaries of the body appear fragile and susceptible to penetration. Here, again, Bibidji arrives seconds too late to save the baby's life,[10] but cries that he has witnessed the most terrible war crime known to man. And, in a further disturbance of identities, the face of the infanticide becomes confused with that of the woman on the boat, suggesting a connection in the slave imaginary between these three key sites of trauma: infant death, suicide and infanticide.

Cathy Caruth, as we saw in Chapter 1, has argued that traumatic experience may be stored in the body without mediation or consciousness, and return as flashbacks, or through the compulsion to repeat. She reminds us that 'what returns in the flashback is not simply an overwhelming experience that has been obstructed by a later repression or amnesia, but an event that is itself constituted, in part, by its lack of integration into consciousness'. In other words, it is precisely that which escapes full consciousness as it happens which is destined for this sort of return. Caruth continues, 'Not having been fully integrated as it occurred, the event cannot become, as Janet says, a "narrative memory" that is integrated into a completed story of the past'.[11] Of course, the 'dix-huit paroles' of Afoukal in *Chronique*, which constitute a lyrical distillation of the slave past, sit outside the main narrative frame stylistically, typographically and diegetically. But *Biblique* explores this un-integrated memory at much greater length than the earlier novel, showing how trauma cannot be consigned to the past but is relived in the present through nightmares and hallucinations.

The deaths of the adult slave and of the baby, like the horror of the ship itself, are on a diegetic level experiences which have been literally 'missed' by the protagonist; he explicitly acknowledges later in the novel that he has invented these episodes (pp. 252–53). These events have thus been experienced 'out of time' in two respects: first, they belong to the mythical collective past of the Antilles, rather than to the twentieth-century narrative framework of the novel. Moreover, these are precisely the experiences which, because of their traumatic nature, have been most deeply repressed in the collective psyche. Caruth talks of 'the story of a wound that cries out, that addresses us in the attempt to tell us of a reality or truth that is not otherwise available', and continues, 'This truth, in its delayed appearance and its belated address, cannot be linked only to what is known, but also to what remains unknown in our very actions and our language'.[12] Crucially, then, trauma makes itself evident only in another place, in another time, because of the latency inherent in its structure. Bibidji, as we have seen, embodies a collective Antillean consciousness, marked by the horrors of the Middle Passage, slavery and oppression, but the 'real time' of his testimony is in a relatively affluent and peaceful late twentieth-century Martinique, in whose 'opulences de surface, il [Bibidji] ne voyait aucune violence contre laquelle il auraut pu sortir ses armes' (p. 699). As a by-product of assimilation, as we have seen throughout this study, Martinique has lapsed into passive dependence, repressing the memory of its brutal genesis. Through Bibidji's expansive memory, what Caruth calls the 'unclaimed experience' of the past is excavated in the oblivious, late-capitalist present of the novel.

If the novel sets up in its opening section these primal scenes of wounding and collapse, it goes on to explore the relics and residues of these foundational experiences in the collective unconscious. Slavery is known, euphemistically, as 'la Malédiction', and is literally silenced: the elder midwives of the community are typical, for example, in that 'pas une ne prononçait le mot *esclavage*' (p. 416, italics in original). Yet, as the italics suggest, the very act of repression serves only to intensify the pernicious effects of the past, for 'les miasmes de la vieille Malédiction étaient d'autant plus virulents que tout le monde s'efforçait d'oublier le passé' (p. 593). This memory is largely disinterred through the relationship between Man L'Oubliée (whose name gestures towards a lost world of slave memory) and Bibidji. The former's main concern in mentoring the young boy is precisely to unearth the buried narratives of collective memory, particularly with regard to conquest and slavery:

> Man L'Oubliée ne remontait point dans une mémoire qui lui serait personnelle, mais dans un passé collectif, accessible à chacun d'entre nous, donc

d'abord à lui-même, Balthazar-Bodule Jules [...] cette mémoire provenait de l'esclavage et de la traversée des bateaux négriers:... nous l'avons refoulée, et nous cherchons à l'effacer, mais Man L'Oubliée savait la retrouver à chaque sucée de sa vieille pipe. (p. 251)

Memory is shown to be both a nurturing and a dangerous force, and it carries its own promises and pitfalls, 'car la mémoire est comme une sève! Elle nourrit comme un feu et peut détruire autant!' (p. 252). There is, moreover, a sense in which memory improves with practice. Characters such as Bibidji and Man L'Oubliée are not endowed with superior capacities; rather, their sustained attention to, and exercise of, memory – Bibidji's 'memory work' is at one point likened to gymnastics (p. 252) – ensures that both personal and collective memory can be enhanced. This in turn explains why memory is so fragile in the contemporary period described at the beginning of the novel. It is not just the initial fractures wrought by transplantation and enslavement which have weakened collective memory, but also, as we have seen, the fact that there is no outlet for memory in the late capitalist present of the island. The DOM-TOMs may have escaped the massacres, assassinations and summary executions of the decolonization process. However, the repression of key foundational events (the extermination of the indigenous peoples, the Middle Passage, slavery), coupled with the contemporary lack of an outwardly violent colonizer calling for revolutionary resistance, is portrayed as a damaging and debilitating void.

As Caruth reminds us, the term 'trauma', although now generally understood to refer to a psychological condition, originally referred to a wound inflicted on the body, and is related to the Greek verb *titrosko*, to pierce or to penetrate. In *Beyond the Pleasure Principle*, Freud deploys images of *physical* penetration to offer a definition of psychological trauma, suggesting that traumatic experience results from 'any excitations from outside which are powerful enough to break through the protective shield [...]. The concept of trauma necessarily implies a connection of this kind with a breach in an otherwise efficacious barrier against stimuli.'[13] The three episodes discussed above explore incidents in which this (physical) barrier breaks down or comes under siege, and the implication is that the experience of corporeal fragility or wounding has a strong psychological dimension. The suicide and the infanticide call forth issues of connection and separation in the mother–child relationship as it developed under slavery, while the evocation of the Middle Passage explores, in a particularly graphic way, anxieties around inter-penetration, fusion, delimitation, detachment and violation. For, as Kathryn Robson argues in another context, the image of the bodily wound 'in turn points to the vulnerability and lack of self-containment of the traumatized psyche'.[14]

As Bibidji's education progresses, the boy accompanies his mentor while she cures the victims of a range of curious symptoms and illnesses in a section entitled 'Œuvre et malédiction'. And it is during these visits that the long-term effects of the slave past are shown most vividly, once again through images of corporeal dysfunction. Freud's 'protective shield' is starkly broken in a vast array of characters whose wounds are shown to derive directly from the condition of slavery. The sufferings of the past are thus inscribed on the body, which bears the imprint of collective psychic disorder through open wounds and festering sores. For example, Man L'Oubliée tends to an old plantation worker whose eyes are 'métallisés par une blessure jamais bien refermée' (p. 447), and to a young boy whose neck, fists and ankles have begun to decompose. His suffering is linked back to the physical torture of slavery, as the child experiences this corporeal decay on the precise sites of the 'chaînes d'esclavage, colliers de servitude, bracelets mangeurs de chair, carcans qui défolmantent les vertèbres du cou' (p. 477). Man L'Oubliée comments '*c'est charroie qu'il charroie la mémoire dans ses chairs*' (p. 477, italics in original), once more linking flesh and memory. This description uncannily echoes that of Bibidji's identical experience on the slave ship (p. 59), a point to which I shall return later.

In yet another example of physical dysfunction in the novel, the narrator describes the common phenomenon of babies born with a 'tête fendue', and who die in early infancy as their skull bones never knit together. These wounded children are described as 'dépositaires d'une mémoire impossible à loger' (p. 442), hinting at the unhomely, or unhousable, quality of the memory of slavery. The formulation resonates with Homi Bhabha's elaboration in *The Location of Culture* of 'the unhomely', a condition which he describes as the 'paradigmatic colonial and post-colonial condition'.[15] Bhabha is working out of Freud's description of the 'unheimlich' as 'the name for everything that ought to have remained secret and hidden... but has come to light'. He argues that texts such as Nadine Gordimer's *My Son's Story* and Toni Morrison's *Beloved* offer a kind of working out in fiction of 'the unspoken, underrepresented pasts that haunt the historical present': 'The recesses of the domestic space become sites for history's most intricate invasions. In that displacement, the borders between home and world become confused; and, uncannily, the private and the public become part of each other, forcing upon us a vision that is as divided as it is disorienting.'[16]

In addition to the corporeal symptoms discussed above, in *Biblique* the homes of numerous characters exemplify what Bhabha calls 'the metaphoricity of the houses of racial memory'.[17] In yet another instance of boundaries being breached, these houses have been rendered unhomely by the confusion of private and public, and by the return of the repressed memories of the past.[18] For example, the Vénéré family is struck down mysteriously, from generation to generation, by physical and mental handicap, premature death and infertility. Man L'Oubliée digs up from the family's garden a conch shell dating from the period of the Amerindian genocide at European hands. The shell stands as a relic of a deeply buried narrative of decimation and trauma, a kind of original sin which continues to stain the island environment. Man L'Oubliée warns the family to counteract its curse by trying to 'garder mémoire des souffrances premières' (pp. 464–65). She is later summoned by a family whose home has been showered by sudden bursts of icy water and horse urine. She establishes that the house is built on the site of an infirmary for injured slaves; so infected is the residence that its reserves of wine and rum have soured. In a rite of purification, these bottles and their gruesome contents are discarded en masse: 'à chaque fois ce n'était pas du vin ou du rhum vieux […] mais des concrétions opaques semblables à des fœtus' (p. 468). Similarly, the shoemaker's wife, who loses successive newborns 'en fausses couches, hémorragies brutales, descentes d'organes et autres désastres' (p. 471) is eventually cured because of Man L'Oubliée's intervention. The couple's house has been built on the site of a slave cemetery, 'un de ces coins inqualifiables où planteurs et jésuites balançaient la dépouille de tout esclave non-baptisé'. She unearths clavicles, skulls, tibias, ribs, femurs, jawbones and coccyx, in a process chillingly described as a harvest of bones (p. 474). This unearthing, and subsequent reburial, of the remains of dead slaves, results in a resounding catharsis, so that the woman proceeds to bear a child for every bone exhumed.

These unhomely homes, which we could call, after Pierre Nora, 'lieux d'oubli', have never known 'l'onction d'un châtiment, la caresse apaisante d'une commémoration ou d'un hommage aux victimes de l'endroit' (p. 467). In all of these examples drawn from the 'pays enterré', memory – manifest in a physical trace – is figured as having gone underground. Man L'Oubliée effects a very literal unearthing of the long-repressed and painful memories of the 'pays enterré'. Through her agency, the unhomely place is rendered homely and, as a corollary to this catharsis, the wounded body is healed.

Uncanny Memories: Sex and Childbirth

Bhabha's reading of Freud's essay on 'The "Uncanny"' is a selective one, as Celia Britton has pointed out.[19] One of the most important aspects of Freud's argument, which is not mentioned by Bhabha, is the notion of the 'double', a phenomenon in which

> the subject identifies himself with someone else, so that he is in doubt as to which his self is, or substitutes the extraneous self for his own. In other words, there is a doubling, dividing and interchanging of the self. And finally there is the constant recurrence of the same thing – the repetition of the same features or character traits or vicissitudes, of the same crimes, or even the same names through several consecutive generations.[20]

Freud's insights shed light on one of the most enigmatic and troubling aspects of the novel. More than in any other Chamoiseau text, identity in *Biblique* is rendered fluid and uncertain through spectral reappearances, crossings and what Freud calls, in the above quotation, the continual 'doubling, dividing and interchanging of the self'. For Bibidji, at the start of the novel, Man L'Oubliée, the infanticide and the slave woman on the boat are interchangeable. Man L'Oubliée is described as a 'reflet incertain' (p. 146), and later Bibidji obsessively identifies himself with her, to the extent that he feels he becomes Man L'Oubliée (p. 166; p. 427). At the novel's end, the narrator proclaims that he has become his subject, Bibidji (p. 765). In his anti-colonial odyssey the women he meets are consistently likened to Man L'Oubliée, and to each other. Indeed Bibidji vows at several points that he is incapable of distinguishing between these women, so much do their identities overlap with each other. During his apprenticeship, he lives with a round of shapeshifting and intermelding characters, whose lack of a discrete and determinate identity is signalled in the impacted hyphens which conjoin their ever more complex names. Nicol Timoléon, the Marxist revolutionary who teaches Bibidji about armed struggle, is revealed to be a woman, Déborah-Nicol Timoléon. But the indeterminacy of the character is such that she 'se mouvait à l'aise entre les deux personnes'. Déborah lives with a young girl, Anaïs-Alicia, conceived through the violent rape of Déborah's now-dead twin, Sarah, by a zombie, a classic manifestation of the uncanny. Sarah had been obsessed with mirrors – yet another symptom of the Freudian uncanny – and her identity is continually, if unevenly, refracted through that of both her daughter and her sister. Thus, Déborah's personality has to some extent been taken over by that of her dead sister, whom she loved 'd'un sentiment bien plus que fraternel. C'était un attachement total, une osmose majeure' (p. 504). Sarah, in both life and death, is in turn 'en connivence totale' with her daughter, to the extent that the latter's name eventually metamorphoses into Sarah-Anaïs-Alicia. Mother and daughter are so similar that it seems that 'ce sang quittait les artères de Sarah, traversait l'air pour atteindre le corps d'Anaïs-Alicia afin d'y faire un petit tour complet, puis rejoignait l'organisme maternel pour un autre petit tour, et ainsi de suite' (p. 366). The family constitutes a very literal realization of Freud's notion that the uncanny can result in the same names and character traits being reproduced through several consecutive generations.

Crucially, then, in this series of overlapping, chiastic crossings, there is a strong corporeal dimension, and it is in the episodes of (sometimes only attempted) physical interpenetration and fusion that the trauma narrative and the uncanny can be seen to coincide. After all, trauma shares certain structural similarities with the uncanny – both have to do with the breaching of boundaries, both suggest a return of the repressed, and in both repetition is a key device.[21] In *Biblique*, the uncanny and the traumatic can be seen to be intimately interrelated: the traumatic is almost always uncanny, while uncanny effects in the novel often have a traumatic edge. In the previous chapter, I briefly alluded to the uncanny nature of the stones found in *L'Esclave vieil homme et le molosse*. In *Biblique*, this uncanniness is a much more pervasive feature of the novel. Here, however, it takes on a disturbing, highly gendered, and hence more problematic form.

Freud argues that 'The uncanny is that class of the frightening which leads back to what is known of old and long familiar [...] something which has undergone repression and then returned from it'. But he goes further in his elaboration of the concept, linking the uncanny specifically – in what reads almost as a tantalizing afterthought to his line of argument – to female genitalia:

> It often happens that neurotic men declare that they feel that there is something uncanny about the female genital organs. This *unheimlich* place, however, is the entrance to the former *Heim* [home] of all human beings, to the place where each of us lived once upon a time and at the beginning. There is a joking saying that 'Love is home-sickness'; and whenever a man dreams of a place or a country he says to himself, while he is still dreaming: 'this place is familiar to me, I've been here before', we may interpret the place as being his mother's genitals or her body. In this case too, then, the *unheimlich* is what was once *heimisch*, familiar; the prefix '*un*' is the token of repression.[22]

Understood in this light, the uncanny is itself a symptom of the unending quest for origins, a central theme in this novel as elsewhere, and this quest can be seen to underlie Bibidji's priapic conquest of women in the colonized world.[23] Freud's linking of (foreign) countries, female genitals and the uncanny can be seen in a telling synecdoche, when Bibidji acknowledges that in his relationship with women throughout the colonized world, 'il ne les avait pas assez regardées, pas assez soupesées, pas assez estimées, il avait toujours considéré la prise de leur coucoune comme une prise de l'ensemble' (p. 395).[24] And even as a child, his relationship with Man L'Oubliée is described as 'jouissive mais maternelle' (p. 192). Although she is not his biological mother, his instincts suggest an acute desire to enter the maternal body: he wants to reduce the distance between her body and his, is frustrated by the fact that she will not allow him to 'entrer en fusion' with her, and is consequently projected into 'l'immense solitude de son corps' (pp. 166–67). Later he expresses the desire to 's'installer dans ses chairs, rechercher une place entre ses os, se répandre sur la couche de son sang' (p. 248). The desire to penetrate and to occupy the mother-figure's body is an obsessive one, and the female sexual organs simultaneously call to and repel the protagonist.

In his detailed study of the phenomenon, Nicholas Royle argues that '[the] uncanny is bound up with generative, creative uncertainties about sexual identity'.[25] Among the multiple instances of uncanniness that *Biblique* provides, it is perhaps in these anxieties around gender and sexuality that the undercurrents of slavery are most powerfully present, and it is on this aspect that I shall focus in the remainder of this chapter. The novel suggests that one of the key sites of traumatic memory remains the female body (specifically, female genitalia), and inevitably, then, sexuality and procreation are key arenas in which this memory is played out. The most graphic explorations of the bodily vulnerability explored above concern the numerous women ripped open in childbirth. The damaging of the mother–child bond through slavery is of course a familiar theme in Caribbean writing. As Bibidji comments, '*L'esclavage avait tout infecté, et c'est dans cette infection que l'enfant s'apprêtait à tomber*' (p. 417, italics in original). But in *Biblique*, pregnancy and birth are consistently described in such a way as to emphasize the permeability of the body and its organs, so that a sense of the horrific and monstrous physicality of femininity permeates the text. The hero himself, according to Yvonette Cléoste, '*devait se construire dans deux matrices disjointes*' (p. 119, italics in original). Symphorine Massidor's womb is the site of a horrific and indeterminate growth, which spills out from her genitals. The narrator describes an octopus-like creature (a 'chatrou') growing in her womb: 'Il voulait absolument sortir entre ses jambes, à croire que son ventre se dévidait par là. Une masse rose, molle, sanglante' (p. 423). Both

Man L'Oubliée and Yvonnette Cléoste – respectively the good and bad witches of Bibidji's childhood – are midwives, who attend particularly traumatic and complicated births. Children are born too early or too late, women frequently experience prolapse, and birth and death are often conjoined, so that 'Les enfants qui détruisaient leur mère étaient nombreux' (p. 409). Traumatic memory again originates in, and remains inscribed on, the female body, which is presented as both an archive and as an active witness, bearing stubborn and unique testimony to the horrors of the past.

Thus, the uncanny is itself an effect of memory, however repressed, and through it the latent strata of the past – that which 'ought to have remained hidden but which has come to light' – re-echoes in the horrors of the present. And crucially, the uncanniness of these passages is not only an effect of sexual indeterminacy or of gender disturbance. It is also an effect of reading, so that on the *textual* level the descriptions of the decomposing, overflowing, wounded or grotesque (female) body arouse the reader's distant memory of the beginning of the novel, and the terrifying scenes of trauma – transportation, infanticide, suicide – discussed above.

This tissue of repetitions, recurrences and uncanny echoes can be seen in many episodes which occur much later in the novel,[26] but I shall concentrate here on only three. In one of the most disturbing descriptions in *Biblique* Sarah, Déborah's sister, finds herself pregnant with 156 babies, having been seduced by a zombie. These fœtuses, many of whom are 'au sexe pas très fixé', attempt to devour the maternal body from the inside:

> Le pire n'était même pas la question de leur nombre, mais celle de leur appétit. [...] les bébés avalaient pour de bon l'intérieur de la dame, ils lui dévoraient les ovaires, lui dégrappaient les trompes, buvaient ses eaux, rongeaient l'ampoule rectale, grignotaient ses boyaux, aspiraient son sang à travers les membranes, bref menaient des agapes de nature cannibale... (pp. 324–25)

The cannibalizing tendencies of the unborn babies, and the sadistic undertones of the description, again gesture towards a profound perversion of the mother–child relationship. As well as recalling, by inversion, the infanticide of the opening, this passage resonates at the textual level with the imagery and language of the original boat journey. The self-consuming, womb-like space of the boat had also been characterized, as we saw above, by verbs of decomposition, consumption and asphyxiation.

More strikingly still, towards the end of the novel, indeterminate gender identities are once more in play, when the hero encounters

Kalamati, a girl from a Martinican fishing commune. What begins as a love scene degenerates into a hallucinatory encounter – set, significantly, on a boat – in which he is penetrated by her:

> Ces humeurs se mêlaient [...] pour lui couvrir la peau de chaleur et de glace. Il crut même qu'elle avait pissé plusieurs fois et se sentit traversé par des urines bouillantes, il dut pisser aussi et déféquer aussi, à tel point que leurs corps emmêlés baignaient dans une bouillie qui remplissait tout le fond du gommier. [...]. Elle le renversait à son tour, et (avec ses doigts, ses orteils et sa langue) le pénétrait de partout, l'explorait comme lui-meme l'explorait. (pp. 647–49)

The description, in all of its abject physicality, uncannily echoes the descriptions of the Middle Passage quoted earlier in this chapter, in which the hold of the vessel was similarly filled with human waste and in which the body overflowed its own boundaries. The vocabulary of the extract is remarkably similar to that deployed in the earlier passage: terms such as *urine*, *glace*, *langue* and *bouillie* occur in both episodes, which share, moreover, an eerie atmosphere of seduction and horror. Here, again, in the blurred boundaries between self and other, male and female, penetrator and penetrated, sexual desire is underwritten by a generalized drive towards incorporation and invasion, and the threat of death is overwhelmingly present.

And from this perspective, finally, it is clear that the relationship between Déborah-Nicol Timoléon and her sister Sarah has not escaped the abjection which prevails in the novel. In a parallel scene to the one just discussed, set in a bed that is likened to a boat, Déborah attempts to seduce her sleeping sister. The scene inevitably recalls the abusive instincts of a previous seducer, the *dorlis*, but this time it is a lesbian and incestuous desire which is in play. The initial tenderness of the scene evoked by Déborah – the sisters lie like a pair of spoons – quickly degenerates as she forces herself on Sarah. In the description of a sexual encounter with an unwilling other, the imagery of the Middle Passage is once again mobilized to portray a sense of perversion and exploitation:

> Ce lit d'acajou [...] s'était transformé en un fragile bateau [...] je [Déborah] fus emportée dans un vertige d'ondes et de vaguelettes, tout semblait être en eau, les draps, les oreillers, les coussins, la moustiquaire, les colonnes qui ondulaient comme des anguilles de mer, et [le corps de Sarah] semblait être prêt à se décomposer en une coulée d'eau tiède [...]. Tout était distendu douloureux, en conflit permanent. Sarah, qui ne s'était pas réveillée, se mit à gémir, à pleurer, à refuser ma présence auprès d'elle, le contact de mon corps contre le sien. (pp. 506–507)

This is less a scene of symbiotic and mutually fulfilling love than an evocation of sexual dysfunction and violation; the longed-for decomposition of the borders of Sarah's body is denied, and Déborah is rejected by her sleeping sister. Here, again, the desire to fuse with, melt into, penetrate or possess the other, which is explored through various characters in the course of the novel, remains unhealthy, obsessive, unfulfilled or, in some cases, unfulfilling.

Throughout *Biblique*, as we have seen, the endemic anxiety around the limits and thresholds of the body mirrors a similar anxiety concerning any sense of autonomous selfhood. The body is repeatedly figured as vulnerable, abject, scatological, fragmented or excessive, and these states are discursively linked to the trauma of slavery itself. For slavery has ensured that the experience of identity flounders, so that characters are engaged in an urgent and ongoing negotiation of the boundary between inside and outside, male and female, subjectivity and objectivity, and life and death itself. This is what gives meaning to the grotesque scenes of interpenetration, consumption and dispersal which were examined above. These scenes of instability, considered alongside the excessive drive to penetration experienced by the hero, and the literal instances of wounding and injury, can be read in terms of a wider repertoire of images of dysfunction, abjection and trauma. In other words, the breaking down of the boundaries of the body – the piercing of Freud's protective shield – and the consequent elusiveness of any secure identity, whether corporeal or sexual, is explored through a whole series of motifs and images which link back to the primordial trauma of the slave ship and its immediate aftermath.

There is, however, a residual uneasiness in the portrayal of the female body, which remains unresolved by the novel's end. I have until now steered away from the subject of gender as a primary concern in this study, largely because the topic has been so amply treated by other critics, notably with regard to *Texaco*.[27] But in *Biblique* the representation of gender and sexuality departs from the already controversial treatment of that theme in the previous novels. Critics have objected to the stereotypical view of femininity expressed in *Texaco* and elsewhere, or for example to the privileging of the male anatomy in the designation of Marie-Sophie as a *femme-à-graines*. In *Biblique*, however, the discomfort of the reader is of quite a different order, and derives primarily from two factors. First, the female body is repeatedly figured as the key site (and sight) of horror, and a constant threat to the integrity of the male. Secondly, there is a glaring disparity between the hero's apparent sympathy for the subaltern or the oppressed – his activism in enlightened anti-colonial struggle – and his priapic conquest of unindividuated women in the colonized world. This disparity is all the more surprising from an author who is highly conscious of the objections expressed by critics concerning his portrayal of gender – critics dismissed too readily, perhaps, as 'des critiques américains qui m'ont accusé d'être machiste' – and who has claimed that all his novels are 'des romans féminins'.[28]

Biblique is more than any other Chamoiseau novel concerned with the act of seeing, rather than of listening, and one of the novel's most uncomfortable aspects is the obsessive or voyeuristic gaze on female sexuality. It is certainly true that wounding and pain are shown to be widespread relics of the slave past, and thus afflict both men and women. But while the wounds of male characters affect eyes, neck and wrists, for example, and while the hero is injured in armed struggles against various colonial powers, women are associated with an unheroic, and often horrific, kind of trauma, in their experience of sex, pregnancy and childbirth. And in turn, woman constitutes a constant threat to the bodily integrity of the male. Throughout the text, she is aligned with the 'ventouse', the suction pad or cupping-glass. The hero fears her 'pièges aspirants, [ses] gouffres de désordre' (p. 237), while even his father had his flesh devoured by Yvonnette Cléoste so that he becomes a 'plaie vive' (p. 99). Furthermore, there is an uneasy sense of indulgence (and even, perhaps, explicit misogyny) in the extended descriptions of the devastated female body: devoured ovaries, traumatized vaginas and punctured rectums are evoked in queasy detail. Woman is dubiously aligned with both victim and monster.

Writing in 1987, Ernest Pépin argued that the Antillean author 'ne regarde pas la femme antillaise, craignant sans doute de tomber dans l'exotisme'.[29] Rather than shying away from the female anatomy, since the late 1980s the *créolité* authors (Pépin himself, Confiant most notably, and Chamoiseau to a remarkable degree in this novel) have resolutely oriented their gaze towards the female body. But in so doing, it seems that they have in their turn reproduced an exoticizing or stereotypical version of femininity.[30] Dominique Chancé, in a critical article on *Biblique*, compares the novel to a cartoon, but I would argue in closing that the text also has similarities with the horror movie. In her study of *The Monstrous-Feminine*, Barbara Creed identifies a number of stereotypical roles ascribed to women in the horror genre, almost all of which can be found in *Biblique*: the amoral primeval mother (Yvonnette Cléoste), witch (Man L'Oubliée and L'Yvonnette Cléoste), woman as monstrous womb (Sarah, Symphorine Massidor and many others), monstrous girl-boy (Déborah; Kalamati).[31] These characters are primarily associated with orifices, hollows and openings, and can be seen to embody the primary disturbances of colonialism, as either the instigators or the victims (and frequently both) of penetration and possession. For it remains a remarkably persistent trope of Caribbean discourse to figure the traumatic memory of slavery in terms of the wounded, or wounding, female body. As such, it could be argued that the 'aggressive heterosexual eroticism' criticized by A. James Arnold in a relatively early article on *Texaco* finds it fullest, and most phantastic, realization in Chamoiseau's *Biblique des derniers gestes*.[32]

Finally, from the point of view of the current situation of the island, this monstrosity could be read in socio-political, as well as psychoanalytic, terms. For as Creed notes, 'when confronted by the sight of the monstrous, the viewing subject is put into crisis – boundaries, designed to keep the abject at bay, threaten to disintegrate, collapse'.[33] The opening section can perhaps be read from this perspective, as an exploration of the acute separation anxiety that obtains between colonial *département* and metropolitan parent. The monstrous, all-engulfing displays of *maternalistic* affection in the opening of the novel permeate discourse, iconography and metaphor. This can be seen in proverbs ('mère patrie est lointaine mais elle n'est pas ingrate', p. 20), in the references to the Virgin Mary, which link her to the 'chère Métropole' (p. 19), and in the general feminization of Martinican culture and politics, embodied in the Grande Dame of Creole song and the female minister described as follows: 'Nous aimions cette ministre [...] *un visage au Pouvoir, qui nous ressemblait tant!...*' (p. 20, italics in original). It is perhaps in this grotesque and excessive novel that the emasculating logic or the threat of castration which underlies the colonial situation is most discernible, and in which Martinique's current relationship with France is most provocatively, and disturbingly, criticized.

Afterword

In the transition that has been traced in this monograph, from an æsthetics of re-collection and transcription to a poetics of materiality, the body has emerged as a primary site of both fictional and autobiographical memory, an archive and an active witness. It is appropriate that this study should end with further consideration of *Biblique* because, as we have seen, this novel focuses on the body to an unprecedented degree, and because the text exemplifies many of the tensions which have lain at the heart of my analysis more generally, such as the fraught borderline between nostalgia and 'authentic' memory, or the disconnection between contemporary Martinique and its buried slave past. The novel at first sight seems to explore a further tension, identified by Mary Gallagher as being one of the most persistent preoccupations in French Caribbean writing, 'the tension between reaching out and looking within'.[1] But the sense of nomadism, displacement, or Glissantian *errance* which the text appears to espouse is in the end more apparent than real, for in this novel Chamoiseau reaches out only in order to look in more intently. *Biblique* may well be the only Chamoiseau novel to date which extends in any significant way beyond the geographical confines of Martinique, so that the hero moves through many of the most notorious sites of imperial aggression: Vietnam, the Congo, Algeria. However, within the economy of the text, these countries act primarily as a foil to Martinique, just as the unindividuated female lovers who haunt the text – La Bolivenne, L'Indienne – are unapologetically instrumentalized to shore up and to shed light on Bibidji's character.

The hero's experience in the many independence struggles described in the novel suggests that in those countries in which the colonial presence was a temporary, albeit devastating, phenomenon, the traumas of the past can be more effectively confronted and overcome. Martinique thus constitutes an archetype, a culmination and an anomaly in terms of the colonial experience more generally, by virtue of its early conquest, which precedes by centuries the 'Age of Empire', its uniquely complete experience of colonialism,[2] and its ambivalent contemporary status. To return to the opening section of the novel, the exceptionally brutal experience of the Caribbean is underlined: 'C'est ce qui caractérise la Traite des nègres et l'esclavage aux Amériques: son absence de limites' (p. 57). The hero finds in his native land a kind of template for the horrors of imperial aggression which he will encounter throughout his odyssey: 'Lui qui verrait tant d'infirmités [...] découvrait là, sans le savoir, l'inventaire prophétique des horreurs de ses guerres' (p. 462). Slave resistance to the exploitative structure of the plantation has prefigured the anti-colonial struggles of the post-World War II era, and has allowed the geographically isolated – and historically anomalous – Martinique to position itself as a global pioneer 'sur cette ligne du monde où tant de peuples résistent' (p. 494).

When Bibidji, rather incongruously, becomes a *matrone* in Algeria, he describes the delivery of a newborn in terms that are self-consciously allegorical: '*je me retrouvai soudain avec l'enfant entre les mains, un petit Algérien nouveau dans cette Algérie qui s'efforçait de renaître*' (p. 426, italics in original). This sense of renewal and rebirth is shown to be unimaginable in the Antilles: procreation is, as we have seen, fraught with difficulty, and the genesis of the islands is radically different from that of other postcolonial nations, meaning that trauma and oblivion have assumed a structural and epistemic centrality. The repression of this multiply violent past has resulted in the dysfunctions of the present, so that *Biblique* is above all a lament for the current stagnation of the island. In other words, despite its wider sociopolitical framework, it carries a similar ideological message to all Chamoiseau's other novels.

The geographical displacement of *Biblique*, coupled with its repeated upholding of postmodern 'incertitudes', may have led the reader to expect a new predisposition towards instability or fluidity, or a widening of the literary and ethical concerns of the novel. In fact, the overwhelming impression is of a return to already charted territory. This reinforcement of a primarily insular consciousness – as opposed to the 'roman monde' which Chamoiseau has vaunted in recent writings and interviews, and which one might have expected to find in *Biblique* – can also be seen in the intertextual networks established in the novel. The key echoes are with Antillean writers such as Saint-John Perse, Glissant and Césaire, although Fanon's presence is also, for the first time, manifestly in evidence.[3] Intertextuality in *Biblique* is frequently overt and self-conscious, as extended passages of the novel see the hero or narrator commenting on and responding to the 'classics' of French Caribbean writing. But intertexts also circulate in a subtle, fitful and teasing way, so that other Antillean writers echo uncannily throughout the narrative. To choose two examples among many, Bibidji at one point describes the landscape in a ludic manner that recalls Fanon's *Peau noire, masques blancs*: 'Eau blanche, roche noire. Eau noire, roche blanche. Roche d'eau et eau de roche' (p. 195). When aboard the slave ship, Bibidji hears a dull song which is inaudible to the sailors, but which resonates throughout the hold: '*À té néfè Odono!... À té néfè Odono!...*' (p. 60, italics in original). Odono is the name of the mythical and mysterious ancestor mentioned in several Glissant novels, and the scene can be read as an oblique address to the literary ancestor, who will be an increasingly discernible presence as the novel continues.

Glissant's striking prominence as a point of intertextual and paratextual reference in Chamoiseau's work is a device which has been discussed throughout this study. But in *Biblique*, for the first time, he makes an appearance as a *character* within the fictional narrative, as in the closing pages of the novel both he and Césaire (the latter, of course, an almost obligatory presence in the Chamoiseau novel) come to visit Bibidji in his last agony. Glissant's diegetic début is worth considering here in the conclusion to the study, as his sudden intrusion appears to mark yet another departure in *Biblique*. Both writers make their visit late in Balthazar's 'agonie', which is an occasion for mutual acknowledgement; the writers profess their admiration for the dying man, just as Bibidji has, in turn, been steeped in their work. The text even hints at the possibility that Bibidji and Glissant may have met as political activists during the Algerian War.

Césaire arrives first, and the narrator comments that he and Balthazar 'n'avaient jamais été du même bord ni du même combat'. He adds dismissively that the poet-statesman 'ne faisait plus partie (sinon par sa poésie qui rayonnait encore) du pays enterré'. Césaire refuses the chair that is offered to him, stays only briefly and leaves the gathering 'de son pas devenu hésitant. Tellement amer' (pp. 766–67). Such a belittling description is consistent with other Chamoiseau novels, reinforcing the impression of a feeble old man who is out of touch, remote and embittered. Unsurprisingly, Glissant's intervention as character is of quite a different order, and the contrast with Césaire is emphasized to the point of overstatement. Glissant, we are told, has come all the way from the United States in order to pay his respects to Bibidji. His presence elicits a smile, the first the narrator has seen grace Bibidji's lips, and this reaction contrasts with 'les yeux troubles' provoked by Césaire. Glissant's physique – 'cette tête de commandeur qui nouait autant de doutes que de hautes certitudes' (p. 770) – suggests height, strength and, crucially, an authority which admits of doubt and uncertainty. And the sense of profound sympathy and understanding between the two is such that 'A lui l'agonisant n'avait presque rien à révéler. Glissant savait déjà. Ils se serrèrent les mains, dans tous les sens, comme pour calmer émotions'. As if to drive home the absolute contrast with Césaire, the narrator states that Glissant 'était du pays enterré' (p. 770).

The exclusionary logic which has been at work in the novel[4] – and frequently, as I have suggested, in Chamoiseau's work more generally – means that both writers are pressed into the service of a polarizing and value-laden distinction. The rather too categorical opposition between surface and depth is already implicit in the obsessive celebration of the 'pays enterré', to which Balthazar and Glissant are attuned, but to which Césaire cannot accede.[5] This closing scene reinscribes the rather limiting distinction between the two overbearing literary ancestors, who have been pitted against each other throughout Chamoiseau's writing, and indeed throughout the work of the *créolité* writers more generally. *Biblique*, which began with an ironic exposé of the excessive reverence in which Césaire is held, ends 750 pages later with a yet more emphatic sidelining of the *négritude* poet. The overwhelming impression in this closing scene is of a closed, self-referential and somewhat reactionary literary world. In this sense, the observations of Michel Beniamino, in a relatively early article on the *créolité* movement, have been fully borne out by later writings. Beniamino observes that all too often in contemporary writing, it is in fact Glissant who 'établit la théorie de la créolité, [...] P. Chamoiseau et R. Confiant qui la textualisent et [...] enfin, la critique qui produit un texte sur ces romans'. Beniamino asks whether '[le] texte ne court-il pas le risque de n'être qu'un détour dont l'utilité ne serait que de vérifier la bonne application des principes et de leur applicabilité?'[6] But while Beniamino's primary target here is the critic, who simply reads from theory to text and back, it could equally be argued that in a novel such as *Biblique*, Chamoiseau has effected a similarly reductive manœuvre. It could of course be added that in the obsessive recourse to Césaire, and in the explicit assertion, in the *Eloge* and elsewhere, of *créolité* as a counter-discourse to *negritude*, Chamoiseau merely reinforces the importance of the elder writer. *Créolité*'s reliance on the discourses and the personalities it denies, in order to formulate its own distinct agenda, might even be said to replicate *négritude*'s much-criticized reliance on an oppositional Manichean model for its own self-constitution.

If the closing of *Biblique* suggests, to this reader at least, the risk of an introverted and polarizing æsthetics, it also points undoubtedly to the deep and entangled imbrication of theoretical and creative writing which characterizes Martinican literature, and which is a particularly strong feature of Chamoiseau's work. If this study has relied less than others on the home-grown theories of Caribbean (and, specifically, Martinican) identity politics, and has instead attempted to position Chamoiseau's work within a wider framework of writing and theorizing on the subject of memory, this is not just because of the sense of restriction alluded to above. It is also because of the remarkable consonances that can be seen to link a highly localized identity politics with important debates on memory throughout the world. The urgent questions around how best to remember the traumas of slavery in the Caribbean find strong parallels elsewhere, notably in the ongoing attempt to deal with the legacy of the Holocaust. In this renewed attention to memory, the words of Primo Levi chime with reservations expressed in the Antillean context. Levi argues that an overly familiar or too frequently narrated memory can take on a distorted form: 'it is also true that a memory evoked too often, and expressed in the form of a story, tends to become fixed in stereotype, in a form tested by experience, crystallised, perfected, adorned, which installs itself in the place of raw memory and grows at its expense'.[7] In other words, and paradoxically, in the continual return to the same narratives and to the same events, one risks neutralizing the power of memory. A past that cannot be relinquished may even act as a defence against memory. Similarly, a past which is wilfully recruited in the light of the vagaries of the present can be diluted, or rendered routine by the 'memory industry'. In the ongoing grappling with the memory of slavery in Caribbean writing over the last two decades, these ethical issues remain deeply linked to questions around æsthetics and poetics. In Chamoiseau's fiction, and notably in a work such as *Biblique*, the reader senses a straining against precisely the threat of palatability and dilution. That this novel raises such difficult questions, however, around its obsessive gaze on the female body, testifies to the difficulty of representing the horror and trauma of the past in written narrative.

Whatever my reservations regarding the problematic oppositions which underlie Chamoiseau's representation of memory, his writing undoubtedly makes a unique contribution to contemporary postcolonial literature, and to the ongoing project of 'recovering memory' which characterizes the Antilles today. His is a self-conscious art, which is linguistically and formally experimental, and which, in the demands that it makes upon its reader, might be seen to conform to a 'highbrow' postcolonial literature, as practised by writers such as Salman Rushdie. To this extent, it could be argued that Chamoiseau 'fits' the current academic climate, characterized by what Benita Parry, cited in my introduction, calls the 'linguistic turn',[8] or what Chris Bongie terms the 'value-affirming critical context' of postcolonial studies. Bongie suggests that certain variants of postcolonial writing, in their reaffirmation of the importance of textuality (and difficulty), can be seen to have more in common with the modernist agenda than has been previously recognized. He identifies the 'twin directives' of modernism as 'æsthetic resistance (promoting stylistic difficulty) and political resistance (promoting radical social change)', and mentions a number of writers who privilege one or the other of these directives.[9] Bongie's argument is an important one, as it addresses head-on the unfashionable question of literary quality. He suggests that 'middlebrow', popular authors – he focuses particularly on Maryse Condé, although a writer such as Confiant might also fit his argument – pose something of an embarrassment for postcolonial critics, who find themselves having to ignore popularity in order to underscore a sense of literary seriousness. It is true to say that the reader of Chamoiseau, for whom one of the primary delights is the sheer pleasure of poetic and æsthetic exuberance, encounters no such embarrassment. It is also true that one of Chamoiseau's most resounding achievements has been to work simultaneously, and with equal vigour, between the two modernist poles identified by Bongie above. For this is undoubtedly a writer for whom 'high seriousness' (literary ambition) and 'resistance' (political intervention) are inextricably linked.

Notes

Introduction

1 See in particular Serge Chalons et al., *De l'esclavage aux réparations* (Paris: Karthala, 2000), Christine Chaulet-Achour and R.-B. Fonkoua (eds), *Esclavage: Libérations, abolitions, commémorations* (Paris: Séguier, 2001) and Françoise Vergès, *Abolir l'esclavage – une utopie coloniale: Les ambiguïtés d'une politique humanitaire* (Paris: Albin Michel, 2001).

2 Christiane Taubira-Delannon is a Guyanese deputy, representing the 'Parti radical de gauche' in the French parliament.

3 The reaction was such that on 6 December 2005, Nicolas Sarkozy had to cancel a high-profile trip to Martinique. Aimé Césaire – to whom all manner of visitors, from footballers to statesmen, are routinely presented – for the first time ever declared himself unavailable for such a meeting. The snub, a direct result of the 'loi de la honte', was deeply embarrassing to Sarkozy. Commentators were quick to note that it was on the same day in 1987 that Jean-Marie Le Pen was famously unable to disembark from his plane, which had landed in Lamentin airport, Martinique.

4 Other members of the committee – which includes representatives from Réunion and French Guyana, as well as from the Antilles – include the literary critic Françoise Vergès and the historian Nelly Schmidt.

5 See, for example, the joint interview with Chamoiseau and Glissant, *Libération*, 8th December 2005. See too Marion Van Renterg's 'La Mémoire blessée de la Martinique', *Le Monde*, 15th December 2005.

6 See for example *Le Nouvel Observateur*, 30 January 2006.

7 The current vogue for autobiography in the Antilles will be discussed in Chapter 2.

8 Marianne Hirsch, *Family Frames: Photography, Narrative and Postmemory* (Cambridge, MA, and London: Harvard University Press, 1997).

9 Henri Rousso, *Le Syndrome de Vichy: de 1940 à nos jours* (Paris: Seuil, 1990).

10 His 'syndrome' has been read on one level as evidence of French repression of the colonial past, according to which, in the aftermath of the Algerian War, attention was diverted from atrocities committed in the overseas colony towards a more distant memory of a different kind of occupation.

11 Derek Walcott, *What the Twilight Says: Essays* (New York and London: Faber and Faber, 1998), p. 37.

12 Aimé Césaire, *Discours sur le colonialisme* (Paris: Présence Africaine, 2004 [1955]), pp. 13–14.

13 Ana Douglass and Thomas A. Vogler (eds), *Witness and Memory: The Discourse of Trauma* (London and New York: Routledge, 2003), 'Introduction', pp. 1–53, p. 53.

14 Michèle Praeger, *The Imaginary Caribbean and the Caribbean Imaginary* (Lincoln, NE, and London: University of Nebraska Press, 2003), p. 4.

15 In *Writing History, Writing Trauma* (Baltimore: The Johns Hopkins University Press, 2001), LaCapra defines a 'limit event' as one exemplifying a contemporary 'vision of history [...] as traumatic, especially as a symptomatic response to

a felt implication in excess and disorientation' (pp. x–xi).

16 Hirsch, *Postmemory*, p. 22.

17 Pierre Nora, 'Between Memory and History: les lieux de mémoire', *Representations* 26 (1989), pp. 7–25.

18 Kerwin Klein, 'On the Emergence of *Memory* in Historical Discourse', *Representations* 69 (2000), pp. 127–50, p. 128.

19 Klein, 'On the Emergence of *Memory*', p. 130.

20 Klein, 'On the Emergence of *Memory*', p. 138.

21 Thomas W. Laqueur, 'Introduction', *Representations* 69 (2000), pp. 1–8, p. 8.

22 Fredric Jameson, *The Political Unconscious: Narrative as Socially Symbolic Act* (Ithaca, NY: Cornell University Press, 1981), p. 102.

23 The notion of the navel metonymically signifying a physiological link to the past, and guaranteeing a sense of continuity in the present, is also undermined by Toni Morrison through Pilate's lack of a navel in *Song of Solomon*. The old man of *L'Esclave vieil homme* is, at the start of the novel, one of the most dispossessed in Chamoiseau's *œuvre*, having forgotten his name 'sans qu'il ait eu le sentiment de l'avoir oublié', and not knowing 's'il était né sur l'Habitation ou s'il avait connu cette traversée en cale', p. 35.

24 Walcott, *What the Twilight Says*, p. 37.

25 Pierre Nora, *Les Lieux de mémoire*, Vol. I (Paris: Gallimard, 1997), p. 23.

26 Eric Hobsbawm, *The Age of Extremes: The Short Twentieth Century* (New York: Pantheon, 1994), p. 3.

27 Ann Rigney, 'Plenitude, Scarcity and the Circulation of Cultural Memory', *Journal of European Studies* 35.1 (2005), pp. 11–28, p. 13.

28 Walcott, *What the Twilight Says*, p. 4.

29 This is one of the most persistent criticisms of the *créolité* movement. See in particular Maryse Condé, 'Order, Disorder, Freedom and the West Indian Writer', *Yale French Studies* 83.2 (1993), pp. 121–35. Special Issue, 'Post/Colonial Conditions: Exiles, Migrations, and Nomadisms', edited by Françoise Lionnet and Ronnie Scharfmann.

30 For a denunciation of this lack of an outwardly aggressive colonizer against whom to rebel, see the closing section of *Biblique des derniers gestes*, 'Incertitudes sur les restants d'amours'.

31 Homi Bhabha, *The Location of Culture* (London and New York: Routledge, 1994), pp. 253–54.

32 Richard Price and Sally Price, 'Shadow-Boxing in the Mangrove', *Cultural Anthropology* 12.1 (1997), pp. 3–36, p. 15.

33 Fredric Jameson, *Postmodernism: or, The Cultural Logic of Late Capitalism* (London and New York: Verso, 1991), p. 20.

34 Eric Santner, *Stranded Objects: Mourning, Memory and Film in Postwar Germany* (Ithaca, NY, and London: Cornell University Press, 1990), pp. 7–8.

35 Martin Munro, '*La discorde antillaise*: Contemporary Debates in Caribbean Criticism', *Paragraph* 24.3 (2001), pp. 117–27, p. 119. Special Issue, 'Francophone Texts and Postcolonial Theory' edited by Celia Britton and Michael Syrotinski.

36 See *The Repeating Island: The Caribbean and the Postmodern Perspective*, trans. James E. Maraniss (Durham, NC: Duke University Press, 1992).

37 Raphaël Confiant, *Aimé Césaire: Une Traversée paradoxale du siècle* (Paris: Stock, 1993), p. 266.

38 J. Michael Dash, *The Other America: Caribbean Literature in a New World Context* (Charlottesville, VA: University Press of Virginia, 1999), p. 108.

39 Robert Young, *Colonial Desire: Hybridity in Theory, Culture and Race*

(London and New York: Routledge, 1995), p. 4.

40 *Texaco* (Granta, 1997); *School Days* (University of Nebraska Press, 1997); *Creole Folktales* (The New Press, 1997); *Strange Words* (Granta, 1998); *Solibo the Magnificent* (Granta, 1999); *Childhood* (Granta, 1999); *Seven Dreams of Elmira* (Zoland Books, 1999); *Chronicle of the Seven Sorrows* (University of Nebraska Press, 1999).

41 Lorna Milne, *Patrick Chamoiseau: Espaces d'une écriture antillaise* (Amsterdam and New York: Rodopi, 2006).

42 The novel was first published in 1986.

43 Eva Sansavior, 'Entretien avec Maryse Condé', *Francophone Postcolonial Studies* 2.2 (2004), pp. 7–33, p. 30.

44 Maryse Condé, *Le Cœur à rire et à pleurer: Contes vrais de mon enfance* (Paris: Hatier, 1999), p. 99.

45 H. Adlai Murdoch, *Creole Identity in the French Caribbean Novel* (Gainesville: University Press of Florida, 2001), p. 197.

46 Joseph Nnadi, 'Mémoire d'Afrique, mémoire biblique: la congruence des mythes du nègre dans *Texaco* de Patrick Chamoiseau', *Etudes francophones* 15.1 (2000), pp. 75–91, p. 75.

47 Edward Said, *Beginnings: Intention and Method* (New York: Basic Books, 1975), p. 82.

48 The *Eloge de la créolité* was the product of a three-way collaboration between Chamoiseau, Raphaël Confiant and Jean Bernabé. *Lettres creoles* was co-authored with Confiant.

49 This was not an entirely new departure, as the coffee-table book *Martinique* (Paris: Richer, Hoa Qua, 1998), as well as the history of the penal colony, *Guyane: Traces-mémoires du bagne* (Caisse nationale des documents et des sites, 1994), were collaborations between Chamoiseau and a number of photographers.

50 This juxtaposition of image and text, in the context of a collaborative project, is a very common practice in contemporary Caribbean cultural production, and no doubt merits further critical attention. Raphaël Confiant's *Les Maîtres de la parole créole* (Paris: Gallimard, 1995) was written with Marcel Labielle, and features photographs of aged storytellers taken by David Damoison. An interesting counterpoint in terms of gender is *Femmes des Antilles: Traces et voix cent cinquante ans après l'abolition* (Paris: Stock, 1998), a (textual) collaboration between Gisèle Pineau and Marie Abraham, and the photographer Thomas Dorn.

51 Jefferson Hunter, *Image and Word: The Interaction of Twentieth-Century Photographs and Texts* (Cambridge, MA: Harvard University Press, 1987), pp. 1–2.

52 Susan Sontag, *On Photography* (London and New York: Penguin, 1977), p. 15.

53 Sontag, *On Photography*, p. 15.

54 Pierre Gamarra, 'La Machine à écrire: La parole de la Martinique', *Europe* 55 (1992), pp. 205–208, p. 206, my italics.

55 Benita Parry, 'The Institutionalization of Postcolonial Studies', in *The Cambridge Companion to Postcolonial Literary Studies*, edited by Neil Lazarus (Cambridge: Cambridge University Press, 2004), pp. 66–80, p. 73.

56 This growing body of critical work is most developed in the case of Toni Morrison, but includes Audre Lorde and, more significantly for our purposes here, includes work on Edwige Danticat and on women writers of the anglophone Caribbean (Jamaica Kincaid; Marlene Nourbese Philip, Jean Rhys). See Bouson 2000; Vickroy 2002; Morton 2002.

1   Beginnings: The Enigma of Origin

1 The *djobeurs* were the barrow boys or odd-job men of the Creole market.

2 See Richard D. E. Burton, '"*Debrouya pa peche*" or "*il y a toujours moyen de moyenner*" : Patterns of Opposition in the Fiction of Patrick Chamoiseau', *Callaloo*, 16.2 (1993), pp. 466–81. See also Renée K. Gosson, 'For What the Land Tells: An Ecocritical Approach to Patrick Chamoiseau's *Chronicle of the Seven Sorrows*', *Callaloo*, 26.1 (2003), pp. 219–34.

3 Valérie Loichot, 'Fort-de-France: Pratiques textuelles et corporelles d'une ville coloniale', *French Cultural Studies* 15.1 (2004), pp. 48–60, p. 56.

4 Lorna Milne, 'From *créolité* to *diversalité*: The Postcolonial Subject in Patrick Chamoiseau's *Texaco*', in *Subject Matters: Subject and Self from Descartes to the Present*, ed. Paul Gifford and Johnnie Gratton (Amsterdam and Atlanta: Rodopi, 2000), pp. 161–80, pp. 164–65. My reading therefore diverges from that of J. Michael Dash, who sees Marie-Sophie as being 'in many ways the female equivalent of the *djobeurs* of the earlier *Chronique* – who as keeper of the community's memories emerges as the mother of the precarious Martiniquan nation'. *The Other America*, p. 144. I would argue that one of the most striking features of these characters is precisely the fragility of their memory.

5 René Depestre, *Hadriana dans tous mes rêves* (Paris: Folio, 1990), p. 138.

6 Celia Britton, '"Eating Their Words": The Consumption of French Caribbean Literature', *ASCALF Yearbook* 1 (1996), pp. 15–23, p. 20.

7 The 'unequalness' of the two forms is made explicit by the *djobeurs*, who observe that 'les postes de télévision regorgeaient de plus d'images que la mémoire d'Elmire', *CSM*, p. 135.

8 Sontag, *On Photography*, p. 110.

9 As we will see, amnesia frequently functions in this way in the autobiographies and in *Texaco*.

10 Equally, though, some stories are told more than once, in strikingly similar terms (e.g. the fate of Bidjoule; the story of Man Elo).

11 Said, *Beginnings*, p. 22.

12 Mary Gallagher, *Soundings in French Caribbean Writing since 1950: The Shock of Space and Time* (Oxford: Oxford University Press, 2002), p. 66.

13 Kathleen Gyssels, 'Du titre au roman: *Texaco* de Patrick Chamoiseau', *Roman 20/50*, 20 (1995), pp. 121–32.

14 Gyssels, 'Du titre', 122.

15 Jay Clayton, *The Pleasures of Babel: Contemporary American Literature and Theory* (New York and Oxford: Oxford University Press, 1993), p. 45.

16 Moreover, there are many points of comparison between *Chronique* and Glissant's first novel, *La Lézarde* (1958). The earlier novel is also centrally concerned with departmentalization, features a number of foretellings and predictions, is structured in meanders and circularities and proceeds through slippages in narrative voice.

17 For a full discussion of this issue in Martinican literature and culture, see Richard D. E. Burton, *La Famille coloniale: La Martinique et la mère-patrie 1789–1992* (Paris: L'Harmattan, 1994).

18 This investment in the all-powerful father figures can be seen too in Haiti, the geographically close but politically distant island, whose most recent leaders include Papa Doc Duvalier and 'le petit père' Aristide.

19 The lines resonate, of course, with the popular war-time song glorifying Pétain, 'Maréchal, nous voilà'.

20 For the most balanced and eloquent articulation of this often controversial subject, see Mireille Rosello, 'The "Césaire Effect", or How to Cultivate One's

Nation', *Research in African Literatures*, 32.4 (2001), pp. 77–91.

21 The fact that this is the funniest of Chamoiseau's novels does not necessarily work against the tragic codes of the text, and indeed in many respects it bolsters the sense of tragedy.

22 The *pacotilleuse* is a kind of travelling saleswoman, or pedlar, in the Antilles.

23 Thus, the text conforms to a persistent model identified by Jean Jonassaint, with reference to the Haitian novel. Jonassaint demonstrates how what he calls 'novels of Haitian tradition' are 'organized around two compulsory sequences: the initial one, which is a prospective narrative or discourse (caution or warning), and the final one, which is a retrospective narrative or discourse (clarification or explanation)'. See Jean Jonassaint, 'Tragic Narratives: The Novels of Haitian Tradition', *Callaloo* 26.1 (2003), pp. 203–18. See also by the same author *Des Romans de tradition haïtienne: Sur un récit tragique* (Paris: L'Harmattan; Montreal: Cidihca, 2002).

24 In his autobiography the Guadeloupean writer Daniel Maximin evokes, from a child's perspective, the superstition which surrounds this myth. See *Tu, c'est l'enfance* (Paris: Gallimard, 2004), p. 106. See, too, Edouard Glissant's *Malemort*.

25 The sealed *jarre de Provence* in *Chronique* can be seen to function in a similar way to Proust's conceptualisation, in *Le Temps retrouvé*, of memory as a multitude of sealed vessels, particularly in the sensual impact of memory: 'Le geste, l'acte le plus simple reste enfermé comme dans mille vases clos dont chacun serait rempli de choses d'une couleur, d'une odeur, d'une température absolument différentes'. *Le Temps retrouvé* (Paris: Folio, 1972), p. 448.

26 Glissant, too, in an often-quoted observation – which, indeed, serves as an epigraph to *Texaco* – links the quest for memory in the Caribbean to the archæological dig: 'Parce que la mémoire historique fut trop souvent raturée, l'écrivain antillais doit "fouiller" cette mémoire à partir de traces parfois latentes, qu'il a repérées dans le réel'. *Le Discours antillais* (Paris: Seuil, 1981), p. 421.

27 For a full discussion of psychoanalysis in the French Caribbean, see Celia Britton, *Race and the Unconscious: Freudianism in French Caribbean Thought* (Oxford: Legenda, 2002).

28 Frantz Fanon, *Peau noire, masques blancs* (Paris: Seuil, 1952), p. 122.

29 Glissant, *Le Discours antillais*, pp. 130–31.

30 Cathy Caruth, *Unclaimed Experience: Trauma, Narrative and History* (Baltimore: The Johns Hopkins University Press, 1996), p. 11.

31 Caruth, *Unclaimed Experience*, p. 91.

32 Ruth Leys, *Trauma: A Genealogy* (Chicago and London: The University of Chicago Press, 2000), p. 9.

33 Caruth, *Unclaimed Experience*, p. 3.

34 Shoshana Felman and Dori Laub, *Testimony: Crises of Witnessing in Literature, Psychoanalysis and History* (London and New York: Routledge, 1993), p. 158.

35 LaCapra, *Writing History*, p. 28.

36 LaCapra, *Writing History*, p. 93.

37 Jacques Derrida, *Spectres de Marx: L'état de la dette, le travail du deuil et la nouvelle internationale* (Paris: Galilée, 1993).

38 Ranjana Khanna, *Dark Continents: Psychoanalysis and Colonialism* (Durham, NC: Duke University Press, 2003), p. 16.

39 Bhabha, *The Location of Culture*, p. 18.

40 LaCapra, *Writing History*, p. 90.

41 Jacques Derrida, *L'Ecriture et la différence* (Paris: Seuil, 1979), p. 292.

2   'Une tracée de survie': Autobiographical Memory

1 Several years after their release, the first two texts were repackaged by Folio as *Une enfance créole* volumes I and II respectively. In this chapter, unless otherwise stated, I refer to their original editions, and the three volumes will be abbreviated as *AE*, *CE* and *BE* respectively.

2 These include Confiant's *Ravines du devant-jour* (1993) and *Le Cahier des romances* (2000); Pépin's *Coulée d'or* (1995); Pineau's *L'Exil selon Julia* (1996); Emile Ollivier's *Mille Eaux* (1999), Condé's *Le Cœur à rire et à pleurer* (1999) and Maximin's *Tu, c'est l'enfance* (2004).

3 Chamoiseau was 37 in 1990, and his most recent volume appeared when he was 49.

4 The quest for beginnings in *Antan d'enfance* is equally presented in a humorous way. See, for example, the *négrillon*'s attempt to retrace the steps of his pregnant mother on her way to hospital to give birth to him: 'Il est arrivé à l'homme de refaire ce chemin de naissance [...]. Il lui est arrivé, enfin, d'examiner les orages nocturnes de décembre quand ils surgissaient un jeudi, avec l'envie d'y percevoir non pas un signe, mais une sensation familière, une résurgence de la primordiale sensation' (*AE*, p. 13).

5 The word 'vie', of course, is contained in both *envie* and *survie*. The fact that the much desired school of 'Envie' becomes something to be survived or recovered from is made explicit in *Chemin-d'école* when le *négrillon* resolves that the only solution is to 'survivre. S'en sortir' (*CE*, p. 104).

6 Derek Walcott, 'Another Life'. Quoted by Edward Baugh, 'The Poet's Fiction of Self: The Schooner *Flight*', *The South Atlantic Quarterly* 96.2 (1997), pp. 311–20, p. 313.

7 See Debra Kelly, *Autobiography and Independence: Selfhood and Creativity in North African Postcolonial Writing in French* (Liverpool: Liverpool University Press, 2004) for a full discussion of this tension. Although Kelly deals specifically with the Maghreb, many of her arguments hold good for the Antillean situation as well.

8 Glissant, *Le Discours antillais*, p. 439.

9 Sandra Pouchet Paquet, 'West Indian Autobiography', in *African-American Autobiography* (Englewood Cliffs, NJ: Prentice Hall, 1993), pp. 196–211, pp. 197–98.

10 Exceptionally, however, the 'je' unambiguously conveys an instance in the past time of the diegesis ('Et parfois, je la vis sourire', *AE*, p. 58). Likewise, although the third person 'il' is usually associated with le *négrillon* in the past, the interventions from 'l'homme d'aujourd'hui' introduce the perspective of the adult.

11 Michael Sheringham, *French Autobiography: Devices and Desires* (Oxford: Clarendon Press, 1993), pp. 6–7.

12 Sheringham, *French Autobiography*, pp. 6–7.

13 Sheringham, *French Autobiography*, p. 290.

14 Again, *A Bout d'enfance* diverges from the other two texts. Here, the jostling for position seems to have been resolved into a mutually enriching three-way negotiation between memory, le *négrillon* and the 'je' of the narrator: '...*et voilà mémoire qui cherche mon négrillon... te voilà mon négrillon qui nourrit ma mémoire... me voilà, vous construisant ensemble, vous inventant sans doute comme vous me concevez...*' (*BE*, p. 73, italics and ellipses in original).

15 Like the untaken photograph with which Duras's *L'Amant* opens, so the unwritten memory remains 'juste', intact and uncontaminated; both attain a kind of absolute status precisely because they remain virtual, unrealized, and therefore of

undiminished potential.

16 Like Marie-Sophie, 'l'informatrice' in *Texaco*, Man Ninotte ('la haute confidante') is a privileged source of the oral history of the community. Both women transmit this past to an eager younger recipient, *le négrillon*/Oiseau de Cham.

17 Philippe Lejeune, *Le Pacte autobiographique* (Paris: Seuil, 1975), p. 37.

18 It is significant that poetry has disappeared from *A Bout d'enfance*, given the co-implication of poetry and childhood. The narrator of *Antan d'enfance* comments: 'Le poète [...] ne grandit jamais, ou si peu', *AE*, p. 79.

19 They bear comparison, indeed, with the italicized passages in *Roland Barthes par Roland Barthes*, which Barthes himself compares to the haiku, in their compactness, their lack of dramatic significance and their resistance to signification. See *Roland Barthes par Roland Barthes* (Paris: Seuil, 1975), p. 113.

20 The immediacy of the fragment contrasts with the more reflective 'Les mains adultes se souviennent en cicatrices' of *A Bout d'enfance*, p. 91.

21 The *deliberate* attempt to recover the past proves ineffectual, however. When the narrator retraces the steps of his mother's journey to hospital to give birth, he is forced to conclude that he has been unable to retrieve 'une sensation familière, une résurrection de la primordiale sensation' (*AE*, pp. 13–14).

22 Rosemary Lloyd, *The Land of Lost Content: Children and Childhood in Nineteenth-Century French Literature* (Oxford: Clarendon Press, 1992), p. 26

23 Without wanting to push the comparison with that great chronicler of childhood memory too far, it might even be suggested that, as with the famous madeleine, the lusciousness of these descriptions suggests that the fruits act as something of a mother substitute. For this second section of *Antan d'enfance* is above all concerned with the *négrillon*'s progressive distancing himself from the intimacy of the maternal relationship, and from the Creole culture she represents.

24 Indeed, in *Antan d'enfance*, the *négrillon* progresses through a number of developmental stages – the Fire Age, the Tool Age, the Blade Age – which replicate and reinvent the progression of Ancient Man.

25 Petroglyphs will be examined in greater depth in both *Ecrire en pays dominé* and *L'Esclave vieil homme et le molosse*. See Chapter 4.

26 The word 'fer' is also deeply connected to the plantation experience, denoting the iron chains in which slaves were bound.

27 See Philippe Lejeune, 'Paroles d'enfance', *Revue des sciences humaines* 93. 217 (1990), pp. 23–38.

28 Man Ninotte's stance here can be seen to contrast with her retort in the earlier text, 'C'est pas tant pis, c'est un mentir' (*AE*, p. 34).

29 While Sarraute's orality is of a different order, it is interesting that Lejeune highlights this aspect of her text as well: '*Enfance* est un livre à entendre. Une chambre d'échos. Un travail sur la voix', 'Paroles d'enfance', p. 23.

30 In a few cases in the autobiographies, the notes assume their conventionally informative – if sometimes wryly pedantic – function (for example '1. En langue créole le chapardeur est appelé "voleur-de-poules" quel que soit l'objet de son délit', *CE*, p. 75; see also p. 80). Characteristically, however, even this straightforward explanatory role is quickly destabilized by the irony of a narrator who has shown himself to be anything but all-knowing ('*Note de l'Omniscient*', p. 80; '*Traduction de l'Omniscient*', p. 114).

31 For a full discussion of the politics and poetics of Glissant's concept of opacity, see Celia M. Britton, *Edouard Glissant and Postcolonial Theory: Strategies of Language and Resistance* (Charlottesville, VA, and London: The University Press of Virginia, 1999), pp. 18–25.

32 Suzanne Crosta, *Le Récit de vie de l'Afrique et des Antilles* (Sainte Foy:

GRELCA, 1998), p. 2.

33 For a fuller elaboration of this argument, see Maeve McCusker, '"Troubler l'ordre de l'oubli": Memory and Forgetting in French Caribbean Autobiography of the 1990s', *Forum for Modern Language Studies* 40 (2004), pp. 438–50. Special Issue, 'Caribbean Connections', edited by Lorna Milne.

34 Suzette Henke, *Shattered Subjects: Trauma and Testimony in Women's Life Writing* (London: Macmillan, 2000), p. xv.

35 Mary Gallagher, 'Re-membering Caribbean Childhoods: Saint-John Perse's "Eloges" and Patrick Chamoiseau's *Antan d'enfance*', in *The Francophone Caribbean Today: Literature, Language, Culture*, edited by Gertrud Aub-Buscher and Beverley Ormerod Noakes (Kingston: The University of the West Indies Press, 2003), pp. 45–59, p. 45.

36 Maximin, *Tu, c'est l'enfance*, p. 48.

37 See McCusker, '"Troubler l'ordre le l'oubli"', pp. 441–43.

38 While the *récits d'enfance* of Maximin and Ollivier devote considerable space to memory as a theme, they have a more pronounced socio-historical dimension. Maximin's notion that childhood imagination serves to compensate for the gaps in history differs from Chamoiseau's more intimate approach.

39 For a full discussion of this practice, see Mireille Rosello, *Littérature et identité créole aux Antilles* (Paris: Karthala, 1992), pp. 121–25.

40 Zobel's classic coming-of-age novel *La Rue Cases-Nègres* (Paris: Présence Africaine, 1974 [1950]) is the most significant intertextual counterpoint to *Chemin-d'école*, an association reinforced by the cover of the latter, which features a still image of the schoolmaster from Euhzan Palcy's film version of the novel. Zobel, as one of the first generation of Martinicans to have access to formal education, promotes a very positive view of schooling here. For an account of this perspective, inevitably very prevalent in the 1940s and 1950s, see the chapter 'The Plantation as Hell: School in the Novels of Joseph Zobel and Michèle Lacrosil', in Beverley Ormerod's *An Introduction to the French Caribbean Novel* (London: Heinemann, 1985), pp. 56–86.

41 For example the first teacher, Man Salinière, is 'une autre manière de Man Ninotte' (*CE*, p. 39).

42 So significant is the name that, in one of the very few direct transpositions from one work to another, we are again told in *A Bout d'enfance* that 'Le négrillon répondait à un nom compliqué qui mélangeait les chats, les chamois, les chameaux et les oiseaux' (*BE*, p. 134).

43 Patrick Crowley, 'The *Etat Civil*: Post/colonial Identities and Genre', *French Forum* 29.3 (2004), pp. 79–94, p. 90.

44 Contrary to my argument here, Crowley suggests that Chamoiseau's word-play means that 'the filial relationship between author and text is undone', and that the autobiographical pact is acknowledged, but remains unsealed.

45 Patrick Chamoiseau and Raphaël Confiant, *Lettres créoles: Tracées antillaises et continentales de la littérature 1635–1976* (Paris: Hatier, 1991), p. 60.

46 Aimé Césaire, *Cahier d'un retour au pays natal* (Paris: Présence Africaine, 1950), p. 22.

47 Fredric Jameson, 'Third World Literature in the Era of Multinational Capitalism', *Social Text* 15 (1986), pp. 65–88, p. 69. It is clear from the context of Jameson's essay that a country such as Martinique, although far removed from what we might call a 'Third World' economy, fits within the field of writing he is exploring.

48 It could indeed be argued that novels such as *Solibo Magnifique*, *Texaco* and *Biblique des derniers gestes*, by virtue of the manifestly representative nature of their heroes, also conform to Jameson's discredited, but too quickly dismissed, theory.

49 This device, indeed, resonates with the titles of two of the best known autobiographies of black childhood: Camara Laye's *L'Enfant noir* and Richard Wright's *Black Boy*.

50 See Britton, '"Eating Their Words"'.

51 There is here a further parallel with Sarraute's *Enfance*, in which the narrator – also torn between cultures – at one point describes her horror at the introduction of calomel into the strawberry jam: 'L'impression un peu inquiétante de quelque chose de répugnant sournoisement introduit, caché sous l'apparence de ce qui est exquis, ne s'est pas effacée' (*Enfance* (Paris: Gallimard, 1983), p. 46). In both cases, the refusal to ingest and absorb the apparently beneficial product signals a more general cultural resistance.

52 It is interesting, in this context, that the semantically unspecific name 'Gros-Lombric' is translated into English as 'Big Bellybutton'. See Linda Coverdale's translation of *Chemin-d'école*, *Schooldays* (Lincoln, NE: University of Nebraska Press, 1997).

3   Memory Re-collected: Witnesses and Words

1 Dominique Chancé, *L'Auteur en souffrance: Essai sur la position et la représentation de l'auteur dans le roman antillais contemporain (1981–1992)* (Paris: Presses Universitaires de France, 2000), p. 10.

2 Walcott, *What the Twilight Says*, p. 37.

3 Chancé, *L'Auteur*, pp. 36–37.

4 David Cowart explains that this semantic link (less pronounced in English) is common to many languages: 'History and fiction [...] have affinities, and in many languages the words for story and history coincide. Italian *storia*, French *histoire*, Spanish *historia*, Russian *istorya*, German *Geschichte* – all demonstrate the linguistic tendency to obscure the distinction between veracious and imagined narrative.' *History and the Contemporary Novel* (Carbondale, IL: Southern Illinois University Press, 1989) p. 17.

5 Poetry is given precedence over fiction here, despite the fact that both Confiant and Chamoiseau are novelists. This testifies to what Mary Gallagher has identified as the 'reverence' and the 'cultural weight' afforded to poetry by contemporary novelists. 'Contemporary French Caribbean Poetry: The Poetics of Reference', *Forum for Modern Language Studies* (2004), pp. 451–62, 451. Special Issue, 'Caribbean Connections', edited by Lorna Milne.

6 See Nicolas Abraham and Maria Torok, *L'Ecorce et le noyau* (Paris: Flammarion, 1987).

7 This reflection also recalls an observation made by Glissant in *Le Discours antillais*: '[L'histoire officielle] de la Martinique a été conçue à partir de la liste des découvreurs et des gouverneurs de ce pays, sans compter les souveraines . . .' (p. 139).

8 The term is scattered throughout Nora's introduction. See *Les Lieux de mémoire*, Vol. 1, pp. 24; 26; 30 and passim. See also the *Eloge*, pp. 36–38, and *Ecrire en pays dominé*, p. 271.

9 Nora, *Les Lieux de mémoire*, Vol. I, p. 24.

10 Nora, *Les Lieux de mémiore*, Vol. I, p. 23.

11 Jameson, *Postmodernism*, p. 37.

12 In addition to Solibo's 'strangling' by the word, Oiseau de Cham is asthmatic, he describes his tape recorder as 'bronchitic', and worries that his text 'ne transmet rien du *souffle*' (pp. 43–45).

13 Price and Price, 'Shadow-Boxing in the Mangrove', p. 15.

14 Roy Chandler Caldwell Jnr, 'Creole Voice, Creole Time: Narrative Strategies in Chamoiseau's *Chronique des sept misères*', *Romance Quarterly* 47.2 (2000), pp. 103–11, p. 110.

15 See also, for example, Robert Aldrich, 'From *francité* to *créolité*: French West Indian Literature Comes Home', in *Writing Across Worlds: Literature and Migration*, edited by Russell King, John Connell and Paul White (London and New York: Routledge, 1995), pp. 101–24.

16 'Order, Disorder', p. 130.

17 René Ménil, *Antilles déjà jadis* (Paris: Jean Michel Place, 1999), p. 279. Ménil's argument, unusually, suggests that the choice of subject matter has in fact led to an impoverishment of the literary language in which it is expressed, an argument which counters the dominant view of these novels as linguistically rich and inventive.

18 See, for example, Maeve McCusker, 'De la problématique du territoire à la problématique du lieu: Un entretien avec Patrick Chamoiseau', *The French Review* 73.4 (2000), pp. 724–33, pp. 726–27.

19 Nicola King, *Memory, Narrative, Identity: Remembering the Self* (Edinburgh: Edinburgh University Press, 2000), p. 29.

20 Richard Burton, '*Ki Moun Nou Ye?* The Idea of Difference in Contemporary French West Indian Thought', *New West Indian Guide* 67, 1&2 (1993), pp. 5–32, p. 23.

21 For example, Solibo calms Man Gnam's pig by talking to it, and his skills in cookery have been transmitted by word of mouth.

22 Kirby Farrell, *Post-Traumatic Culture: Injury and Interpretation in the Nineties* (Baltimore and London: The Johns Hopkins University Press, 1998), p. 54.

23 Walter Benjamin, 'The Storyteller', in *Illuminations*, translated by Harry Zohn, edited by Hannah Arendt (London: Fontana, 1992), pp. 83–110.

24 Nora, *Les Lieux de mémoire*, Vol. I, p. 29.

25 Jacques Derrida, *Mal d'archive: une impression freudienne* (Paris: Galilée, 1995), p. 11.

26 Indeed, read against Derrida's reflections, the epigraph from Italo Calvino at the outset of *Solibo Magnifique*, celebrating as it does 'le dessin, la symétrie, le réseau d'images qui se posent autour [du fait bizarre], comme dans la formation d'un cristal', becomes itself suffused with irony. For it is precisely the lack of order and transparency, and the absolute impossibility of explaining the 'fait bizarre', which besets the investigation from the start.

27 Derrida, *Mal d'archive*, p. 24.

28 See for example Maeve McCusker, 'An Interview with Patrick Chamoiseau', *International Journal of Francophone Studies* 1,3 (1998), pp. 176–84, p. 178. See also Michaël Plumecocq, 'Entretien avec Patrick Chamoiseau autour de *Solibo Magnifique*', *Roman 20/50* 27 (1999), pp. 125–35, p. 129. Joyce is one of the most frequently invoked authors in the 'Sentimenthèque' of *Ecrire en pays dominé* (see for example pp. 216, 291, 310), and is referred to in *Texaco* and *Biblique*.

29 Declan Kiberd, *Inventing Ireland: The Literature of the Modern Nation* (London: Vintage, 1996), p. 355. Just as Chamoiseau does in *Solibo*, in this quotation Kiberd links writing and human waste.

30 The notion of re-membering as a process of putting the body back together has been mobilized by a number of critics of Caribbean writing. See, for example, Mary Gallagher, 'Re-membering Caribbean Childhoods', J. Michael Dash, 'Writing the Body: Edouard Glissant's Poetics of Re-membering', or April Shemak, 'Re-membering Hispaniola: Edwige Danticat's *The Farming of Bones*', *Modern Fiction Studies* 48.1 (2002), pp. 83–112.

31 Edouard Glissant, 'Le Chaos-monde, l'oral et l'écrit', in *Ecrire la parole de nuit. La nouvelle littérature antillaise*, ed. Ralph Ludwig (Paris: Folio, 1994), pp. 111, 129, 117.

32 In addition to the *marqueur*–source relationship, Marie-Sophie has also converted her father's spoken word into written form, while Ti-Cirique acts as a kind of public writer for the community. Moreover, the town planner's reflections on the nature of the Creole town are frequently conveyed in literary terms.

33 The association with textuality – whose etymology links to the notion of weaving – is of course mobilized specifically in the terms 'maille' and 'fil', and is perhaps suggested obliquely in the title *Texaco*.

34 These three versions are not openly in conflict with each other. Rather, in the manner of the Gospels which they recall ('L'Arrivée du Christ selon Sonore' etc.) they supplement each other, and provide differing emphases.

35 Michelle R. Warren, 'Post-Philology', in *Postcolonial Moves: Medieval Through Modern*, ed. Patricia Clare Ingham and Michelle R. Warren (Basingstoke: Palgrave Macmillan, 2002), pp. 19–45, p. 21.

36 Jean-François Lyotard, *La Condition postmoderne* (Paris: Minuit, 1998 [1979]).

37 It is beyond the scope of this chapter to enter the critical minefield which is the debate around postmodern referentiality in any greater detail. 'Postmodernism' is a highly contested term when applied to history (and perhaps particularly to post-colonial history), due to a common conception that it is a non-referential and ahistorical discourse which glibly dismisses the material reality of the past. Something of the ferocity of the debate surrounding the application of postmodern theories to the writing of history can be gleaned from Keith Jenkins' *The Postmodern History Reader* (London and New York: Routledge, 1998). Elizabeth Wesseling's *Writing History as a Prophet: Postmodernist Innovations of the Historical Novel* (Amsterdam and Philadelphia: John Benjamins, 1991), a title which chimes nicely with Glissant's advocacy of the Antillean writer's 'vision prophétique du passé', also provides a useful overview of the problematics and dilemmas involved in a more strictly literary context.

38 '[W]ith the collapse of the modernist project in ways which, metaphorically speaking, sink right down to its once ostensible roots, so we have witnessed the atten-dant collapse of histories in the upper case; nobody believes in those particular fantasies any more'. Keith Jenkins, Introduction to *The Postmodern History Reader*, pp. 1–30, p. 5.

39 Hayden White is the historian who has most thoroughly theorized the 'emplotment' (or the story*line*) of history, a rhetorical strategy, invented more than discovered, to facilitate comprehension. See in particular White's *Metahistory* (Baltimore: The Johns Hopkins University Press, 1973) and *The Content of the Form* (Baltimore: The Johns Hopkins University Press, 1978).

40 Linda Hutcheon, *The Poetics of Postmodernism* (New York and London: Routledge, 1988).

41 Hutcheon, *Poetics*, p. 5.

42 Hutcheon, *Poetics*, p. 5.

43 In this sense she has a quite different view of the movement from, say, Terry Eagleton, whose work she frequently criticises.

44 Hutcheon, *Poetics*, p. 117.

45 Glissant, *Le Discours antillais*, p. 157.

46 This non-totalizing project is already suggested by the fact that the chronology proceeds in 'élans', in fitful starts and surges, rather than in clearly defined and staged *étapes*.

47 Hutcheon, *Poetics*, p. 114.

48 It is entirely consistent with the non-linear and rhizomatic model that this relationship, which occupies such a weighty section of the story, is not the significant one in terms of the novel's teleology. The relationship with Marie-Sophie's mother, Idoménée, is given considerably less narrative space.

49 Gallagher, *Soundings*, p. 11.

50 Hutcheon, *Poetics*, p. 114.

51 Even Césaire, a local statesman (although distanced by his implication in the project of assimilation and his status as *député* to the French parliament) is hopelessly detached from the people he represents, incapable of communicating with, or being understood by, them. Marie-Sophie and Esternome are unable to see or hear him when he addresses them in the context of a political speech. Ironically, Esternome concludes 'C'est un mulâtre' (*Texaco*, p. 276). Later, when Césaire finally visits Texaco (the section describing his visit is pointedly entitled 'L'effet-Césaire', p. 390), his difference from his people is emphasized. Again, mutual misunderstanding characterizes the event. Césaire asks Marie-Sophie whether she has read the *Cahier*, or whether she just knows an isolated quotation. When Marie-Sophie responds that she has read it, 'il ne dut pas me croire' (p. 403).

52 For a fascinating discussion of the significance of these dates, 'two master narratives of abolition that have for the last few decades uneasily shared the historical stage', see Chris Bongie, 'A Street Named Bissette: Nostalgia, Memory and the *Cent-Cinquantenaire* of the Abolition of Slavery in Martinique', *The South Atlantic Quarterly* 100.1 (2001), pp. 215–57, p. 231.

53 Hutcheon, *Poetics*, p. 48.

54 See Hutcheon, *Poetics*, pp. 122–23. Hutcheon refers specifically to the role of footnotes, a feature of Chamoiseau's work which is worth commenting on at this point. His first novel, *Chronique des sept misères*, includes frequent explanatory notes to illuminate the often obscure references of the *djobeurs*, as well as to provide occasional translations of Creole expressions: 'les djobeurs évoquent là Georges Robert, haut-commissaire aux Antilles françaises' (p. 54); 'les djobeurs évoquent là la loi 46-51 du 19 mars 1946 "tendant au classement comme départements français"' (p. 133). In all subsequent novels, however, the notes lose this explanatory function, acting rather as a sort of supplement to the main body of the text. This would seem to suggest either that from the first novel onwards, Chamoiseau envisages an exclusively Caribbean readership, who do not need these explanations, or, perhaps more convincingly, that the desire for transparency has been reduced.

55 Jameson, *Postmodernism*, p. 18.

4 Memory Materialized: Traces of the Past

1 Klein, 'On the Emergence of *Memory*', p. 136.

2 The obvious exception to this rule is the book, which is valued firstly as an object, and imbued with a highly sensual and tactile charge. See in particular *Écrire en pays dominé*, pp. 24–44, and *Texaco*, in which Marie-Sophie treasures a number of books, including *Alice in Wonderland* and Montaigne's *Essais*.

3 In the more contemporary perspective, one could cite Ollivier's paternal photograph and the Parker pen in *Mille Eaux*, or Daniel Maximin's broken spinning top in *Tu, c'est l'enfance*.

4 There is significant overlap in Chamoiseau's use of the words *tracée* and *trace*. The former, however, tends to carry a spatial signification, and is usually linked to the maroon past. In *Antan d'enfance* it is evoked thus: 'Aller tout droit n'était pas le

meilleur moyen d'arriver aux endroits, et si les Tracées tournoyaient dans les bois, il fallait savoir tournoyer avec elles. [...] Il fallait prendre les Tracées, gribouiller leur ordre d'une déraison marronne' (*AE*, pp. 109–10, p. 110). Elsewhere, however, the *trace* is defined in precisely these terms. The slipperiness of both signifiers is further emphasized in the photo-text *Tracées de mélancolies*, in which the substantive of the title is entirely absent from the text, which mentions only 'traces'. This text suggests, moreover, that the meaning of the terms has been expanded to encompass almost any local practice (hairdressing, cock-fighting, chocolate-making).

5 Paul Ricœur, *Temps et récit III: Le Temps raconté* (Paris: Seuil, 1985), pp. 181–82.

6 Ricœur, *Temps et récit III*, p. 219.

7 Michel Foucault, *Power/Knowledge: Selected Interviews and Other Writings 1972–1977*, edited by Colin Gordon (New York: Pantheon, 1980), p. 149.

8 bell hooks, *Yearning: Race, Gender and Cultural Politics* (London: Turnaround, 1991), p. 42.

9 Sigmund Freud, 'The "Uncanny"', *Standard Edition*, Vol. XVII, trans. James Strachey (London: Hogarth Press, 1955), pp. 217–56.

10 Gaston Bachelard, *La Poétique de l'espace* (Paris: Presses Universitaires de France, 1974), p. 18. It is not insignificant that Bachelard is mainly concerned with the bourgeois novelistic world of Marcel Proust.

11 Alain Robbe-Grillet, *Pour un nouveau roman* (Paris: Minuit, 1963), p. 125.

12 Edward Brathwaite, 'Houses in the West Indian Novel', *The Literary Half Yearly* 17.1 (1976), pp. 111–21, p. 111.

13 Incidentally, the associated emphases suggested by Robbe-Grillet, such as the detailed description of characters' physical appearance, are also relatively muted in Chamoiseau's work.

14 Glissant, *Le Discours antillais*, p. 439.

15 There is perhaps a gendered distinction to be made in the treatment of interior spaces. Evelyn O'Callaghan has commented on the prevalence of the protective space of the 'Kumbla' in Caribbean women's writing. This cocoon-like space can shelter the vulnerable woman, although O'Callaghan acknowledges that it has the potential to entrap them too. For Chamoiseau's female characters, any such retreat is rare, short-lived and relatively easily ended. See 'Interior Schisms Dramatized: The Treatment of the "Mad" Woman in the Work of Some Female Caribbean Novelists', in *Out of the Kumbla: Caribbean Women and Literature*, edited by Carole Boyce Davies and Elaine Savory Fido (Trenton, NJ: Africa World Press, 1990), pp. 89–109.

16 For example, in *Chronique des sept misères*, on finding herself pregnant by a *dorlis*, Héloïse hides away in the *case*, 'soustrayant sa honte à la parole malveillante' (*CSM*, p. 35). Later Clarine retreats to the house built by Gogo in order to mourn his death (*CSM*, p. 66). When, towards the end of *Texaco*, Marie-Sophie abandons herself to alcohol, it is almost as though the house is complicit in her degeneration, as she remarks that she 'cachai[t] [les bouteilles de Neisson] dans les trous de la case' (*Texaco*, p. 395). Retiring to the private sphere is seen by Chamoiseau as a kind of last resort, and even then represents a temporary withdrawal rather than a definitive break with society.

17 On this point, see Ormerod, *Introduction to the French Caribbean Novel*, pp. 60–63.

18 See the chapter 'The Other Question' in *The Location of Culture*, pp. 66–84, in particular pp. 81–83.

19 In *L'Esclave vieil homme et le molosse*, the *Grand-case* is presented as a sickly, stagnant and damaged environment. The master's sons are 'blêmes et criards'; his daughter 'bat de la paupière sur des pupilles trop fixes'; his wife endures an 'aphone

mélancolie' interrupted occasionally by a 'vieux rire dramatique' (pp. 19–20).

20 Cited and referenced in the epigraph to this section.

21 Pierre Bourdieu and Jean-Claude Passeron, *Reproduction in Education, Society and Culture*, translated by Richard Nice (London and Beverly Hills: Sage, 1978), p. 78.

22 Régis Antoine, *Rayonnants écrivains de la Caraïbe* (Paris: Maisonneuve & Larose, 1998), p. 125.

23 In *Antan d'enfance*, the communal wooden house is constantly under attack from the elements. The carpenter claims to have read 'dans quelque ouvrage philosophique une affaire de petits cochons [...]. Et il concluait : le seul petit cochon qui échappa ainsi au loup fut bâtisseur d'une maison en ciment' (*AE*, p. 32). The Barbadian poet Marlene Nourbese Phillips also draws on the fable in her poem 'How to build your house safe and build it right'. *She Tries Her Tongue, Her Silence Softly Breaks* (London: The Women's Press, 1993), p. 63.

24 Jacques André, *Caraïbales: Essais sur la littérature antillaise* (Paris: Editions Caribbéennes, 1981), p. 115.

25 A fuller discussion of this association (which can be traced back to Plato) can be found in Walter Ong's *Orality and Literacy: The Technologizing of the Word* (London: Methuen, 1982). See in particular p. 81.

26 Chris Bongie, *Islands and Exiles: The Creole Identities of Post/Colonial Literatures* (Stanford: Stanford University Press, 1998), pp. 171–72.

27 Gallagher, *Soundings*, p. 85.

28 Roger Caillois, *Pierres*, quoted in Sourour Ben Ali Memdouh, 'Préface', *L'Esprit créateur* XLV.II (2005), pp. 3–9, p. 8. Special Issue, 'Ecriture des pierres, pierres écrites: territoires de l'imaginaire minéral dans la littérature du XXe siècle'.

29 For a convincing reading of this aspect of the novel, see Lorna Milne, 'The *marron* and the *marqueur*: Physical Space and Imaginary Displacement in Patrick Chamoiseau's *L'esclave vieil homme et le molosse*', in *Ici-là: Place and Displacement in Caribbean Writing in French*, edited by Mary Gallagher (Amsterdam and New York: Rodopi, 2003), pp. 61–82.

30 Caillois, *Pierres*, p. 8. Quoted in Memdouh, 'Préface', p. 5.

31 Douglas Smith, 'Beyond the Cave: Lascaux and the Prehistoric in Post-War French Culture', *French Studies* LVII.2 (2004), pp. 219–32.

32 Smith, 'Beyond the Cave', p. 224. Bataille, as Smith notes, is implicitly referring to Johan Huizinga's groundbreaking study, *Homo Ludens*.

33 This lament for a lack of creative ancestry is a common rhetorical device in Caribbean writing, and is exemplified by the declaration, early in the *Eloge*, that 'nous sommes encore dans un état de prélittérature' (p. 14).

34 Ricœur, *Temps et récit III*, p. 219.

35 The two works, the first a novel, the second a discursive essay, were published on the same day, and they can in many ways be read as complementary and mutually illustrative. Lorna Milne describes a 'dynamic of identification' which runs through both works. See 'The *marron* and the *marqueur*', p. 70.

36 The reader will note in passing the palimpsestic reference to Césaire's volume of poetry *Moi laminaire*, itself described in a recent study as 'une poésie de la minéralité et du roc'. See Jean Khalfa, 'Césaire volcanique', in *L'Esprit créateur* XLV.II (2005), pp. 52–61, p. 52. Special Issue on 'Ecritures de pierres, pierres écrites: territoires de l'imaginaire minéral dans la littérature du XX siècle', edited by Sourour Ben Ali Memdouh.

37 The name 'Carib' itself, as we saw above, was endowed by the colonizers and etymologically linked to cannibalism.

38 Freud, 'The "Uncanny"', p. 220.

39 Freud, 'The "Uncanny"', p. 225.

40 Susan Stewart, *On Longing: Narratives of the Miniature, the Gigantic, the Souvenir, the Collection* (Durham, NC, and London: Duke University Press, 1993), p. 31.

5   Flesh Made Word: Traumatic Memory in *Biblique des derniers gestes*

1 All parenthetical references in this chapter, unless otherwise stated, are to *Biblique des derniers gestes* (Paris: Gallimard, 2002).

2 The similarities with *Texaco* are manifold and repeatedly accentuated. For example, both novels begin with a section entitled 'Annonciation', and a strong undertow of biblical reference underlies both: Bibidji, like Marie-Sophie, is figured as a sort of saviour figure, and his parents are compared to Mary and Joseph. Certain structural principles are also common. In both cases, Oiseau de Cham acknowledges the extent to which his own literary devices have shaped the story. See for example *Texaco*, when he acknowledges that 'je réorganisai la foisonnante parole de l'Informatrice, autour de l'idée messianique d'un Christ' (p. 497), and *Biblique*, when he states '*Gasdo, vous n'aviez accordé pièce importance au calebassier, mais je le replace au centre de cette mort comme vecteur des effets de fiction*' (p. 128, italics in original).

3 The selection and attribution of epigraphs on this opening page follows a similar pattern to other texts in integrating literary and local wisdom. Glissant, as always, takes precedence, and the second epigraph comes from Paul's Letter to the Corinthians, the first biblical epigraph in an *œuvre* which none the less resonates with biblical reference. The last is a Creole proverb, presumably from a local Martinican woman. Similarly, *Antan d'enfance*, *Texaco* and *Solibo* juxtapose the strictly literary quotation with the oral, Creole wisdom. *Biblique* is peppered with quotations from the *conteur* Isomène Calypso.

4 Milne, *Patrick Chamoiseau*, p. 184.

5 This recalls the privileged place afforded to the body in both *Antan d'enfance* and *Chemin-d'école*.

6 Paul Ricœur, *La Mémoire, l'histoire, l'oubli* (Paris: Seuil, 2000), p. 1.

7 The formulation has been used already in *Ecrire en pays dominé* to describe slavery. See *EPD*, p. 119, and my discussion of this collocation in Chapter 4.

8 Although this version too is suffused with magical realism: in it, for example, Bibidji's mother Manotte is eleven months pregnant when she gives birth.

9 This recalls Benítez-Rojo's description of the colonial plantation system as 'the big bang of the Caribbean universe, whose slow explosion throughout modern history threw out billions and billions of cultural fragments in all directions – fragments of diverse kinds that, in their endless voyage, come together in an instant to form a dance step, a linguistic trope, the line of a poem, and afterward repel each other to re-form and pull apart once more, and so on.' *The Repeating Island*, p. 55.

10 These episodes can be seen to enact a key feature of trauma, belatedness: in the case of both the suicide and the infanticide, the stimulus or fright comes too quickly for Balthazar to recognize or to act upon it. To quote Caruth again: 'The breach in the mind – the conscious awareness of the threat to life – is not caused by a pure quantity of stimulus, Freud suggests, but by "fright", the lack of preparedness to take in a stimulus that comes too quickly. It is not simply, that is, the literal threatening of bodily life, but the fact that the threat is recognized as such by the mind *one moment too late*'. *Unclaimed Experience*, p. 62, italics in original.

11 Cathy Caruth, 'Introduction' to the second section of *Trauma: Explorations in Memory* (Baltimore, MD: Johns Hopkins University Press, 1995), pp. 151–57, p. 152.

12 Caruth, *Unclaimed Experience*, p. 4.

13 Sigmund Freud, *Beyond the Pleasure Principle* (New York: Norton, 1961), p. 23.

14 Kathryn Robson, *Writing Wounds: The Inscription of Trauma in Post-1968 French Women's Life-Writing* (Amsterdam and New York: Rodopi, 2004), p. 33.

15 Interestingly, Nicholas Royle notes the Scottish origins of the English word 'uncanny', and links it to 'uncertainties at the origin concerning colonization and the foreign body, and a mixing of what is at once old and long familiar with what is strangely "fresh" and new'. See *The Uncanny* (Manchester: Manchester University Press, 2003), p. 12.

16 Bhabha, *The Location of Culture*, p. 9.

17 Bhabha, *The Location of Culture*, p. 13.

18 This unhomely quality contrasts with the reassuring properties of the *case créole* as described in *Texaco* and elsewhere, and which were discussed in the previous chapter.

19 See Britton's very useful analysis of Bhabha's appropriation of Freud in *Edouard Glissant and Postcolonial Theory*, pp. 119–23.

20 Freud, 'The "Uncanny"', p. 234.

21 Anneleen Masschelein, developing an argument by Mieke Bal, would also caution that the terms have become fashionable, and risk becoming meaningless. See 'The Concept as Ghost: Conceptualization of the Uncanny in Late-Twentieth-Century Theory', *Mosaic* 35.1 (2002), pp. 53–68.

22 Freud, 'The "Uncanny"', p. 245.

23 For a fuller discussion of this problematic presentation of gender, see Maeve McCusker, 'Carnal Knowledge: Trauma, Memory and the Body in Patrick Chamoiseau's *Biblique des derniers gestes*', in *Violence, Culture and Identity in the Francophone Ex-Colonies*, edited by Lorna Milne (forthcoming, Peter Lang, 2007).

24 The Creole word 'coucoune' denotes the female genitals.

25 Royle, *The Uncanny*, p. 43.

26 Sarah later falls pregnant to the mysterious 'spectre-personne' whose penis, due to overexcitement, becomes phenomenally large and divides up, allowing him to enter his victims from every possible angle: 'Les excréments qu'il expulsait alors se mêlaient au sperme cyclopéen [...]. Il vécut dans des poils fourragés aux extrêmes, disparaissait presque entier dans des vagins traumatisés, transformait des sphincters en soleils offusqués. Il restait encollé à des ventres par les sucres du désir, suçait des dents, mordait des amygdales, dévastait les seins ensorcelés sous des succions pharaoniques et des morsures de Léviathan [...]. Sa victime se réveillait avec le corps tout bleu, les entrailles à l'envers et une fatigue de trente-trois siècles' (pp. 369–70). This description of brutalizing sex, in its excessive and visceral qualities, strongly recalls the above evocation of pregnancy, suggesting that both experiences have been irreparably damaged.

27 For criticism of this characterization, see Thomas Spear, 'Jouissances carnavalesques: représentations de la sexualité' and A. James Arnold, 'The Gendering of *créolité*: The Erotics of Colonialism', in *Penser la créolité*, ed. Maryse Condé and Madeleine Cottenet-Hage (Paris: Karthala, 1996), pp. 135–52 and pp. 21–40 respectively. For a nuanced critique of their articles, and an incisive reading of the role of gender in Chamoiseau's work more generally, see Lorna Milne, 'Sex, Gender and the Right to Write: Patrick Chamoiseau and the Erotics of Colonialism', *Paragraph* 24.3 (2001), pp. 59–75.

28 McCusker, 'De la poétique du lieu à la poétique du territoire: Un entretien avec Patrick Chamoiseau', p. 731.

29 Ernest Pépin, 'La Femme antillaise et son corps', *Présence Africaine* 141 (1987), pp. 181–93.

30 And this discourse is not an isolated one; witness Benítez-Rojo's construction of the Atlantic as 'the painfully delivered child of the Caribbean, whose vagina was stretched between continental clamps, all Europe pulling on the forceps to help at the birth of the Atlantic. After the blood and saltwater spurts, quickly sew up the torn flesh and apply the antisceptic tinctures, the gauze and the surgical plaster; then the febrile wait through the forming of a scar: suppurating, always suppurating'. *The Repeating Island*, p. 5.

31 Barbara Creed, *The Monstrous-Feminine: Film, Feminism and Psychoanalysis* (London: Routledge, 1993), p. 1.

32 See Arnold, 'The Gendering of *créolité*', p. 37.

33 Creed, *The Monstrous-Feminine*, p. 29.

Afterword

1 Gallagher, *Soundings*, p. 269.

2 For an interesting discussion of Martinique's uniquely complete experience of colonization, see Tony Delsham, *Gueule de journaliste* (Schoelcher: Editions MGG, 1998).

3 See for example p. 43, p. 345.

4 Dominique Chancé suggests another facet of this polarizing approach when she criticizes 'la linéarité du récit, un monolithisme du point de vue, une simplification de la pensée et des enjeux de sens', and entitles one of the sections of her article 'Un monde binaire'. She argues that the fundamental distinction in the novel is between good and evil, a distinction embodied in Man L'Oubliée and Yvonnette Cléoste. See Dominique Chancé, 'De *Chronique des sept misères* à *Biblique des derniers gestes*: Patrick Chamoiseau est-il baroque?', *Modern Language Notes* 118 (2003), pp. 867–94.

5 Earlier in the novel, Bibidji finds that the distinction between the 'pays rêvé' and the 'pays réel', as elaborated in Glissant's *Poétique de la relation*, confirms his own distinction 'entre pays enterré et pays officiel' (p. 737).

6 Michel Beniamino, 'Pour une poétique de la xénologie à propos de la création lexicale dans la littérature franco-créole: comparaisons et hypothèses', *Etudes créoles* 20.1 (1997), pp. 29–45.

7 Primo Levi, *The Drowned and the Saved* (New York: Vintage, 1989), pp. 11–12.

8 Parry, 'The Institutionalization of Postcolonial Studies', p. 206.

9 See Bongie, 'Exiles on Main Stream: Valuing the Popularity of Postcolonial Literature', *Postmodern Culture* 14.1 (2003), online publication, http://www3.iath. virginia.edu/pmc/text-only/issue.903/14.1bongie.txt

Bibliography

Works by Patrick Chamoiseau

ManMan Dlo Contre la Fée Carabosse (Paris: Editions Caribéennes, 1981).
Chronique des sept misères (Paris: Folio, 1988 [1986]).
Solibo Magnifique (Paris: Folio, 1988).
Au temps de l'antan (Paris: Hatier, 1988).
Martinique (Paris: Editions Hoa-Qui/Richer, 1988).
(with Raphaël Confiant), *Lettres creoles: Tracées antillaises et continentales de la littérature 1635–1976* (Paris: Hatier, 1991).
'Reflections on Maryse Condé's *Traversée de la Mangrove*', *Callaloo* 14.2 (1991), pp. 389–95.
Texaco (Paris: Gallimard, 1992).
Antan d'enfance (Paris: Gallimard, 1993).
Une enfance créole I (Paris: Folio, 1996 [1993]).
'Le dernier coup de dent d'un voleur de banane' in *Ecrire la parole de nuit: La nouvelle littérature antillaise*, edited by Ralph Ludwig (Paris: Folio, 1993), pp. 29–38.
'Que faire de la parole? Dans la tracée mystérieuse de l'oral à l'écrit', in *Ecrire la parole de nuit*, edited by Ralph Ludwig (Paris: Gallimard, 1994), pp. 151–58.
Chemin-d'école (Paris: Gallimard, 1994).
Guyane: Traces-mémoires du bagne, with photographs by Randolphe Hammadi (Paris: Caisse nationale des monuments historiques et des sites, 1994).
Ecrire en pays dominé (Paris: Gallimard, 1997).
L'Esclave vieil homme et le molosse (Paris: Gallimard, 1997).
Elmire des sept bonheurs, with photographs by Jean-Luc de Laguarigue (Paris: Gallimard, 1998).
Emerveilles (Paris: Gallimard, 1998).
Tracées de mélancolies, with photographs by Jean-Luc de Laguarigue (Habitation Saint-Etienne: Editions Traces, 1999).
Cases en pays-mêlés, with photographs by Jean-Luc de Laguarigue (Habitation Saint-Etienne: Editions Traces, 2000).
Livret des villes du deuxième monde (Paris: Centre des documents nationaux, 2002).
Biblique des derniers gestes (Paris: Gallimard, 2002).
'De la mémoire obscure à la mémoire consciente', in S. Chalons et al., *De l'esclavage aux réparations* (Paris: Karthala, 2000), pp. 109–16.
A Bout d'enfance (Paris: Gallimard, 2005).

Interviews with Patrick Chamoiseau

Broussillon, Odile and Michèle Desbordes, 'Un entretien avec Patrick Chamoiseau', *Notes bibliographiques caraïbes* 48 (1988), pp. 10–22.
Ette, Ottmar and Ralph Ludwig, 'En guise d'introduction: Points de vue sur l'évolution de la littérature antillaise: Entretien avec les écrivains martiniquais Patrick

Chamoiseau et Raphaël Confiant', *Lendemains* 67 (1992), pp. 6–16.

Gauvin, Lise, 'Un rapport problématique: Patrick Chamoiseau' in Lise Gauvin, *L'Ecrivain français à la croisée des langues: Entretiens* (Paris: Karthala, 1997), pp. 35–47.

Martinez, Juan, 'Rencontre avec Patrick Chamoiseau', *La Tribune des Antilles* (December 1997, no. 6), pp. 28–31.

McCusker, Maeve, 'An Interview with Patrick Chamoiseau', *International Journal of Francophone Studies* 1.3 (1998), pp. 176–84.

—— 'De la problématique du territoire à la problématique du lieu: Un entretien avec Patrick Chamoiseau', *The French Review* 73.4 (2000), pp. 724–33.

Pausch, Marion, 'Exprimer la complexité antillaise à l'aide de la tradition orale', *Matatu* 12 (1994), pp. 151–58.

Plumecocq, Michaël, 'Entretien avec Patrick Chamoiseau autour de *Solibo Magnifique*', *Roman 20/50* 27 (1999), pp. 125–35.

Réjouis, Rose-Myriam, 'A Reader in the Room: Rose-Myriam Réjouis meets Patrick Chamoiseau', *Callaloo* 22.2 (1999), pp. 346–50.

Secondary sources

Abraham, Nicolas and Maria Torok, *L'Ecorce et le noyau* (Paris: Flammarion, 1987).

Aldrich, Robert, 'From *francité* to *créolité*: French West Indian Literature Comes Home', in *Writing Across Worlds: Literature and Migration*, edited by Russell King, John Connell and Paul White (London and New York: Routledge, 1995), pp. 101–24.

André, Jacques, *Caraïbales: Essais sur la littérature antillaise* (Paris: Editions Caribbéennes, 1981).

Andrews, William L. (ed.), *African American Autobiography* (Englewood Cliffs, NJ: Prentice Hall, 1993).

Antoine, Régis, *La Littérature franco-antillaise* (Paris: Karthala, 1992).

—— *Rayonnants écrivains de la Caraïbe* (Paris: Maisonneuve & Larose, 1998).

Antze, Paul and Michael Lambek (eds), *Tense Past: Cultural Essays in Trauma and Memory* (New York and London: Routledge, 1996).

Arnold, A. James, 'The Gendering of *créolité*: The Erotics of Colonialism', in *Penser la créolité*, edited by Maryse Condé and Madeleine Cottenet-Hage (Paris: Karthala, 1995), pp. 21–40.

Ashcroft, Bill, Gareth Griffiths and Helen Tiffin, *The Empire Writes Back: Theory and Practice in Post-Colonial Literatures* (New York and London: Routledge, 1992).

Bachelard, Gaston, *La Poétique de l'espace* (Paris: Presses Universitaires de France, 1974).

Barthes, Roland, *Le plaisir du texte* (Paris: Seuil, 1973).

—— *Roland Barthes par Roland Barthes* (Paris: Seuil, 1975).

Baugh, Edward, 'The Poet's Fiction of Self: The Schooner *Flight*', *South Atlantic Quarterly* 96.2 (1997), pp. 311–20.

Beniamino, Michel, 'Pour une poétique de la xénologie à propos de la création lexicale dans la littérature franco-créole: comparaisons et hypothèses', *Etudes créoles* 20.1 (1997), pp. 29–45.

Benítez-Rojo, Antonio, *The Repeating Island: The Caribbean and the Postmodern Perspective*, translated by James E. Maraniss (Durham, NC: Duke University Press, 1992).

Benjamin, Walter, 'The Storyteller', in *Illuminations*, translated by Harry Zohn, edited with an introduction by Hannah Arendt (London: Fontana, 1992), pp. 83–110.

Bernabé, Jean, Patrick Chamoiseau and Raphael Confiant, *Éloge de la créolité* (Paris: Gallimard, 1989).

Bhabha, Homi K. (ed.), *Nation and Narration* (London and New York: Routledge, 1990).

—— *The Location of Culture* (London and New York: Routledge, 1994).

Bongie, Chris, *Islands and Exiles: The Creole Identities of Post/Colonial Literature* (Stanford: Stanford University Press, 1998).

—— 'A Street Named Bissette: Nostalgia, Memory and the Cent-Cinquantenaire of the Abolition of Slavery in Martinique', *The South Atlantic Quarterly* 100.1 (2001), pp. 215–57.

—— 'Exiles on Main Stream: Valuing the Popularity of Postcolonial Literature', *Postmodern Culture* 14.1 (2003). Online publication.

Bourdieu, Pierre and Jean-Claude Passeron, *Reproduction in Education, Society and Culture*, translated by Richard Nice (London and Beverly Hills: Sage, 1978).

Bouson, J. Brooks, *Quiet As It's Kept. Shame, Trauma and Race in the Novels of Toni Morrison* (Albany, NY: SUNY Press, 2000).

Brathwaite, Edward, 'Houses in the West Indian Novel', *The Literary Half Yearly* 17.1 (1976), pp. 111–21.

Britton, Celia, '"Eating Their Words": The Consumption of French Caribbean Literature', *ASCALF Yearbook* 1 (1996), pp. 15–23.

—— *Edouard Glissant and Postcolonial Theory: Strategies of Language and Resistance* (Charlottesville, VA, and London: The University Press of Virginia, 1999).

—— *Race and the Unconscious: Freudianism in French Caribbean Thought* (Oxford: Legenda, 2002).

Burrows, Victoria, *Whiteness and Trauma. The Mother–Daughter Knot in the Fiction of Jean Rhys, Jamaica Kincaid and Toni Morrison* (Basingstoke and New York: Palgrave Macmillan, 2004).

Burton, Richard D.E., 'Between the Particular and the Universal: Dilemmas of the Martinican Intellectual', in *Intellectuals in the Twentieth-Century Caribbean*, Vol. 2, edited by Alistair Hennessy (London: Macmillan, 1992), pp. 186–210.

—— '*Debrouya pa peche* or *Il y a toujours moyen de moyenner*: Patterns of Opposition in the Fiction of Patrick Chamoiseau', *Callaloo* 16 (1993), pp. 466–81.

—— '*Ki Moun Nou Ye*? The Idea of Difference in Contemporary French West Indian Thought', *New West Indian Guide* 67, 1&2 (1993), pp. 5–32.

—— *La Famille Coloniale: La Martinique et la Mère Patrie 1789–1992* (Paris: L'Harmattan, 1994).

—— *Le Roman Marron: Etudes sur la littérature martiniquaise contemporaine* (Paris: L'Harmattan, 1997).

Caldwell, Roy Chandler Jr, 'Creole Voice, Creole Time: Narrative Strategies in Chamoiseau's *Chronique des sept misères*', *Romance Quarterly* 47.2 (2000), pp. 103–11.

Caruth, Cathy, *Unclaimed Experience: Trauma, Narrative and History* (Baltimore: The Johns Hopkins University Press, 1996).

—— (ed. and introduction to) *Trauma: Explorations in Memory* (Baltimore: The Johns Hopkins University Press, 1995).

Césaire, Aimé, *Cahier d'un retour au pays natal* (Paris: Présence Africaine, 1950).

—— *Discours sur le colonialisme* (Paris: Présence Africaine, 2004 [1955]).

Chalons, Serge et al., *De l'esclavage aux réparations* (Paris: Karthala, 2000).

Chancé, Dominique, *L'Auteur en souffrance: Essai sur la position et la représenta-tion de l'auteur dans le roman antillais contemporain (1981–1992)* (Paris: Presses Universitaires de France, 2000).

—— 'De *Chronique des sept misères* à *Biblique des derniers gestes*: Patrick Chamoiseau est-il baroque?', *Modern Language Notes* 118 (2003), pp. 867–94.

Chaulet-Achour, Christine and R.-B. Fonkoua (eds), *Esclavage: Libérations, abolitions, commémorations* (Paris: Séguier, 2001).

Clayton, Jay, *The Pleasures of Babel: Contemporary American Literature and Theory* (New York and Oxford: Oxford University Press, 1993).

Condé, Maryse, 'Order, Disorder, Freedom and the West Indian Writer', *Yale French Studies* 83.2, Special Issue on 'Post/Colonial Conditions: Exiles, Migrations, and Nomadisms', ed. Françoise Lionnet and Ronnie Scharfmann (1993), pp. 121–35.

—— (ed., with Madeleine Cottenet-Hage), *Penser la créolité* (Paris: Karthala, 1995).

—— 'Littérature et créolité', in *Créoles de la Caraïbe*, edited by Alain Jacou (Paris: Karthala, 1996), pp. 91–93.

—— *Le Cœur à rire et à pleurer: Contes vrais de mon enfance* (Paris: Hatier, 1999).

Confiant, Raphaël, *Aimé Césaire: Une Traversée paradoxale du siècle* (Paris: Stock, 1993).

—— *Ravines du devant-jour* (Paris: Gallimard, 1993).

—— with Marcel Lebielle, *Les Maîtres de la parole créole* (Paris: Gallimard, 1995). Photographs by David Damoison.

—— *Le Cahier des romances* (Paris: Gallimard, 1999).

Cowart, David, *History and the Contemporary Novel* (Carbondale, IL: Southern Illinois University Press, 1989).

Creed, Barbara, *The Monstrous-Feminine: Film, Feminism, Psychoanalysis* (London and New York: Routledge, 1993).

Crosta, Suzanne, *Le Recit de vie de l'Afrique et des Antilles* (Sainte Foy: GRELCA, 1998).

Crowley, Patrick, 'The *Etat Civil*: Post/colonial Identities and Genre', *French Forum* 29.3 (2004), pp. 79–94.

Dash, J. Michael, 'Writing the Body. Edouard Glissant's Poetics of Re-Membering', in *L'Heritage de Caliban*, ed. Maryse Condé (Pointe-à-Pitre: Jasor, 1992), pp. 75–83.

—— *The Other America: Caribbean Literature in a New World Context* (Charlottesville, VA: University Press of Virginia, 1999).

Davies, Carole Boyce and Elaine Savory Fido (eds), *Out of the Kumbla: Caribbean Women and Literature* (Trenton, NJ: African World Press, 1990).

Delsham, Tony, *Gueule de journaliste* (Schoelcher: Editions MGG, 1998).

Depestre, René, *Hadriana dans tous mes rêves* (Paris: Folio, 1990).

Derrida, Jacques, *L'Ecriture et la Différence* (Paris: Seuil, 1979).

—— *Spectres de Marx: L'état de la dette, le travail du deuil et la nouvelle interna-tionale* (Paris: Galilée, 1993).

—— *Mal d'archive: Une impression freudienne* (Paris: Galilée, 1995).

Douglass, Ana and Thomas A. Vogler (eds), *Witness and Memory: The Discourse of Trauma* (London and New York: Routledge, 2003).

Dow Adams, Timothy, *Light Writing and Life Writing: Photography in Autobiography* (Chapel Hill, NC, and London: The University of North Carolina Press, 2000).

Fanon, Frantz, *Peau noire, masques blancs* (Paris: Seuil, 1952).

—— *Les Damnés de la terre* (Paris: François Maspero, 1961).

Farrell, Kirby, *Post-Traumatic Culture: Injury and Interpretation in the Nineties*

(Baltimore and London: The Johns Hopkins University Press, 1998).

Felman, Shoshana, and Dori Laub, *Testimony: Crises of Witnessing in Literature, Psychoanalysis and History* (London and New York: Routledge, 1993).

Foucault, Michel, *Power/Knowledge: Selected Interviews and Other Writings 1972–1977*, edited by Colin Gordon (New York: Pantheon, 1980).

Freud, Sigmund, 'The "Uncanny"', *Standard Edition*, Vol. XVII, translated by James Strachey (London: Hogarth Press, 1955), pp. 219–56.

—— *Beyond the Pleasure Principle* (New York: Norton, 1961).

Gallagher, Mary, 'Whence and Whither the French Caribbean "créolité" Movement?', *ASCALF Bulletin* 9 (1994), pp. 3–19.

—— *Soundings in French Caribbean Literature since 1950: The Shock of Space and Time* (Oxford: Clarendon Press, 2002).

—— (ed.), *Ici-là: Place and Displacement in Caribbean Writing in French* (Amsterdam and New York: Rodopi, 2003).

—— 'Re-membering Caribbean Childhoods: Saint-John Perse's "Eloges" and Patrick Chamoiseau's *Antan d'enfance*', in *The Francophone Caribbean Today*, edited by Gertrud Aub-Buscher and Beverley Ormerod Noakes (Kingston: The University of the West Indies Press, 2003), pp. 45–59.

—— 'Contemporary French Caribbean Poetry: The Poetics of Reference', *Forum for Modern Language Studies* 40.4 (2004), pp. 451–62. Special Issue, 'Caribbean Connections', edited by Lorna Milne.

Gamarra, Pierre, 'La Machine à écrire: La Parole de la Martinique', *Europe* 55 (November/December 1992), pp. 205–208.

Gauvin, Lise, *L'Ecrivain français à la croisée des langues* (Paris: Karthala, 1997).

Genette, Gérard, *Palimpsestes* (Paris: Seuil, 1982).

George, Rosemary, *The Politics of Home* (Cambridge: Cambridge University Press, 1996).

Gikandi, Simon, *Writing in Limbo: Modernism and Caribbean Literature* (Ithaca, NY, and London: Cornell University Press, 1992).

Gilroy, Paul, *The Black Atlantic: Modernity and Double Consciousness* (London: Verso, 1992).

Giraud, Michel, 'La créolité: une rupture en trompe-l'œil', *Cahiers d'études africaines* 148 (1997), pp. 795–812.

Glissant, Edouard, *L'Intention poétique* (Paris: Seuil, 1969).

—— *Le Discours antillais* (Paris: Seuil, 1981).

—— *La Case du commandeur* (Paris: Seuil, 1981).

—— *Poétique de la relation* (Paris: Gallimard, 1990).

—— *Tout-monde* (Paris: Gallimard, 1993).

—— 'Le Chaos-monde, l'oral et l'écrit', in *Ecrire la parole de nuit*, edited by Ralph Ludwig (Paris: Folio, 1994), pp. 111–29.

Gosson, Renée K., 'For What the Land Tells: An Ecocritical Approach to Patrick Chamoiseau's *Chronicle of the Seven Sorrows*', *Callaloo* 26.1 (2003), pp. 219–34.

Gusdorf, Georges, 'Conditions and Limits of Autobiography', in *Autobiography: Essays Theoretical and Critical*, edited by James Olney (Princeton: Princeton University Press, 1980), pp. 28–48.

Gyssels, Kathleen, 'Du Titre au Roman: *Texaco* de Patrick Chamoiseau', *Roman 20/50* 20 (1995), pp. 121–32.

Haigh, Sam (ed.), *An Introduction to Caribbean Francophone Writing: Guadeloupe and Martinique* (Oxford and New York: Berg, 1999).

Henke, Suzette, *Shattered Subjects: Trauma and Testimony in Women's Life-Writing* (London: Macmillan, 2000).

Hirsch, Marianne, *Family Frames: Photography, Narrative and Postmemory* (Cambridge, MA, and London: Harvard University Press, 1997).

Hobsbawm, Eric, *The Age of Extremes: The Short Twentieth Century* (New York: Pantheon, 1994).

hooks, bell, *Ain't I a Woman: Black Women and Feminism* (London: Pluto, 1982).

—— *Yearning: Race, Gender, and Cultural Politics* (London: Turnaround, 1991).

Hulme, Peter, *Colonial Encounters: Europe and the Native Caribbean, 1492–1797* (London: Methuen, 1986).

Hunter, Jefferson, *Image and Word: The Interaction of Twentieth-Century Photographs and Texts* (Cambridge, MA: Harvard University Press, 1987).

Hutcheon, Linda, *A Poetics of Postmodernism* (New York and London: Routledge, 1988).

Ingham, Patricia Clare and Michelle R. Warren (eds), *Postcolonial Moves: Medieval Through Modern* (Basingstoke: Palgrave Macmillan, 2002).

Jameson, Fredric, *The Political Unconscious: Narrative as a Socially Symbolic Act* (Ithaca, NY: Cornell University Press, 1981).

—— 'Third World Literature in the Era of Multinational Capitalism', *Social Text* 15 (1986), pp. 65–88.

—— *Postmodernism, or the Cultural Logic of Late Capitalism* (London and New York: Verso, 1991).

Jenkins, Keith (ed. and introduction to), *The Postmodern History Reader* (London and New York: Routledge, 1998).

Jonassaint, Jean, 'Tragic Narratives: The Novels of Haitian Tradition', *Callaloo* 26.1 (2003), pp. 203–18.

—— *Des Romans de tradition haïtienne: Sur un récit tragique* (Paris: L'Harmattan; Montreal: Cidihca, 2002).

Khalfa, Jean, 'Césaire volcanique', *L'Esprit créateur* XL.II (2005), pp. 52–61. Special Issue on 'Ecritures de pierres, pierres écrites: terroitoires de l'imaginaire minéral dans la littérature du XX siècle', edited by Sourour Ben Ali Memdouh.

Khanna, Ranjana, *Dark Continents: Psychoanalysis and Colonialism* (Durham, NC: Duke University Press, 2003).

Kiberd, Declan, *Inventing Ireland: The Literature of the Modern Nation* (London: Vintage, 1996).

King, Nicola, *Memory, Narrative, Identity: Remembering the Self* (Edinburgh: Edinburgh University Press, 2000).

King, Russell, John Connell and Paul White (eds), *Writing Across Worlds: Literature and Migration* (London and New York: Routledge, 1995).

Klein, Kerwin Lee, 'On the Emergence of *Memory* in Historical Discourse', *Representations* 69 (2000), pp. 127–50.

LaCapra, Dominick (ed.), *History, Politics and the Novel* (Ithaca, NY, and London: Cornell University Press, 1987).

—— *Representing the Holocaust. History, Theory, Trauma* (Ithaca, NY: Cornell University Press, 1994).

—— *History and Memory after Auschwitz* (Ithaca, NY, and London: Cornell University Press, 1998).

—— *Writing History, Writing Trauma* (Baltimore: The Johns Hopkins University Press, 2001).

Laqueur, Thomas W., 'Introduction', *Representations* 69 (2000), pp. 1–8.

Lejeune, Philippe, *L'Autobiographie en France* (Paris: Armand Colin, 1971).

—— *Le Pacte autobiographique* (Paris: Seuil, 1975).

—— 'Paroles d'enfance', *Revue des sciences humaines* 93.217 (1990), pp. 23–38.

Levi, Primo, *The Drowned and the Saved* (New York: Vintage, 1989).
Leys, Ruth, *Trauma: A Genealogy* (Chicago and London: The University of Chicago Press, 2000).
Lloyd, Rosemarie, *The Land of Lost Content: Children and Childhood in Nineteenth-Century French Literature* (Oxford: Clarendon Press, 1992).
Loichot, Valérie, 'Fort-de-France: Pratiques textuelles et corporelles d'une ville coloniale', *French Cultural Studies*, 15.1 (2004), pp. 48–60.
Lyotard, Jean-François, *La Condition postmoderne* (Paris: Minuit, 1998).
Masschelein, Anneleen, 'The Concept as Ghost: Conceptualization of the Uncanny in Late-Twentieth-Century Theory', *Mosaic* 35.1 (2002), pp. 53–68.
Maximin, Daniel, *Tu, c'est l'enfance* (Paris: Gallimard, 2004).
Mazama, Ama, 'Critique afrocentrique de l'*Eloge de la créolité*', in *Penser la créolité*, edited by Maryse Condé and Madeleine Cottenet-Hage (Paris: Karthala, 1995), pp. 85–99.
McCusker, Maeve, 'No Place Like Home? Constructions of Identity in Patrick Chamoiseau's *Texaco*', in *Ici-là: Place and Displacement in Caribbean Writing in French*, edited by Mary Gallagher (Amsterdam and New York: Rodopi, 2003), pp. 41–60.
—— '"This Creole Culture, Miraculously Forged": The Contradictions of *créolité*', in *Francophone Studies/Postcolonial Theory*, edited by Charles Forsdick and David Murphy (London and New York: Arnold, 2003), pp. 112–21.
—— '"Troubler l'ordre de l'oubli": Memory and Forgetting in French Caribbean Autobiography of the 1990s', *Forum for Modern Language Studies* 40.4 (2004), pp. 438–50. Special Issue, 'Caribbean Connections', edited by Lorna Milne.
Memdouh, Sourour Ben Ali, 'Préface', *L'Esprit créateur* XLV.2 (2005), pp. 3–9. Special Issue, 'Ecriture des pierres, pierres écrites: territoires de l'imaginaire minéral dans la littérature du XXe siècle'.
Ménil, René, *Tracées: Identité, Négritude, Esthétique aux Antilles* (Paris: Laffont, 1981).
—— *Antilles déjà jadis* (Paris: Jean Michel Place, 1999).
Milne, Lorna, 'From *Créolité* to *Diversalité*: The Postcolonial Subject in Patrick Chamoiseau's *Texaco*', in *Subject Matters*, edited by Johnnie Gratton and Paul Gifford (Amsterdam and Atlanta: Rodopi, 2000), pp. 162–80.
—— 'Sex, Gender and the Right to Write: Patrick Chamoiseau and the Erotics of Colonialism', *Paragraph* 24.3 (2001), pp. 59–75.
—— 'The *marron* and the *marqueur*: Physical Space and Imaginary Displacement in Patrick Chamoiseau's *L'Esclave vieil homme et le molosse*', in *Ici-là: Place and Displacement in Caribbean Writing in French*, edited by Mary Gallagher (Amsterdam and New York: Rodopi, 2003), pp. 61–82.
—— *Patrick Chamoiseau: Espaces d'une écriture antillaise* (Amsterdam and New York: Rodopi, 2006).
Minh-ha, Trinh T., 'Other than Myself/My Other Self', in *Travellers' Tales: Narratives of Home and Displacement*, edited by George Robertson et al. (New York and London: Routledge, 1994), pp. 9–22.
Morrison, Toni, *Beloved* (London: Picador, 1988).
—— *Song of Solomon* (London: Vintage, 1998).
Morton, Stephen, 'Slavery and the Poetics of Trauma – Marlene Nourbese Philip's *She Tries her Tongue, Her Silence Softly Breaks*', *Atlantic Literary Review* 3.2 (2002), pp. 92–109.
Moudileno, Lydie, 'Ecrire l'écrivain: créolité et spécularité' in *Penser la créolité*, edited by Maryse Condé and Madeleine Cottenet-Hage (Paris: Karthala, 1995), pp. 85–99.

—— *L'Ecrivain antillais au miroir de sa littérature* (Paris: Karthala, 1997).

Munro, Martin, '*La Discorde antillaise*: Contemporary Debates in Caribbean Criticism', *Paragraph* 24.3 (2001), pp. 117–27.

Murdoch, H. Adlai, *Creole Identity in the French Caribbean Novel* (Gainesville: University Press of Florida, 2001).

Nnadi, Joseph, 'Mémoire d'Afrique, mémoire biblique: la congruence des mythes du nègre dans *Texaco* de Patrick Chamoiseau', *Etudes francophones* 15.1 (2000), pp. 75–91.

Nora, Pierre, *Les Lieux de mémoire*, 3 volumes (Paris: Gallimard, 1997).

Ollivier, Emile, *Mille Eaux* (Paris: Gallimard, 1999).

Ong, Walter, *Orality and Literature: The Technologizing of the Word* (London: Methuen, 1982).

Ormerod, Beverley, *An Introduction to the French Caribbean Novel* (London: Heinemann, 1985).

Palcy, Euhzan (dir.), *La Rue Cases-nègres* (1983).

Parry, Benita, 'The Institutionalization of Postcolonial Studies', in *The Cambridge Companion to Postcolonial Literary Studies*, edited by Neil Lazarus (Cambridge: Cambridge University Press, 2004), pp. 66–80.

Perret, Delphine, 'Lire Chamoiseau', in *Penser la créolité*, edited by Maryse Condé and Madeleine Cottenet-Hage (Paris: Karthala, 1995), pp. 153–72.

Pineau, Gisèle, and Marie Abraham, *Femmes des Antilles: Traces et voix cent cinquante ans après l'abolition* (Paris: Stock, 1998). With photographs by Thomas Dorn.

Pouchet Paquet, Sandra, 'West Indian Autobiography', in *African-American Autobiography*, edited by William L. Andrews (Englewood Cliffs, NJ: Prentice Hall, 1993), pp. 196–211.

Praeger, Michèle, *The Imaginary Caribbean and the Caribbean Imaginary* (Lincoln, NE, and London: University of Nebraska Press, 2003).

Price, Richard and Sally Price, 'Shadow-Boxing in the Mangrove', *Cultural Anthropology* 12.1 (1997), pp. 3–36.

Proust, Marcel, *Le Temps retrouvé* (Paris: Folio, 1972).

Ricœur, Paul, *Temps et récit III: Le Temps raconté* (Paris: Seuil, 1985).

—— *La Mémoire, l'histoire, l'oubli* (Paris: Seuil, 2000).

Rigney, Ann, 'Plenitude, Scarcity and the Circulation of Cultural Memory', *Journal of European Studies* 35.1 (2005), pp. 11–28.

Robbe-Grillet, Alain, *Pour un nouveau roman* (Paris: Editions de Minuit, 1963).

Robertson, George et al., *Travellers' Tales: Narratives of Home and Displacement* (London and New York: Routledge, 1994).

Robson, Kathryn, *Writing Wounds: The Inscription of Trauma in Post-1968 French Women's Life-Writing* (Amsterdam and New York: Rodopi, 2004).

Rosello, Mireille, *Littérature et identité créole aux Antilles* (Paris: Karthala, 1992).

—— 'The "Césaire Effect", or How to Cultivate One's Nation', *Research in African Literatures* 32.4 (2001), pp. 77–91.

Rousso, Henri, *Le Syndrome de Vichy: de 1940 à nos jours* (Paris: Seuil, 1990).

Royle, Nicholas, *The Uncanny* (Manchester: Manchester University Press, 2003).

Said, Edward, *Culture and Imperialism* (London: Vintage, 1993).

—— *Beginnings: Intention and Method* (New York: Basic Books, 1975).

Santner, Eric, *Stranded Objects: Mourning, Memory and Film in Postwar Germany* (Ithaca, NY: Cornell University Press, 1990).

Sarraute, Nathalie, *Enfance* (Paris: Gallimard, 1983).

Sheringham, Michael, *French Autobiography: Devices and Desires* (Oxford: Clarendon Press, 1993).

Shemak, April, 'Re-membering Hispaniola: Edwige Danticat's *The Farming of Bones*', *Modern Fiction Studies* 48.1 (2002), pp. 83–112.

Smith, Douglas, 'Beyond the Cave: Lascaux and the Prehistoric in Post-War French Culture', *French Studies* LVII.2 (2004), pp. 219–32.

Smith, Sidonie and Julia Watson (eds), *De/Colonizing the Subject* (Minneapolis: University of Minnesota Press, 1992).

Sonsavior, Eva, 'Entretien avec Maryse Condé', *Francophone Postcolonial Studies* 2.2 (2004), pp. 7–33.

Sontag, Susan, *On Photography* (London and New York: Penguin, 1977).

The South Atlantic Quarterly 96.2 (1997), Special Issue, *The Poetics of Derek Walcott: Intertextual Perspectives*.

Spear, Thomas C., 'Jouissances carnavalesques: représentations de la sexualité', in *Penser la créolité*, edited by Maryse Condé and Madeleine Cottenet-Hage (Paris: Karthala, 1995), pp. 135–52.

Stewart, Susan, *On Longing: Narratives of the Miniature, the Gigantic, the Souvenir, the Collection* (Durham, NC, and London: Duke University Press, 1993).

Tiffin, Helen, Ian Adam et al., 'Introduction', in *Past the Last Post: Theorising Postcolonialism and Postmodernism* (Calgary: University of Calgary Press, 1990), pp. i–xv.

Vergès, Françoise, *Abolir l'esclavage – une utopie coloniale: Les ambiguïtés d'une politique humanitaire* (Paris: Albin Michel, 2001).

Vickroy, Laurie, *Trauma and Survival in Contemporary Fiction* (Charlottesville, VA: University of Virginia Press, 2002).

Vogler, Thomas and Ana Douglass (eds), *Witness and Memory: The Discourse of Trauma* (London and New York: Routledge, 2003).

Walcott, Derek, 'The Sea is History', in *Frontiers of Caribbean Literature in English*, edited by Frank Birbalsingh (New York: St Martin's Press, 1996), pp. 22–28.

—— 'A Letter to Chamoiseau', *The New York Review of Books*, 14 August 1997, pp. 45–48.

—— *What the Twilight Says: Essays* (New York and London: Faber and Faber, 1998).

Warren, Michelle R., 'Post-Philology', in *Postcolonial Moves: Medieval Through Modern*, edited by Patricia Clare Ingham and Michelle R. Warren (Basingstoke: Palgrave Macmillan, 2002), pp. 19–45.

Watts, Richard, '"*Toutes ces eaux!*": Ecology and Empire in Patrick Chamoiseau's *Biblique des derniers gestes*', *Modern Language Notes* 118 (2003), pp. 895–910.

Webb, Barbara, *Myth and History in the Caribbean* (Amherst: University of Massachusetts Press, 1992).

Weintraub, Karl, 'Autobiography and Historical Consciousness', *Critical Enquiry* 1 (1975), pp. 821–47.

Wesseling, Elizabeth, *Writing History as a Prophet: Postmodernist Innovations of the Historical Novel* (Amsterdam and Philadelphia: John Benjamins Publishing Company, 1991).

White, Hayden, *Metahistory* (Baltimore: The Johns Hopkins University Press, 1973).

—— *The Content of the Form* (Baltimore: The Johns Hopkins University Press, 1987).

Young, Robert, *Colonial Desire: Hybridity in Theory, Culture and Race* (London and New York: Routledge, 1995).

Zobel, Joseph, *La Rue Cases-Nègres* (Paris: Présence Africaine, 1974).

Index

Abraham, Nicolas, 78
Africa, 5, 45, 78
  Maghreb, 2, 8, 64, 87, 151
André, Jacques, 111–12
Antoine, Régis, 111
Arnold, A. James, 149

Bachelard, Gaston, 104–05, 116
Beniamino, Michel, 153
Benítez-Rojo, Antonio, 13, 158
Benjamin, Walter, 84
Bhabha, Homi, 4, 11, 44, 107, 133,
  140–42
Bongie, Chris, 113, 155
Bourdieu, Pierre, 109, 114
Brathwaite, Edward, 104–05, 110, 133
Britton, Celia, 24, 71, 142
Burton, Richard D.E., 22, 33, 160, n. 17

Caillois, Roger, 117
Caldwell, Roy Jr., 81
Caruth, Cathy, 19, 40, 41, 42, 137–38,
  139
Césaire, Aimé, 1, 3, 5, 11, 35, 70, 80,
  81, 113, 130, 132, 151–53
Chamoiseau, Patrick:
  Chronique des sept misères, 15, 19,
    21–46, 47, 64
  Solibo Magnifique, 19, 26, 46, 77,
    78, 79, 80, 83–90, 93, 127, 129
  Lettres créoles, 73, 117, 159, n. 48
  Texaco, 19, 26, 77, 78, 79, 83, 85,
    89, 90–100, 102, 103–16, 129
  Antan d'enfance, 47, 48, 49, 50, 51,
    52, 53, 54, 55, 56, 57, 58, 59,
    63, 64, 66, 69, 72, 115
  Chemin-d'école, 47, 48, 49, 51, 54,
    55, 57, 58, 60, 61, 62, 63, 64,
    66, 67, 68, 69, 70, 71, 73, 74,
    129
  Guyane: Traces-mémoires du bagne,
    102, 103
  Une enfance créole I, 115
  Ecrire en pays dominé, 4, 5, 102,
    118–20
  L'Esclave vieil homme et le molosse,
    8, 102, 120–26, 129, 158, n. 23
  Elmire des sept bonheurs, 16, 21
  Cases en pays mêlés, 16, 102, 104,
    113
  Tracées de mélancolies, 16
  Biblique des derniers gestes, 15, 16,
    18, 19, 21, 26, 78, 79, 80, 81,
    82, 86, 101, 127–49, 158, n. 30
  A Bout d'enfance 47, 48, 49, 50, 51,
    58, 66, 69, 73
Chancé, Dominique, 76, 148
Chirac, Jacques, 3
Clayton, Jay, 31
Condé, Maryse, 3, 14, 47, 65, 81, 154
Confiant, Raphaël, 11, 13, 47, 50, 65,
  69, 77, 117, 148, 154
Creed, Barbara, 148–49
créolité, 10–13, 16, 45–46, 70–75, 93,
  116, 125, 153
  Eloge de la créolité, 4–12, 70, 73,
    77, 78, 92, 93, 110, 116, 153,
    159, n. 48
Crosta, Suzanne, 64–65
Crowley, Patrick, 68

Dash, J. Michael, 13, 160, n. 4
departmentalization, 1, 24
Depestre, René, 23
Derrida, Jacques, 43, 45, 77, 87
Douglass, Ana, 5

Fanon, Frantz, 1, 40, 151–52
Farrell, Kirby, 84
Felman, Shoshana, 43
Foucault, Michel, 103, 111
France, 2, 3, 4, 13, 72, 79
Freud, Sigmund, 103, 123, 133, 139–43

Gallagher, Mary, 30, 65, 95, 116, 150
Gamarra, Pierre, 17
Gaulle, Charles de, 29, 34, 95
Gilroy, Paul, 4

Glissant, Edouard, 1, 3, 4, 14, 17, 31, 40, 53, 56, 64, 76, 88, 92, 93, 96, 105, 113, 120, 125, 128, 133, 134, 151–53
Gyssels, Kathleen, 30, 50

Haiti, 1, 160, n. 18
Henke, Suzette, 65
Hirsch, Marianne, 4, 6, 134
Hobsbawm, Eric, 9–10
Holocaust, 4, 5, 6, 7, 154
hooks, bell, 103
Hunter, Jefferson, 16
Hutcheon, Linda, 92–100

intertextuality, 17, 83, 110, 121, 151–52

Jameson, Fredric, 7, 12, 71, 73, 79, 80, 82, 100
Jonassaint, Jean, 161, n. 23
Joyce, James, 76, 88

Khanna, Ranjana, 43
Kiberd, Declan, 88
King, Nicola, 82
Klein, Kerwin Lee, 6–7, 101

Lacan, Jacques, 67
LaCapra, Dominick, 4, 6, 19, 43, 44, 157, n. 15, 161, n. 35, 36, 40
Laguarigue, Jean-Luc de, 16
Laqueur, Thomas W., 7
Lejeune, Philippe, 56, 68
Letchimy, Serge, 100
Levi, Primo, 154
Leys, Ruth, 41
Lloyd, Rosemary, 59–60
Loichot, Valérie, 20, 22
Lyotard, Jean-François, 4

Maghreb, 2, 64, 87, 151
Márquez, Gabriel García, 17–18, 99
Maximin, Daniel, 3, 47, 50, 65, 161, n. 24
McCusker, Maeve, 173, n. 28
Ménil, René, 81
Milne, Lorna, 14, 23, 128
Morrison, Toni, 45, 140
Munro, Martin, 12
Murdoch, H. Adlai, 14

names, 23, 67, 68, 69

négritude, 70–75, 132, 153
Nnadi, Joseph, 14–15
Nora, Pierre, 6, 9, 10, 78–80, 82, 86, 128, 141

Ollivier, Emile, 47, 65

Parry, Benita, 17, 155
Pépin, Ernest, 47, 148
Pineau, Gisèle, 47, 65, 159, n. 50
Pouchet Paquet, Sandra, 50
Praeger, Michèle, 5–6
Price, Richard, 12, 81
Price, Sally, 12, 81
Proust, Marcel, 161, n. 25

Ricœur, Paul, 103, 119, 132
Rigney, Ann, 10
Robbe-Grillet, 104–05
Robson, Kathryn, 140
Rosello, Mireille, 160–61, n. 20, 164, n. 39
Rousso, Henri, 4, 9, 157, n. 10
Royle, Nicholas, 144
Rushdie, Salman, 17, 76, 154

Said, Edward, 15, 30, 159, n. 47
Saint-John Perse, 151
Santner, Eric, 12
Sarraute, Nathalie, 56–57, 62
Sheringham, Michael, 51–52
slavery, 1–6, 8, 19, 22, 39, 64–70, 103, 123–25, 135–49, 154
abolition of, 1–6
Smith, Douglas, 117–18
Sonsavior, Eva, 159, n. 43
Sontag, Susan, 16, 25
Stewart, Susan, 124

Taubira, 1, 3
Torok, Maria, 78
trauma, 4, 8, 10, 19, 22, 39–46, 135–41

uncanny, 103, 123–24, 135, 140, 142–49
Vogler, Thomas A., 5

Walcott, Derek, 1, 5, 8, 10, 50, 76, 133, 157
White, Hayden, 92

Young, Robert, 13

Zobel, Joseph, 66, 101